Study Guide

Fundamentals of Economics

SECOND EDITION

Boyes/Melvin

James E. Clark
Wichita State University

Janet L. Wolcutt
Wichita State University

HOUGHTON MIFFLIN COMPANY   BOSTON   NEW YORK

Sponsoring Editor: Ann West
Editorial Associate: Tonya Lobato
Senior Manufacturing Coordinator: Marie Barnes

Printed in the U.S.A.

ISBN: 0-618-24686X

123456789 – CRS – 06 05 04 03 02

Contents

USING THE *STUDY GUIDE* EFFECTIVELY

WHAT'S IN THE STUDY GUIDE

All *Study Guide* chapters are organized the same way; each includes the following:

- *Fundamental Questions* are repeated from the text chapter and are briefly answered. The questions and their answers give you an overview of the chapter's main points.

- *Key Terms* from the chapter are listed to remind you of new vocabulary presented in the chapter.

- *A Quick-Check Quiz* focuses on vocabulary and key concepts from the chapter. These multiple-choice questions allow you to see whether you understand the material and are ready to move on or whether you need to review some of the text before continuing.

- *Practice Questions and Problems* provide in-depth coverage of important ideas from the chapter and give you the opportunity to apply concepts and work out problems.

- *The Thinking About and Applying* section covers one or more topics in greater depth and will help you learn to apply economics to real-world situations. This section will also show you how various economic concepts are related to one another and, as a result, will help you to think economically.

- *The Answers* section may be the most important part of the *Study Guide*. Answers to all questions and problems are provided with explanations of how to arrive at the correct answer. In many cases, explanations are given for what you did wrong if you arrived at certain wrong answers.

HOW TO STUDY ECONOMICS

No one ever said that economics is an easy subject, and many students tell us it is the most challenging subject they have studied. Despite the challenge, most students manage to learn a great deal of economics, and we're sure you can too. But doing well in economics requires a commitment from you to *keep up* your studying and to *study properly*.

Keeping up: Although there may be subjects that can be learned reasonably well by cramming the night before an exam, economics is *not* one of them. Learning economics is like building a house: first you need to lay a solid foundation, and then you must carefully build the walls. To master economics you must first learn the early concepts, vocabulary, and ideas; if you do not, the later ones will not make any sense.

Studying properly: Listening in class, reading the text, and going through the *Study Guide* are not really enough to learn economics—you must also organize your studying. The textbook and the *Study Guide* have been designed to help you organize your thinking and your studying. Used together, they will help you learn. You can create a mini-notebook with *Study Guide* sheets in the chapter sequence recommended by your instructor. Handouts from your instructor or newspaper articles that you've clipped might also be included here.

Following these steps for each chapter is an effective way to learn economics.

1. Skim the text chapter before your instructor discusses it in class to get a general idea of what the chapter covers.

   a. Read through the Fundamental Questions and the Preview to get a sense of what is to come.

   b. Skim through the chapter, looking only at the section headings and the section Recaps.

    c.   Read the chapter Summary. By this point, you should have a good idea of what topics the chapter covers.

2.   Read the text chapter and *Study Guide* one section at a time. Both the text and the *Study Guide* break down each chapter into several sections so that you will not need to juggle too many new ideas at once.

    a.   Read through one section of the text chapter. Pay attention to the marginal notes containing definitions of Key Terms.

    b.   Study the section Recap. If parts of the Recap are not clear to you, review those parts of the section.

    c.   In the *Study Guide,* read the answers to the Fundamental Questions covered in the section you are studying.

    d.   Take the Quick-Check Quiz for the section. Write your answers on a separate sheet of paper so that you can use the quiz again later. If you missed any questions, review the applicable section in the text.

    e.   Work through the Practice Questions and Problems for the section, writing your answers in the spaces provided. Check your answers, and then review what you missed. Read through the explanations in the Answers section, even if you answered the question or problem correctly.

    f.   If there are ideas that are not clear or problems you do not understand, talk to your instructor. Economics instructors are interested in helping their students.

3.   Review the chapter as a whole. Although each section should initially be studied alone, you will need to put the pieces together.

    a.   Read through the chapter again, paying special attention to the Fundamental Questions, the section Recaps, the Economic Insight boxes, and the chapter Summary. If you like to outline chapters on paper, now is the time to do so. The section headings and subheadings provide an ideal framework for outlining the text.

    b.   In the *Study Guide,* read through the Fundamental Questions and their answers.

    c.   Review the list of Key Terms. Write down the definition of each one at this point, and check your definitions against the marginal notes or the glossary. Study any terms you missed.

    d.   Work through the Exercises at the end of the text chapter.

    e.   Work through the Thinking About and Applying section of the *Study Guide.*

    f.   Read through and carry out the Internet Exercise at the end of the chapter to get current information to reinforce your knowledge of the chapter's topics.

4.   Ideally, studying for exams should be a repetition of steps 1, 2, and 3. However, economists recognize the existence of opportunity costs, and you have many other things to do with your time in addition to studying economics. If you cannot study for an exam as thoroughly as you should, you can use some techniques to help refresh your memory. These techniques assume that you *did* study the materials at least once. (There is no magic way to learn economics without doing some serious studying.)

    a.   Review the Fundamental Questions, the section Recaps, the Key Terms lists, and the chapter Summaries in the text.

    b.   Read again the Fundamental Questions and their answers in the *Study Guide.*

    c. Take the Quick-Check Quiz again, writing your answers in the *Study Guide* this time. Questions that you miss will direct you to the areas you need to study most.

If you follow these suggestions, you are sure to meet with success in your study of economics.

USE THE TEXT AS A SYSTEM

The text presents all the key concepts of economics. In addition it explains how people use these concepts—in business, in government, and in ordinary households. In both the world of theory and the real world of application, knowing the relationships of ideas is crucial. No one can move about in either world without knowing the pathways that relationships form. The features of the text provide these pathways; taking advantage of them will help your studying immensely. The *Fundamental Questions* point to main issues and help you categorize details, examples, and theories accordingly. Colors in the *graphs* help you classify curves and see relationships to data in the *tables*. The *Recaps* reinforce overarching ideas; they orient you before you go on to the next big section. The *system of referencing* sections and headings by number will help you group concepts and also keep track of what level of ideas you are working with. If you use the features of the text, the text can be more than an authoritative source of information—it can be a system for comprehension.

TAKE MORE THAN ONE VIEW

As you work through the chapters of this book, you will examine in close-up each particular concept. Yet to understand the material and to get a feel for how economists think, you need to have a second point of view too—an overview. Keeping yourself "up above it" at the same time you are "down in it" will help you remember what you are reading much better and also help you understand and use the concepts you learn more easily. Taking more than one view of your subject has another benefit; it is an ingredient of good critical thinking.

J.E.C.

J.L.W.

CHAPTER 1

Economics and the World Around You

FUNDAMENTAL QUESTIONS

1. Why study economics?

   Economics is the study of how people choose to allocate scarce **resources** to satisfy their unlimited wants. There are several words in this definition that should be emphasized. First, people allocate *scarce* resources. If there were enough of a resource to go around so that everyone could have as much as he or she wanted, there would be no need to allocate.

   The definition states that people have *unlimited* wants. Notice that it says wants, not needs. People *act* on the basis of their wants, not necessarily on the basis of their needs. (Otherwise they would not buy strawberry sundaes.) If each of us made a list right now of the top ten things we would like to have and our fairy godmother popped out of the air and gave us what we wanted, most of us immediately would find that there are ten *more* things we'd like to have. Because resources are scarce and wants are unlimited, economics studies the best way to allocate resources so that none are wasted.

2. What are opportunity costs?

   Because **scarcity** is universal, people must make choices. The **opportunity cost** of something is what you need to give up in order to get it. For example, if you would prefer to be sleeping now instead of studying economics, the opportunity cost of studying is the sleep you could be enjoying. Opportunity costs are a key element in the way economists look at the world.

3. How are specialization and opportunity costs related?

   Opportunity costs determine which activities people should specialize in. For example, think about a small law office with just one lawyer and one secretary. The lawyer earns $100 per hour working as a lawyer, and the secretary earns $15 per hour for typing. Even if the lawyer types faster than the secretary, it wouldn't make sense for the lawyer to do her own typing— every hour spent typing has an opportunity cost of $100 to the lawyer. It is more efficient for the lawyer to specialize in practicing law, and let the secretary do the typing.

4. Why does specialization occur?

   It pays to specialize whenever opportunity costs are *different*. Two parties can specialize and then trade, which makes both parties better off. Even if one person or nation does something more efficiently than another in the production of a good or service, it does not mean that person or nation should produce that good or service. Specialization occurs as a result of **comparative**, not absolute, **advantage**. Specialization according to comparative advantage minimizes opportunity costs.

5.   What are the benefits of trade?

If both parties specialize according to comparative advantage, trading enables them to acquire more of the goods and services they want.

KEY TERMS

scarcity	capital	comparative
resources	financial capital	gains from trade
land	opportunity costs	barter
labor	tradeoffs	exchange rate

QUICK-CHECK QUIZ

Section 1: The Definition of Economics

1.   If an item is scarce,
   a.   it is not an economic good.
   b.   at a zero price, the amount of the item that people want is less than the amount that is available.
   c.   there is not enough of the item to satisfy everyone who wants it.
   d.   there is enough to satisfy wants even at a zero price.
   e.   it must be a resource as opposed to an input.

2.   Which of the following is *not* one of the categories of resources?
   a.   land
   b.   labor
   c.   capital
   d.   stocks and bonds
   e.   All of the above are categories of resources.

3.   Janine is an accountant who makes $30,000 a year. Robert is a college student who makes $8,000 a year. All other things being equal, who is more likely to stand in a long line to get a cheap concert ticket?
   a.   Janine, because her opportunity cost is lower
   b.   Janine, because her opportunity cost is higher
   c.   Robert, because his opportunity cost is lower
   d.   Robert, because his opportunity cost is higher
   e.   Janine, because she is better able to afford the cost of the ticket

4.   Economics is the study of the relationship between
   a.   people's unlimited wants and their scarce resources.
   b.   people's limited wants and their scarce resources.
   c.   people's limited wants and their infinite resources.
   d.   people's limited income and their scarce resources.
   e.   human behavior and limited human wants.

5.   The heart of the economic problem is to
   a.   provide for full employment.
   b.   eliminate scarcity.
   c.   increase our standard of living.
   d.   allocate limited resources among unlimited uses.

e.   increase leisure.

 6.   Which of the following is considered to be capital by economists?
a.   stocks
b.   bonds
c.   machinery
d.   money
e.   finished products

 7.   Which of the following do economists call financial capital?
a.   stocks
b.   bonds
c.   money
d.   all of the above
e.   only a and b

8.   Which of the following should *not* be considered an opportunity cost of attending college?
a.   money spent on living expenses that are the same whether or not you attend college
b.   lost salary
c.   business lunches
d.   interest that could have been earned on your money had you put the money into a savings account rather than spent it on tuition
e.   opportunities sacrificed in the decision to attend college

Section 2: Specialization and Exchange - part I

1.   Exchange among people occurs because
a.   everyone involved believes they will all gain.
b.   one person gains, and the others lose.
c.   only one person loses, while everyone else gains.
d.   people have no other choices.
e.   the government requires it.

2.   What must be given up to gain a unit of a good is that good's
a.   utility cost.
b.   opportunity value.
c.   universal value.
d.   opportunity cost.
e.   specialty.

3. Which of the following statements is true?
    a. Individuals, firms, and nations specialize in the production of the good or service that has the highest opportunity cost.
    b. An individual, firm, or nation first must be able to produce more of a good or service before it can have a comparative advantage in the production of that good or service.
    c. Comparative advantage exists whenever one person, firm, or nation engaging in an activity incurs the same costs as some other individual, firm, or nation.
    d. An individual, firm, or nation gains when it specializes according to comparative advantage.
    e. An individual, firm, or nation should trade with parties that have the same opportunity costs for the goods and services produced.

4. You have a comparative advantage in producing something when you
    a. have a higher opportunity cost than someone else.
    b. have a special talent.
    e. have a lower opportunity cost than someone else.
    d. have learned a useful skill.
    e. have the same opportunity cost as someone else.

Section 2: Specialization and Exchange - part II

Use the following table to answer questions 5 though 9.

On a 10-acre farm, one farmer can produce these quantities of corn or wheat in Alpha and Beta.

	Corn	Wheat
Alpha	200	400
Beta	100	300

1. In the preceding table, the opportunity cost of corn in Beta is
    a. 300 wheat.
    b. 1 wheat.
    c. 3 wheat.
    d. 100 corn.
    e. .5 corn.

2. In the preceding table, the opportunity cost of wheat in Beta is
    a. .333 corn.
    b. 1 wheat.
    c. 3 wheat.
    d. 300 wheat.
    e. .5 corn.

3.   In the preceding table, the opportunity cost of corn in Alpha is
    a.   400 wheat.
    b.   2 wheat.
    c.   4 wheat.
    d.   100 corn.
    e.   .5 corn.

4.   In the preceding table, the opportunity cost of wheat in Alpha is
    a.   400 wheat.
    b.   2 wheat.
    c.   4 corn.
    d.   100 corn.
    e.   .5 corn.

5.   Which of the following statements is(are) true?
    a.   Alpha has a comparative advantage in corn, and Beta has a comparative advantage in wheat.
    b.   Alpha has a comparative advantage in wheat, and Beta has a comparative advantage in corn.
    c.   Alpha has a comparative advantage in both corn and wheat.
    d.   Beta has a comparative advantage in both corn and wheat.
    e.   Neither has a comparative advantage in anything.

Section 3: Trade

1.   Why do nations trade with each other?
    a.   Trade makes people worse off.
    b.   Trade makes people better off.
    c.   Trade provides less to consume but more to produce.
    d.   Trade provides less to consume and less to produce.
    e.   Governments insist on it.

2.   The country that trades the most with the U.S. is
    a.   China.
    b.   Japan.
    c.   Mexico.
    d.   Germany.
    e.   Canada.

3.   Canada and Mexico are the two biggest trading partners of the U.S. Why?
    a.   They are geographically close to the U.S.
    b.   They joined with the U.S. in NAFTA to reduce trade barriers.
    c.   They are the only other countries that speak English.
    d.   all of the above
    e.   only a and b

4. Trade without the use of money is called
    a. barkering.
    b. barter.
    c. banter.
    d. simple exchange.
    e. complex exchange.

5. The exchange rate is
    a. the price of imports in terms of exports.
    b. the price of exports in terms of imports.
    c. the price of one currency in terms of another.
    d. the price in developing countries in terms of the price in industrial countries.
    e. the price in industrial countries in terms of the price in developing countries.

PRACTICE QUESTIONS AND PROBLEMS

Section 1: The Definition of Economics

1. _____ exists when less of something is available than people want at a zero price.

2. _____ have to be made because of scarcity.

3. If there is enough of a good available at a zero price to satisfy wants, the good is called a(n) _____ good.

4. A good that people will pay to have less of is called an economic _____.

5. List the three categories of resources and the payments associated with each.

    _____

    _____

    _____

6. _____ includes all natural resources, such as minerals, timber, and water, as well as the land itself.

7. _____ refers to the physical and intellectual services of people.

8. _____ is a manufactured or created product used solely to produce goods and services.

9. _____ capital refers to the money value of capital as represented by stocks and bonds.

10. _____ are forgone opportunities or forgone benefits.

11. The opportunity cost of an activity is the _____-valued alternative that must be forgone.

12. What is economics?

    _____

    _____

    _____

13. Joyce decides to buy a ticket to a classical music concert. The ticket costs $10. She spends 30 minutes driving to the ticket office, 60 minutes waiting in line, and 30 minutes eating a snack after buying the ticket. List her opportunity costs of getting the ticket.

    _____

14. Instead of studying economics right now, you could be watching TV, eating a snack, or talking to a friend on the telephone. What is your opportunity cost of studying economics right now?

    _____

Section 2: Specialization and Exchange

1. Exchange occurs because _____ (one person, everyone involved) believes the exchange can be beneficial.

2. It is in your best interest to specialize where your opportunity costs are _____ (highest, constant, lowest).

3. People specialize according to _____ advantage.

4. A nation has a comparative advantage in those activities in which it has _____ (the highest, constant, the lowest) opportunity costs.

5. Chris works at a part-time job that pays $15 per hour. He wants a new shirt to wear next Friday night. He can buy one at the mall for $30, or he can make one (using materials he already has) with five hours of labor.

    a. If Chris makes the shirt himself, how many hours will he spend on making the shirt?

        _____

    b. If Chris works at his job and uses the money to buy a shirt, how many hours of work does it take to get the money to buy the shirt? _____

    c. What do economists call the three hours Chris saved by working at his job and trading his money for a shirt, instead of making it himself? _____

6. The table below shows the number of shirts or ties that two tailors, Joe and Harry, can make in one day.

	Shirts	**Ties**
Joe	1	4
Harry	2	6

   a. Joe's opportunity cost of making one shirt is _____.

   b. Joe's opportunity cost of making one tie is _____.

   c. Harry's opportunity cost of making one shirt is _____.

   d. Harry's opportunity cost of making one tie is _____.

   e. Who has a comparative advantage in making shirts? _____

   f. Who has a comparative advantage in making ties? _____

   g. Who should specialize in making ties? _____

   h. Who should specialize in making shirts? _____

Section 3: Trade

1. Barter is trade without _____. International trade is sometimes based on barter, but usually involves _____.

2. The price at which currencies are exchanged is called the _____.

3. You are a U.S. tourist in London. Suppose the exchange rate between U.S. dollars and British pounds is $2 = 1 pound. You see a beautiful scarf in a shop window by Trafalgar Square that is priced at 20 pounds. What is the price of the scarf in U.S. dollars? _____

4. A Japanese tourist in the U.S. wants to buy a bottle of soda pop that costs $1. How many yen does it take to equal $1, based on the exchange rate in Table 3? _____.

THINKING ABOUT AND APPLYING ECONOMICS AND THE WORLD AROUND YOU

I.   Scarce Parking in Wichita?

The following is an excerpt from the author's local newspaper, *The Wichita Eagle*:

> It's become part of Wichita lore. Folks in these parts are nutty about parking.
>
> They want it free. They want it at the front door of wherever they're going. They refuse to look for a parking space anywhere for more than eight or 10 seconds. And they think the downtown Wichita parking situation is horrible.
>
> The fact is, there's plenty of parking in the city's core. About 20,000 people work downtown. There are almost 19,000 parking spaces. That nearly 1-to-1 ratio is better than other cities in the region such as Oklahoma City, and it's just as good as Topeka. And the average distance a person has to walk is about a block. That's better than similar-sized cities.

The editorial laments that people don't go downtown for activities because they think they'll have trouble parking and comments on a new report by the Metropolitan Area Planning Commission.

Relying on the information in the editorial, discuss whether parking spaces can be considered a scarce resource in downtown Wichita.

_____

_____

_____

II.   Resource and Income Flows

Complete the figure below.

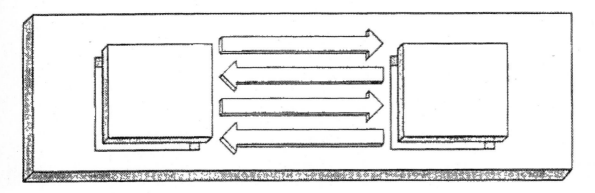

III. Opportunity Costs

Mr. Safi and Mr. Nohr are neighbors. Mr. Safi makes $200 an hour as a consultant, while Mr. Nohr makes $10 an hour as an aerobics instructor. The men are complaining that the grass on their lawns has grown so fast due to recent rainy weather that it is hard to keep their lawns looking nice. Mr. Nohr mows his lawn himself. Mr. Safi comments that he hires a neighbor's child to cut his grass "because it is too expensive for me to cut it myself." Explain Mr. Safi's comment.

_____

_____

_____

ANSWERS

QUICK-CHECK QUIZ

Section 1: The Definition of Economics

1. c;

2. d;

3. c;

4. a;

5. d;

6. c;

7. e;

8. a

If you missed any of these questions, you should go back and review Section 1 in Chapter 1.

Section 2: Specialization and Exchange

1. a;

2. d;

3. d;

4. c;

5. c;

6. a;

7. b;

8. e;

9. a

If you missed any of these questions, you should go back and review Section 2 in Chapter 1.

Section 3: Trade

1. b;

2. e;

3. e;

4. b;

5. c

If you missed any of these questions, you should go back and review Section 3 in Chapter 1.

PRACTICE QUESTIONS AND PROBLEMS

Section 1: The Definition of Economics

1. Scarcity

2. Choices

3. free

4. bad

5. land; rent
   labor; wages
   capital; interest

6. Land

7. Labor

8. Capital

9. Financial

10. Opportunity costs

11. highest

12. Economics is the study of how people choose to use their scarce resources to attempt to satisfy their unlimited wants.

13. $10 and 90 minutes. The 30 minutes for the snack isn't an opportunity cost of the ticket.

14. Whichever *one* of the alternatives you would actually do if you weren't studying economics.

Section 2: Specialization and Exchange

1. everyone involved

2. lowest

3. comparative

4. the lowest

5. a. five
    b. two
    c. gains from trade

6. a. 4 ties
    b. 1/4 shirt
    c. 3 ties (six ties divided by 2 shirts)
    d. 1/3 shirt
    e. Harry. (He has a lower opportunity cost–3 ties–than Joe–4 ties.)
    f. Joe. (He has a lower opportunity cost—1/4 shirt—than Harry—1/3 shirt.)
    g. Joe. (He has a comparative advantage in ties.)
    h. Harry. (He has a comparative advantage in shirts.)

Section 3: International Trade

1. money; money

2. exchange rate

3. $40 ($2 = 1 pound, so the price in dollars is 20 pounds times $2 per pound.)

4. 500 yen (Each yen is worth $.002, so a $1 bottle of soda pop costs $1 divided by .002 dollars per yen.)

THINKING ABOUT AND APPLYING ECONOMICS AND THE WORLD AROUND YOU

I.   Scarce Parking in Wichita?

     If there is not enough of an item to satisfy everyone that wants it at a zero price, then an item is scarce. If people want parking at the front door of wherever they are going and have to walk, on average about a block, parking is scarce.

II. Resource and Income Flows

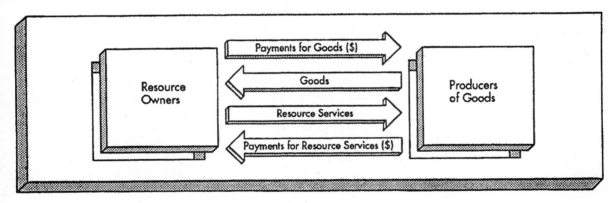

III. Opportunity Costs

     The opportunity cost for Mr. Safi to cut his grass is $200 an hour; that is what he would make in his next best use of time. It is better for him to spend his hour consulting and pay the neighbor's child to cut the grass—unless the neighbor's child charges $200 an hour!

CHAPTER 2

Markets and the Market Process

FUNDAMENTAL QUESTIONS

1. How are goods and services allocated?

   Since resources are scarce, we have to make decisions about how we will allocate the available resources; that is, decide which goods and services will be produced, and who will get what is produced. While there are many different methods that people can use, the market mechanism is one that is frequently used, primarily because it is usually (but not always) the allocation method with the highest **efficiency**.

2. How does a market work?

   A market is a mechanism for bringing together buyers and sellers so that they can exchange goods and services. The market process refers to the way buyers and sellers interact in making decisions that allocate our scarce resources.

3. What is demand?

   Demand is the quantity of a good or service that buyers are willing and able to buy at various prices. People often confuse demand with **quantity demanded**. Demand refers to a list of quantities and prices. Quantity demanded is the amount of a good or service that people are willing and able to buy at *one* specific price. It's correct to say, "If the price of a hair dryer is $15, the *quantity demanded* is 20." It is NOT correct to say, "The demand for hair dryers is 20."

   The **law of demand** states that as the price of a good decreases, people will buy more (and vice versa). That's why stores have sales to get rid of merchandise they can't sell; they know that if they lower the price, people will buy more.

   When economists construct a **demand schedule**, they hold everything except the price constant and determine the quantities consumers will buy at all the possible prices. However, things other than price affect how much of a good or service people are willing to buy. These other **determinants of demand** are income, tastes, prices of related goods and services, consumers' expectations, and the number of buyers. The exchange rate is also a determinant of demand. When one of these determinants of demand changes, the whole demand schedule changes.

   Economists take seriously the adage, "A picture is worth a thousand words," so they draw pictures of demand schedules. These pictures are called **demand curves**. Price is put on the vertical axis and quantity on the horizontal axis. Demand curves slope down from left to right. When one of the determinants of demand changes, the demand curve shifts to the left or to the right.

4. What is supply?

    Supply is the quantity of a good or service that sellers are willing and able to offer for sale at various prices. People often confuse supply with quantity supplied. Supply refers to a list of quantities and prices. Quantity supplied is the amount of a good or service that people are willing and able to offer for sale at *one* specific price. It's correct to say, "If the price of a hair dryer is $15, the *quantity supplied* is 10." It is NOT correct to say, "The supply for hair dryers is 10."

    The **law of supply** states that as the price of a good increases, people will offer more for sale (and vice versa). That's why people offer a seller a higher price for the product when there is a shortage; they know that the higher price will entice the producer to produce more.

    When economists construct a **supply schedule**, they hold everything except the price constant and determine the quantities producers will offer for sale at all the possible prices. However, things other than price affect how much of a good or service people are willing to supply. These other **determinants of supply** are prices of resources, technology and productivity, expectations of producers, the number of producers, and the prices of related goods or services. When one of these determinants of supply changes, the whole supply schedule changes.

    A picture of a supply schedule is called a **supply curve**. Again price is put on the vertical axis and quantity on the horizontal axis. Supply curves slope up from left to right. When one of the determinants of supply changes, the supply curve shifts to the left or to the right.

5. How is price determined by demand and supply?

    The price of a good or service changes until the equilibrium price is reached. **Equilibrium** is the point at which the quantity demanded equals the quantity supplied at a particular price. At prices above the equilibrium price, the quantity supplied is greater than the quantity demanded, so a **surplus** develops. Sellers must lower their prices to get rid of the goods and services that accumulate. At prices below the equilibrium price, the quantity demanded is greater than the quantity supplied, and a **shortage** develops. Sellers see the goods and services quickly disappear and realize they could have asked for a higher price. The price goes up until the shortage disappears.

6. What causes price to change?

    Price may change when demand or supply change. When demand or supply change, they will create either a surplus, leading to a lower price, or a shortage, leading to a higher price.

7. Why isn't the market used to allocate everything?

    While the market is usually an efficient system for making allocation decisions, under some conditions it doesn't work efficiently, or it doesn't make decisions the way people want the decisions made. For example, most people don't like the idea of deciding who gets a heart transplant by seeing which potential recipient is willing to pay the most—that doesn't seem like a fair method to most people.

    Several circumstances can cause problems in relying on markets to make the most efficient decisions. When there are **transactions costs** involved in buying a good or service in the market, firms may decide to provide the good or service themselves, rather than buying it from someone else. For example, if a business needs repairs on some of their equipment, a manager could search the phone book for another firm that fixes that type of equipment, negotiate a contract with that firm, and then make sure the work got done properly. Many times, it's much less expensive and more efficient to just hire a mechanic as a permanent employee.

Market failure can also make markets to work poorly. When no one owns a resource (like fish in the ocean), markets don't allocate resources efficiently (fish get caught faster than they can reproduce, leading to decreased catches in the future). Also, when there are **positive externalities** or **negative externalities**, markets don't take into account all the benefits or cost of producing and consuming a product.

KEY TERMS

efficiency	substitute goods	surplus
demand	complementary goods	shortage
law of demand	supply	transaction costs
demand schedule	law of supply	market failure
demand curve	determinants of supply	negative externality
market demand	supply schedule	positive externality
quantity demanded	supply curve	
determinants of demand	equilibrium	

QUICK-CHECK QUIZ

Section 1: Allocation Mechanisms

1. Economists use the term *allocation* to refer to
    a. deciding how to pay for goods and services.
    b. deciding who gets goods and services.
    c. choosing the best method of production.
    d. choosing who to elect in a democracy.
    e. deciding what to eat for dinner.

2. Which of the following is an example of a random allocation method?
    a. Winning a lottery
    b. The high bidder at an auction gets a valuable painting.
    c. The mayor of a city decides who will be hired.
    d. You decide to wear blue socks tomorrow.
    e. Students who arrive early for class get the best seats.

3. Which of the following is an example of a market allocation method?
    a. Winning a lottery
    b. The high bidder at an auction gets a valuable painting.
    c. The mayor of a city decides who will be hired.
    d. You decide to wear blue socks tomorrow.
    e. Students who arrive early for class get the best seats.

4. Which of the following is an example of a first come, first served allocation method?
    a. Winning a lottery
    b. The high bidder at an auction gets a valuable painting.
    c. The mayor of a city decides who will be hired.
    d. You decide to wear blue socks tomorrow.
    e. Students who arrive early for class get the best seats.

5. Which of the following is an example of a government allocation method?
   a. Winning a lottery
   b. The high bidder at an auction gets a valuable painting.
   c. The mayor of a city decides who will be hired.
   d. You decide to wear blue socks tomorrow.
   e. Students who arrive early for class get the best seats.

6. An efficient economic system is one in which resources are allocated so that
   a. everyone gets the same.
   b. only a few people get most of the output.
   c. no one can be made better off without making someone else worse off.
   d. the government gets a small share of the output.
   e. the government gets a large share of the output.

Section 2: How Markets Function

1. Markets exist
   a. at only one specific location.
   b. at a few specific locations.
   c. at about 100 locations.
   d. whenever buyers and sellers interact.
   e. wherever the government permits them to locate.

2. The market process allocates resources to
   a. the uses specified by the government.
   b. their highest valued uses.
   c. all people equally.
   d. only a few lucky people.
   e. the people who run the market.

Section 3: Demand

1. Which of the following would *not* cause a decrease in the demand for bananas?
   a. Reports surface that imported bananas are infected with a deadly virus.
   b. Consumers' incomes drop.
   c. The price of bananas rises.
   d. A deadly virus kills monkeys in zoos across the United States.
   e. Consumers expect the price of bananas to decrease in the future.

2. Which of the following is a determinant of demand?
   a. the number of sellers
   b. the exchange rate
   c. producers' expectations
   d. an increase in productivity
   e. a change in technology

3. Which of the following is not a determinant of demand?
   a. income
   b. tastes
   c. prices of resources
   d. prices of complements
   e. consumers' expectations

4. A decrease in quantity demanded could be caused by a(n)
    a. decrease in consumers' incomes.
    b. decrease in the price of a substitute good.
    c. increase in the price of a complementary good.
    d. decrease in the price of the good.
    e. increase in the price of the good.

5. A recent Wichita State University study analyzed the effects of anticipated 6,000-plus layoffs at Boeing, a major Wichita employer. As a result of the anticipated layoffs,
    a. the demand for goods and services in Wichita will increase.
    b. the demand for goods and services in Wichita will decrease.
    c. the demand for Boeing airplanes will decrease.
    d. the demand for goods and services in Wichita will shift to the right.
    e. Both a and d are correct.

6. The law of demand states that as the price of a good
    a. rises, the quantity demanded falls.
    b. rises, the quantity supplied falls.
    c. rises, the quantity demanded rises.
    d. rises, the quantity supplied rises.
    e. falls, the quantity demanded falls.

7. Which of the following would cause an increase in the demand for eggs?
    a. The price of eggs drops.
    b. The price of bacon rises.
    c. A government report indicates that eating eggs three times a week increases the chances of having a heart attack.
    d. A decrease in the cost of chicken feed makes eggs less costly to produce.
    e. None of the above would increase the demand for eggs.

8. If the price of barley, an ingredient in beer, increases,
    a. the demand for beer will increase.
    b. the demand for beer will not change.
    c. the demand for beer will decrease.
    d. the quantity of beer demanded will increase.
    e. Both a and d are correct.

9. A freeze in Peru causes the price of coffee to skyrocket. Which of the following will happen?
    a. The demand for coffee will increase, and the demand for tea will increase.
    b. The demand for coffee will increase, and the quantity demanded of tea will increase.
    c. The quantity demanded of coffee will increase, and the demand for tea will increase.
    d. The quantity demanded of coffee will increase, and the quantity demanded of tea will increase.
    e. The quantity demanded of coffee will decrease, and the demand for tea will increase.

Section 4: Supply

1. According to the law of supply, as the price of a good or service
    a. rises, the quantity supplied decreases.
    b. rises, the quantity supplied increases.
    c. rises, the quantity demanded increases.
    d. rises, the quantity demanded decreases.
    e. falls, the quantity supplied increases.

2.   Which of the following is *not* a determinant of supply?
    a.   prices of resources
    b.   technology and productivity
    c.   prices of complements
    d.   producers' expectations
    e.   the number of producers

3.   Japanese producers of a type of microchip offered such low prices that U.S. producers of the chip were driven out of business. As the number of producers decreased,
    a.   the market supply of microchips increased—that is, the supply curve shifted to the right.
    b.   the market supply of microchips increased—that is, the supply curve shifted to the left.
    c.   the market supply of microchips decreased—that is, the supply curve shifted to the right.
    d.   the market supply of microchips decreased—that is, the supply curve shifted to the left.
    e.   there was no change in the supply of microchips. (This event is represented by a movement from one point to another on the same supply curve.)

4.   Electronics firms can produce more than one type of good. Suppose that electronics firms are producing both military radios and microchips. A war breaks out, and the price of military radios skyrockets. The electronics firms throw more resources into making military radios and fewer resources into making microchips. Which of the statements below is true?
    a.   The supply of microchips has decreased, and the quantity supplied of military radios has increased.
    b.   The supply of microchips has decreased, and the supply of military radios has increased.
    c.   The quantity supplied of microchips has decreased, and the supply of military radios has decreased.
    d.   The quantity supplied of microchips has decreased, and the quantity supplied of military radios has decreased.
    e.   There has been no change in the supply of microchips or in the supply of military radios.

5.   Suppose that a change in technology makes car phones cheaper to produce. Which of the following will happen?
    a.   The supply curve will shift to the left.
    b.   The supply curve will shift to the right.
    c.   The supply of car phones will increase.
    d.   The supply of car phones will decrease.
    e.   Both b and c are correct.

6.   Which of the following is a determinant of supply?
    a.   income
    b.   tastes
    c.   number of buyers
    d.   consumers' expectations
    e.   the prices of resources

7.   Suppose that automakers expect car prices to be lower in the future. What will happen now?
    a.   Supply will increase.
    b.   Supply will decrease.
    c.   Supply will not change.
    d.   Demand will increase.
    e.   Demand will decrease.

8. Which of the following would *not* cause an increase in the supply of milk?
    a. an increase in the number of dairy farmers
    b. a change in technology that reduces the cost of milking cows
    c. a decrease in the price of cheese
    d. a decrease in the price of milk
    e. a decrease in the price of cow feed

9. Which of the following would *not* change the supply of beef?
    a. The U.S. government decides to give a subsidy to beef producers.
    b. An epidemic of cow flu renders many cattle unfit for slaughter.
    c. The price of fish increases.
    d. A new hormone makes cows fatter, and they require less feed.
    e. Beef producers expect lower beef prices next year.

Section 5: Equilibrium: Putting Demand & Supply Together - part I

1. If demand increases and supply does not change,
    a. equilibrium price and quantity increase.
    b. equilibrium p rice and quantity decrease.
    c. equilibrium price increases and equilibrium quantity decreases.
    d. equilibrium price decreases and equilibrium quantity increases.
    e. the demand curve shifts to the left.

2. If supply decreases and demand does not change,
    a. equilibrium price and quantity increase.
    b. equilibrium price and quantity decrease.
    c. equilibrium price increases and equilibrium quantity decreases.
    d. equilibrium price decreases and equilibrium quantity increases.
    e. the demand curve shifts to the right.

3. Prices above the equilibrium price cause a(n)
    a. shortage to develop and drive prices up.
    b. shortage to develop and drive prices down
    c. surplus to develop and drive prices up.
    d. surplus to develop and drive prices down.
    e. increase in supply.

4. Prices below the equilibrium price cause a(n)
    a. shortage to develop and drive prices up.
    b. shortage to develop and drive prices down,
    c. surplus to develop and drive prices up.
    d. surplus to develop and drive prices down.
    e. increase in demand.

5. Utility regulators in some states are considering forcing operators of coal-fired generators to be responsible for cleaning up air and water pollution resulting from the generators. Utilities in these states currently do not pay the costs of cleanup. If this law goes into effect,
    a. demand for electricity will increase, and price and quantity will increase.
    b. demand for electricity will decrease, and price and quantity will decrease.
    c. the supply of electricity will decrease, and price and quantity will decrease.
    d. the supply of electricity will increase, price will decrease, and quantity will decrease.
    e. the supply of electricity will decrease, price will increase, and quantity will decrease.

6. Medical research from South Africa indicates that vitamin A may be useful in treating measles. If the research can be substantiated, the
    a. supply of vitamin A will increase, causing equilibrium price and quantity to increase.
    b. supply of vitamin A will increase, causing equilibrium price to fall and quantity to increase.
    c. demand for vitamin A will increase, causing equilibrium price and quantity to increase.
    d. demand for vitamin A will increase, causing equilibrium price to rise and quantity to fall.
    e. supply of vitamin A will increase, causing equilibrium price to rise and quantity to fall.

7. Since 1900, changes in technology have greatly reduced the costs of growing wheat. The population also has increased. If you know that the changes in technology had a greater effect than the increase in population, then since 1900 the
    a. price of wheat has increased and quantity of wheat has decreased.
    b. price and quantity of wheat have increased.
    c. price and quantity of wheat have decreased.
    d. price of wheat has decreased and the quantity of wheat has increased.
    e. quantity of wheat has increased, and you haven't got the faintest idea what happened to the price.

Section 5: Equilibrium: Putting Demand & Supply Together - part II

Use the following table to answer questions 8 through 11.

Price	Quantity Demanded	Quantity Supplied
$0	24	0
1	20	2
2	16	4
3	12	6
4	8	8
5	4	10
6	0	12

8. The equilibrium price is
    a. $1.
    b. $2.
    c. $3.
    d. $4.
    e. $5.

9. The equilibrium quantity is
    a. 2.
    b. 4.
    c. 6.
    d. 8.
    e. 10.

10. If the price is $2, a _____ of _____ units will develop, causing the price to _____.
    a. shortage; 12; increase
    b. shortage; 12; decrease
    c. surplus; 12; increase
    d. surplus; 12; decrease
    e. surplus; 19; decrease

11.   If the price is $5, a _____ of _____ units will develop, causing the price to
      _____.
      a.   shortage; 6; increase
      b.   shortage; 6; decrease
      c.   surplus; 6; increase
      d.   surplus; 6; decrease
      e.   shortage; 12; increase

Section 5: Equilibrium: Putting Demand & Supply Together - part III

Use the following graph to answer questions 12 through 15.

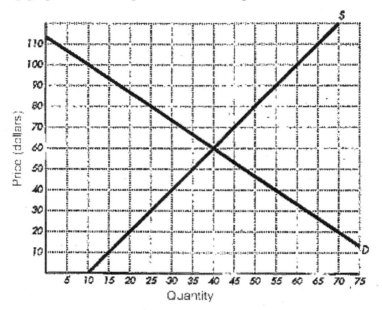

12.   The equilibrium price is
      a. $20.
      b. $40.
      c. $60.
      d. $80.
      e. $100.

13.   The equilibrium quantity is
      a.   25.
      b.   30.
      c.   35.
      d.   40.
      e.   45.

14.   A price of $80 would cause a _____ of _____ units to develop, driving the price
      _____.
      a.   shortage; 6; up
      b.   shortage; 25; up
      c.   surplus; 6; down
      d.   surplus; 25; down
      e.   surplus; 25; up

15. A price of $20 would result in a _____ of _____ units, driving the price
    _____.
    a. shortage; 10; up
    b. shortage; 50; up
    c. surplus; 10; down
    d. surplus; 50; down
    e. shortage; 50; down

16. An increase in demand
    a. shifts the demand curve to the left.
    b. causes an increase in equilibrium price.
    c. causes a decrease in equilibrium price.
    d. causes a decrease in equilibrium quantity.
    e. does not affect equilibrium quantity.

17. When demand decreases,
    a. price and quantity increase.
    b. price and quantity decrease.
    c. price increases and quantity decreases.
    d. price decreases and quantity increases.
    e. supply decreases.

18. When supply decreases,
    a. the supply curve shifts to the right.
    b. equilibrium price and equilibrium quantity both increase.
    c. equilibrium price and equilibrium quantity both decrease.
    d. equilibrium price decreases and equilibrium quantity increases.
    e. equilibrium price increases and equilibrium quantity decreases.

Section 6: Alternatives to Market Allocation

1. The costs involved in making an exchange are called
    a. transfer costs.
    b. transaction costs.
    c. inadvertant costs.
    d. market costs.
    e. exchange costs.

2. Market failure means that the market is unable to
    a. determine demand.
    b. determine supply.
    c. maintain an equilibrium price consistently.
    d. allocate scarce goods, services, or resources.
    e. avoid a shortage or surplus.

3. A *positive externality* occurs when
    a. buyers of a good receive all the benefits of a transaction.
    b. someone not directly involved in a transaction receives benefits from the transaction.
    c. sellers of a good pay all the costs involved in a transaction.
    d. someone not directly involved in a transaction pays some of the costs involved in the
       transaction.
    e. the government receives benefits from a transaction.

4. A *negative externality* occurs when
    a. buyers of a good receive all the benefits of a transaction.
    b. someone not directly involved in a transaction receives benefits from the transaction.
    c. sellers of a good pay all the costs involved in a transaction.
    d. someone not directly involved in a transaction pays some of the costs involved in the transaction.
    e. the government receives benefits from a transaction.

PRACTICE QUESTIONS AND PROBLEMS

Section 1: Allocation Mechanisms

1. _____ refers to choosing how to distribute scarce goods and services.

2. Students at Big Football U. can park on campus without charge, but there aren't enough parking spaces for all students. What kind of allocation mechanism does Big Football U. use to allocate parking spaces? _____

3. Anyone who is willing and able to pay for it can buy stock in General Motors. What kind of allocation mechanism is this? _____

4. The _____ is usually the most efficient method of allocation, because it creates _____ that lead to higher living standards.

5. An efficient allocation of resources is one where _____ can be made better off without harming _____.

6. What factor can make the market system fail to work efficiently?_____ , or when the costs or benefits of a transaction are borne by people not _____ in the tran

Section 2: How Markets Function

1. A market exists when _____ and _____ interact to buy and sell a specific product.

2. The _____ is the term economists use to refer to the _____ and _____ of a good.

3. The market process allocates resources to their _____ uses.

Section 3: Demand

1. _____ refers to the quantities of a well-defined commodity that consumers are willing and able to buy at every possible price during a given time period, *ceteris paribus*.

2. According to the law of demand, if you _____ your price, people will buy more, *ceteris paribus*.

3. List six determinants of demand.

    _____

    _____

    _____

    _____

    _____

    _____

4. Demand curves slope down because of the __________ relationship between price and __________.

5. Suppose that an increase in the price of Nohr Cola causes you to switch to Sooby Cola. You therefore buy less Nohr Cola. Sooby Cola is a(n) __________ for Nohr Cola.

6. The higher people's __________ the more goods they can purchase at any price.

7. A(n) __________ is a graph of a demand schedule.

8. __________ goods can be used in place of each other; these goods would not be consumed at the same time.

9. Goods that are used together are called __________ goods.

10. Dot, Diane, and Mardi are college students who share an apartment. Dot loves strawberries and buys them whenever they are available. Diane is a fair-weather strawberry eater; she only buys them if she thinks she is getting a good price. Mardi eats strawberries for their vitamin C content but isn't crazy about them. The following table shows the individual demand schedules for Dot, Diane, and Mardi. Suppose that these three are the only consumers in the local market for strawberries. Add their individual demands to get the market demand schedule.

	Quantity			
Price per Quart	**Dot**	**Diane**	**Mardi**	**Market**
$0	6.00	4.00	2.00	______
1	5.00	3.50	1.50	______
2	4.00	3.00	1.00	______
3	3.25	2.00	0.75	______
4	2.00	1.50	0.50	______
5	1.25	0.50	0.25	______
6	0	0	0	______

Plot the market demand for strawberries on the following graph

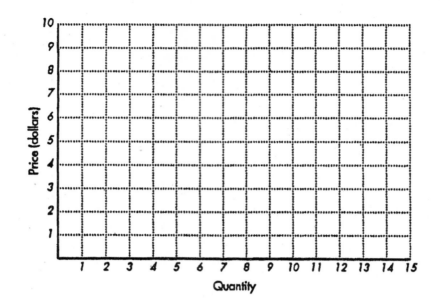

11. Suppose that the price of strawberries increases from $2 to $3 per quart. The increase in price would cause a decrease in the _____ (demand, quantity demanded) of strawberries. Show the effect of this change in the price of strawberries on the preceding graph.

12. Suppose that Dot reads in the paper that eating strawberries increases the health of females. As a group, Dot and her friends decide to buy twice as many strawberries as they did before at any price. Plot the new market demand curve on the preceding graph, and label it D_2. This change in tastes has caused a(n) _____ (increase, decrease) in _____ (demand, quantity demanded).

13. An increase in income _____ (increases, decreases) the _____ (demand, quantity demanded) for haircuts.

14. Many Americans have decreased their consumption of beef and switched to chicken in the belief that eating chicken instead of beef lowers cholesterol. This change in tastes has _____ (increased, decreased) the _____ (demand, quantity demanded) for beef and _____ (increased, decreased) the _____ (demand, quantity demanded) for chicken.

15. In the following graph, the price of good X increased, causing the demand for good Y to change from D_1 to D_2. The demand for good Y _____ (increased, decreased). X and Y are _____ (substitutes, complements).

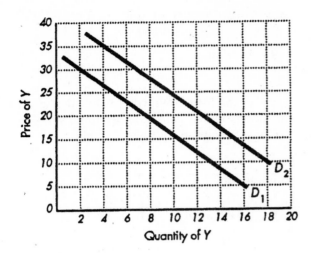

16. Mr. and Mrs. Gertsen are retiring next year and expect that their future income will be less than it is now. If D_1 is their current demand for bacon, show the effect of this expectation on the following graph. Label your new curve D_2. Demand for bacon has _____ (increased, decreased).

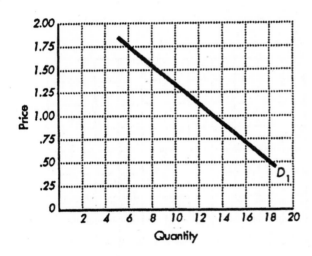

17. A crisis in the Middle East causes people to expect the price of gasoline to increase in the future. The demand for gasoline today will _____ (increase, not change, decrease).

18. If the price of Pepsi increases, the demand for Coke and other substitutes will _____ .

19. People in Mexico buy software produced in the U.S. If the Mexican peso increased in value relative to the dollar, U.S. software in Mexico would _____ (increase, decrease) in price. Mexicans would then buy _____ (more, less) U.S. software, which would _____ (increase, decrease) the demand for U.S. software.

Section 4: Supply

1. _____ is the amount of a good or service that producers are willing and able to offer for sale at each possible price during a period of time, *ceteris paribus*.

2. According to the law of supply, as price _____ , quantity supplied decreases.

3. A table or list of the prices and corresponding quantity supplied of a well-defined good or service is called a(n) _____ .

4. A(n) _____ is a graph of a supply schedule.

5. Market supply curves have _____ slopes.

6. There are only two strawberry producers in the little town where Dot, Diane, and Mardi live. Their individual supply schedules are shown below. Add the individual supplies to get market supply, and then plot market supply (curve S_1) on the following graph.

	Quantity Supplied		
Price per Quart	Farmer Dave	Farmer Ruth	Market
$0	2	2	_____
1	3	3	_____
2	4	4	_____
3	5	5	_____
4	6	6	_____
5	7	7	_____
6	8	8	_____

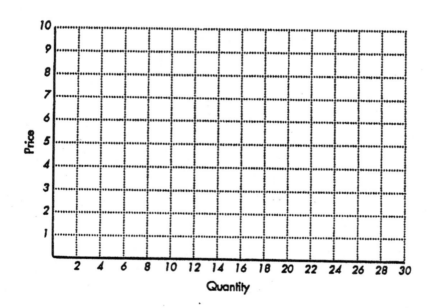

7. List the five determinants of supply.

_____

_____

_____

_____

_____

8. Suppose that a crisis in the Middle East cuts off the supply of oil from Saudi Arabia. If S_1 is the original market supply of oil, draw another supply curve, S_2, on the graph to show the effect of Saudi Arabia's departure from the market. The _____ (quantity supplied, supply) has _____ (increased, decreased).

9. If the price of tomato sauce increases, the _____ (supply, quantity supplied) of pizza will _____ (increase, decrease).

10. _____ is the quantity of output produced per unit of resource.

11. A new process for producing microchips is discovered that will decrease the cost of production by ten percent. The supply of microchips will _____ (increase, decrease, not change), which means the supply curve will _____ (shift to the right, shift to the left, not change).

12. A paper manufacturer can produce notebook paper or wedding invitations. If the price of wedding invitations skyrockets, we can expect the supply of _____ (notebook paper, wedding invitations) to _____ (increase, decrease).

13. A real-estate developer who specializes in two-bedroom homes believes that the incomes of young couples will decline in the future. We can expect the supply of this realtor's two-bedroom homes to _____ (increase, decrease).

14. Changes in quantity supplied are caused by changes in the _____ of the good.

15. A U.S. construction company buys lumber to build houses from a supplier in Canada. If the value of the Canadian dollar decreases relative to the U.S. dollar, it will cost the U.S. company _____ (more, less) U.S. dollars to buy a truckload of lumber. This will _____ (increase, decrease) the cost of building a house, and _____ (increase, decrease) the supply of new houses.

Section 5: Equilibrium: Putting Demand and Supply Together

1. The point at which the quantity demanded equals the quantity supplied at a particular price is known as the point of _____.

2. Whenever the price is greater than the equilibrium price, a(n) _____ arises.

3. A(n) _____ arises when the quantity demanded is greater than the quantity supplied at a particular price.

4. Shortages lead to _____ (increases, decreases) in price and quantity supplied and _____ (increases, decreases) in quantity demanded.

5. Surpluses lead to _____ (increases, decreases) in price and quantity supplied and _____ (increases, decreases) in quantity demanded.

6. The only goods that are not scarce are _____ goods.

7. As long as supply does not change, a change in equilibrium price and quantity is in the _____ (same, opposite) direction as a change in demand.

8. Balloon manufacturers are nervous about a children's movement that may affect their product. The children are lobbying state legislatures to ban launchings of more than ten balloons at a time, citing the danger that balloons can pose to wildlife. If the children are successful, we can expect the _____ (demand for, supply of) balloons to _____ (increase, decrease), causing the equilibrium price to _____ and the equilibrium quantity to _____ .

9. If design changes in the construction of milk cartons cause the cost of production to decrease, we can expect the _____ (demand for, supply of) cartons to _____ (increase, decrease), the equilibrium price to _____ , and the equilibrium quantity to _____ .

10. A decrease in supply leads to a(n) _____ in price and a(n) _____ in quantity.

11. Remember Dot, Diane, and Mardi and the strawberry farmers Dave and Ruth? The local market for strawberries (before Dot read about the effects of strawberries on women's health) is reproduced in the following graph. The original demand is D_1 and original supply S. The equilibrium price is _____ , and the equilibrium quantity is _____ . After Dot read the article on strawberries and health, the market demand curve shifted to D_2. The new equilibrium price is _____ , and the new equilibrium quantity is _____ . There was also a change in _____ (supply, quantity supplied).

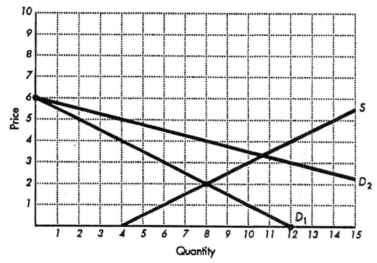

12. _____occurs when the quantity demanded and the quantity supplied are not equal.

13. The following graph shows the market for corn. The equilibrium price is _____, and the equilibrium quantity is _____.

If the price of corn is $14, the quantity demanded will be _____, and the quantity supplied will be_____. A(n) _____ of _____units will develop, causing the price and quantity supplied to _____, and the quantity demanded to_____.

If the price is $4, the quantity demanded will be _____, and the quantity supplied will be _____. A(n) _____of _____units will develop, causing the price and quantity supplied to _____and the quantity demanded to _____.

Section 6: Alternatives to Market Allocation

1. If your car produces so much pollution that it causes other people to have to buy medicines so they can breathe, your car is creating a _____(positive, negative) externality.

2. If you are a parent and get your child immunized against certain diseases, other children are also less likely to get sick. This is an example of a _____(positive, negative) externality.

3. When there are positive externalities, the market system will produce _____(too much, too little) of a product because the buyers and sellers are not receiving or paying all the _____(benefits, costs) of producing and consuming the product.

4. When there are negative externalities, the market system will produce _____(too much, too little) of a product because the buyers and sellers are not receiving or paying all the _____(benefits, costs) of producing and consuming the product.

5. No one owns the whales in the ocean. In the past, governments did not put any restrictions on catching whales, so whalers killed almost all of some species of whales, making it much more expensive to catch whales in the future. This inefficient outcome is an example of market _____ caused by a lack of _____.

6.   A business manager wants an advertising brochure produced for a new product. The manager can have the brochure produced by the company graphic arts department, or an outside artist can be used. If an outside artist is used, the manager will have to spend resources finding an artist, writing a contract, and coordinating the production of the brochure. These extra costs involved in buying the brochure's production in the market, rather than using the company graphic arts department, are called _____.

QUESTIONS: THINKING ABOUT AND APPLYING MARKETS AND THE MARKET PROCESS - QUESTIONS

I.   Changes in Demand

Indicate whether there is an increase or decrease in demand, an increase or decrease in quantity demanded, or no effect on demand. (The market of interest is in italic.)

1.   *TV sets.* The number of producers of TV sets decreases.

2.   *Radios.* The price of radios goes up.

3.   *Cassette recorders.* The price of cassette recorders falls.

4.   *Coffee.* The price of tea falls.

II.   Changes in Supply

Indicate whether the supply curve would shift to the left or right in the following situations. If there is no effect, say so.

		Left	Right	No Effect
1.	The number of producers of the product decreases.			
2.	Consumers expect higher prices in the future.			
3.	The price of the product goes up.			
4.	The cost of an input decreases.			
5.	Consumers' incomes fall.			
6.	A change in technology reduces the costs ofproducing the product.			
7.	A tariff is placed on the product.			
8.	The price of a substitute in production increases.			
9.	A tax on the product is increased.			
10.	The price of the product falls.			

III. Distinguishing Changes in Demand from Changes in Supply

It is important that you be able to distinguish between factors that affect demand and factors that affect supply. Place a D next to items that are determinants of demand and an S next to items that affect supply.

____1. producers' expectations
____2. income
____3. exhange rates
____4. changes in technology
____5. prices of substitutes in production
____6. prices of related goods
____7. number of sellers
____8. tastes
____9. prices of complements
____10. consumers' expectations
____11. number of buyers
____12. changes in productivity
____13. prices of resources
____14. prices of substitutes in consumption

IV. The Market for Battery-Operated Dancing Flowers

For each event below, indicate whether it affects the demand or supply of battery-operated dancing flowers and the direction (increase or decrease) of the change. Also indicate what will happen to equilibrium price and quantity. Remember, the determinants of demand are income, tastes, prices of related goods or services, consumers' expectations, number of buyers, and exchange rates. The determinants of supply are prices of resources, changes in technology or productivity, producers' expectations, number of producers, and prices of related goods or services (goods that are substitutes in production).

1. There is a change in tastes toward battery-operated dancing gorillas.

2. The price of plastic falls.

3. A technological breakthrough makes it cheaper to produce plastic flowers.

4. Consumers' incomes rise.

5. The price of battery-operated dancing gorillas rises.

6. The price of plastic for making flowers skyrockets.

7. A fire destroys a major production facility for dancing flowers.

8. Consumers expect lower prices for dancing flowers in the future.

	Demand	Supply	Price	Quantity
1.				
2.				
3.				
4.				
5.				
6.				
7.				
8.				

V. Drinking and Cancer

The Wichita Eagle reported the results of a recent study that suggest that the anticancer benefit of eating lots of fruits and vegetables is lost if you wash them down with more than two drinks of alcohol.

If people believe this study, you would expect the _____ (demand, supply) for alcoholic drinks will _____ (increase, not change, decrease). The equilibrium price will _____ (increase, not change, decrease), and the equilibrium quantity will _____ (increase, not change, decrease).

Assume the market for alcoholic drinks was in equilibrium before the study, as shown. Illustrate the effects of the research linking the loss of anticancer benefits with alcohol. Be sure your graph matches your answers above.

ANSWERS

QUICK-CHECK QUIZ

Section 1: Allocation Mechanisms

1. b;

2. a;

3. b;

4. e;

5. c;

6. c

If you missed any of these questions, you should go back and review Section 1 in Chapter 2.

Section 2: How Markets Function

1. d

2. b

If you missed any of these questions, you should go back and review Section 2 in Chapter 2

Section 3: Demand

1. c (A change in the price of a good causes movement along the curve-a change in quantity demanded-not a change in demand.);

2. b;

3. c;

4. e (Items a, b, and c are determinants of demand and cause the demand curve to shift. Item d causes an *increase* in quantity demanded.);

5. b;

6. a;

7. e (Item a causes an increase in quantity demanded. Items b and c cause decreases in demand. Item d affects the *supply* of eggs.);

8. b;

9. e (The demand for coffee tells us the quantity demanded when the price changes, so it does not shift when price changes: you move from one price to another on the same curve. Coffee and tea are substitutes in consumption. When the price of coffee rises, people buy less coffee and substitute tea. They buy more tea at every price, so the demand for tea increases.)

If you missed any of these questions, you should go back and review Section 3 in Chapter 2.

Section 4: Supply

1. b;

2. c;

3. d;

4. a (The supply of military radios tells us the quantity of military radios supplied when the price of radios changes. Supply doesn't change when the price changes: you simply move from one price to another on the same curve. Because microchips and military radios are substitutes in production, when the price of military radios increases, the supply of microchips decreases.);

5. e;

6. e;

7. a;

8. d (A change in the price of a good causes a change in quantity supplied, not a change in supply. Cheese and milk are substitutes in production, so if the price of cheese decreases, the supply of milk increases.);

9. c

If you missed any of these questions, you should go back and review Section 4 in Chapter 2.

Section 5: Equilibrium: Putting Demand and Supply Together

1. a;

2. c;

3. d;

4. a;

5. e;

6. c;

7. d (Item e would be correct if you did not know that the supply change was greater than the demand change.);

8. d;

9. d;

10. a;

11. d;

12. c;

13. d;

14. d;

15. b;

16. b;

17. b;

18. e

If you missed any of these questions, you should go back and review Section 5 in Chapter 2.

Section 6: Alternatives to Market Allocation

1. a;

2. d;

3. b;

4. d

PRACTICE QUESTIONS AND PROBLEMS

Section 1: Allocation Mechanisms

1. Allocation

2. first come, first served

3. market

4. market system; incentives

5. no one; someone else

6. imperfect information; involved

Section 2: How Markets Function

1. buyers; sellers

2. market process; buying; selling

3. highest valued

Section 3: Demand

1. Demand

2. lower

3. income;
   tastes;
   prices of related goods or services;
   consumers' expectations;
   number of buyers;
   the exchange rate

4. inverse; quantity

5. substitute good

6. income

7. demand curve

8. Substitute

9. complementary

10. $0 - 12;
    1 - 10;
    2 - 8;
    3 - 6;
    4 - 4;
    5 - 2;
    6 - 0

11. quantity demanded

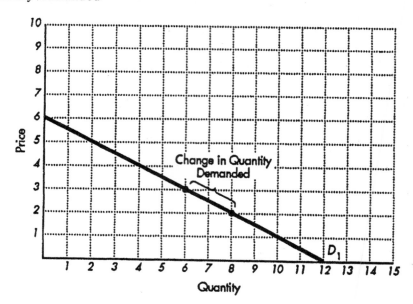

12. increase; demand

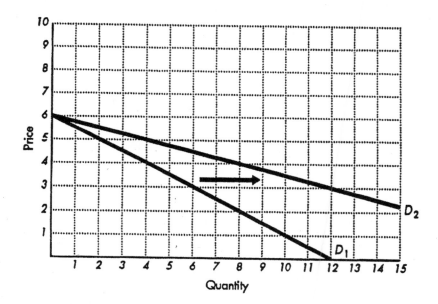

13. increases; demand

14. decreased; demand; increased; demand

15. increased; substitutes

16. decreased

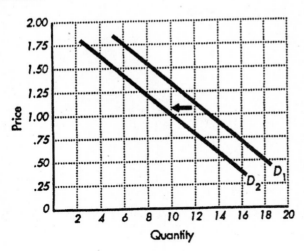

17. increase

18. increase

19. decrease; more; increase

Section 4: Supply

1. Supply

2. decreases

3. supply schedule

4. supply curve

5. positive

6. $0 - 4;
    1 - 6;
    2 - 8;
    3 - 10;
    4 - 12;
    5 - 14;
    6 - 16

7. prices of resources;
    technology and productivity;
    expectations of producers;
    number of producers;
    prices of related goods or services

8. supply; decreased

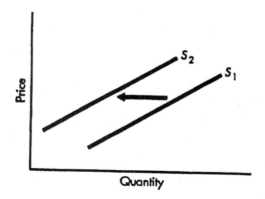

9. supply; decrease

10. Productivity

11. increase; shift to the right

12. notebook paper; decrease

13. increase (The real-estate developer will try to offer as many homes for sale *now*, before incomes drop and the prices of houses drop.)

14. price

15. less; decrease; increase

Section 5: Equilibrium: Putting Demand and Supply Together

1. equilibrium

2. surplus

3. shortage

4. increases; decreases

5. decreases; increases

6. free

7. same

8. demand for; decrease; decrease; decrease

9. supply of; increase; decrease; increase

10. increase; decrease

13. $2; 8; 3 1/3; 10 2/3 (The last two values are eyeballed from the graph.); quantity supplied

12. Disequilibrium

13. $10; 12; 8; 16; surplus; 8; decrease; increase; 18; 6; shortage; 12; increase; decrease

Section 6: Alternatives to Market Allocation

1. negative

2. positive

3. too little; benefits

4. too much; costs

5. failure; private property

6. transaction costs

THINKING ABOUT AND APPLYING MARKETS AND THE MARKET PROCESS

I. Changes in Demand

1. No effect on demand. The decrease in supply causes the price to increase, which ultimately will decrease the quantity demanded.

2. No effect on demand. This movement along the demand curve decreases the quantity demanded.

3. No effect on demand. This movement along the demand curve increases the quantity demanded.

4. The demand for coffee decreases (because some people will switch to tea). The quantity demanded decreases.

II. Changes in Supply

1. Left

2. No effect (Consumers' expectations affect demand.)

3. No effect (This is a movement along the supply curve.)

4. Right

5. No effect (This affects demand.)

6. Right

7. Left (A tariff increases producers' costs.)

8. Left (Producers move out of this product and produce the substitute instead.)

9. Left (Taxes increase producers' costs.)

10. No effect (This is a movement along the curve.)

III. Distinguishing Changes in Demand from Changes in Supply

1. S

2. D

3. D

4. S

5. S

6. D, S

7. S

8. D

9. D

10.D

11.D

12. S

13. S

14. D

IV. The Market for Battery-Operated Dancing Flowers

	Demand	Supply	Price	Quantity
1.	decrease	no change	decrease	decrease
2.	no change	increase	decrease	increase
3.	no change	increase	decrease	increase
4.	increase	no change	increase	increase
5.	increase	no change	increase	increase
6.	no change	decrease	increase	decrease
7.	no change	decrease	increase	decrease
8.	decrease	no change	decrease	decrease

V. Drinking and Cancer

demand; decrease; decrease; decrease

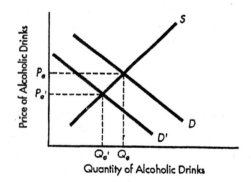

CHAPTER 3

Applications of Demand and Supply

FUNDAMENTAL QUESTIONS

1. In a market system, who determines what is produced?

   In free markets (where there is no government interference), it is the consumers that fundamentally determine what is produced, because businesses respond to consumers' demand for products. When consumers change their preferences, businesses react to those changes by changing what they produce. For example, when many consumers bought DVD players, the demand for movies on DVDs increased and the demand for movies on videotape decreased. Movie studios put more of their movies, even old movies, onto DVDs, and rental outfits started stocking more DVDs and fewer videotapes.

2. Why do different people earn different incomes and why do different jobs pay different wages?

   Different jobs require different sets of skills, knowledge, and abilities, as well as different risks of injury, resulting in many different labor markets. In each labor market, the demand and supply of a specific type of labor determine the equilibrium wage rate. Depending on the demand and supply conditions in different labor markets, wages are very likely to be different. Economists refer to these wage differences due to different risks or job characteristics as **compensating wage differentials.**

3. When the government intervenes in the market by providing a subsidy, what is the result?

   A **subsidy** provided by the government reduces the price consumers actually have to pay for the subsidized good or service. The subsidy increases the demand for the good or service, causing an increase in the market price and the quantity produced and sold.

4. When the government intervenes in the market by setting a price floor or ceiling, what is the result?

   A **price ceiling** occurs when a price is not permitted to rise above a specified amount. If this maximum price is below the equilibrium price, the quantity demanded by consumers at that price will exceed the amount that producers are willing to supply, and a shortage develops. Since the price method cannot be used to allocate the good or service, other methods must be used. A **price floor** occurs when a price is not permitted to fall below a specified amount. If this minimum price is above the equilibrium price, the quantity demanded by consumers at that price will fall short of the amount that producers are willing to supply, and a surplus develops.

5. When the government intervenes in the market with a tariff, what is the result?

   A **tariff** is a tax the government places on products imported from another country. The tax raises the cost of importing the product, reducing the supply of the imported product. Because of the supply reduction, the quantity imported goes down and the price goes up.

KEY TERMS

compensating wage differential   price ceiling   price floor

subsidy   tariff

QUICK-CHECK QUIZ

Section 1: The Market for Fast Foods

1. In the 1980s, people wanted fast food but didn't want to go get it. The _____ for in-restaurant meals _____, causing the price of in-restaurant meals to _____ and the quantity of in-restaurant meals to _____.
    a. demand; increased; increase; increase
    b. supply; increased; increase; increase
    c. demand; decreased; decrease; decrease
    d. supply; decreased; decrease; decrease
    e. supply; decreased; increase; decrease

2. When consumers indicated a preference for meals delivered to their homes, the _____ for delivered food _____, causing the price of delivered food to _____ and the quantity of delivered food to _____.
    a. demand; increased; increase; increase
    b. supply; increased; increase; increase
    c. demand; decreased; decrease; decrease
    d. supply; decreased; decrease; decrease
    e. supply; decreased; increase; decrease

3. A change in tastes away from a good or service causes a(n) _____ in _____.
    a. increase; demand
    b. decrease; demand
    c. increase; supply
    d. decrease; supply
    e. increase; quantity supplied

4. A decrease in demand results in a(n) _____ in quantity demanded at the original price. A _____ develops, causing the equilibrium price to _____.
    a. increase; shortage; increase
    b. increase; surplus; decrease
    c. decrease; shortage; increase
    d. decrease; surplus; decrease
    e. decrease; surplus; increase

5. An increase in demand results in a(n) _____ in quantity demanded at the original price. A _____ develops, causing the equilibrium price to _____.
    a. increase; shortage; increase
    b. increase; surplus; decrease
    c. decrease; shortage; increase
    d. decrease; surplus; decrease
    e. decrease; surplus; increase

6.   The change in tastes away from in-restaurant meals initially resulted in a(n)
     a.   decrease in the supply of in-restaurant meals.
     b.   increase in the supply of in-restaurant meals.
     c.   increase in the quantity supplied of in-restaurant meals.
     d.   decrease in the quantity supplied of in-restaurant meals.
     e.   increase in the supply of delivered foods.

Section 2: The Labor Market

1.   Wage differentials that make up for higher-risk or poor working conditions among different jobs are called
     a.   human capital.
     b.   disparate treatment.
     c.   labor force participation differentials.
     d.   compensating wage differentials.
     e.   affirmative action plans.

2.   Which of the following statements is false?
     a.   The demand for labor slopes down.
     b.   The supply of labor slopes up.
     c.   Younger workers earn higher wages than older workers.
     d.   Riskier jobs pay more than less risky jobs.
     e.   Males earn more than females.

3.   Which statement is true?
     a.   The supply for workers in a less risky occupation is less than the supply for workers in a risky occupation.
     b.   The supply for workers in a less risky occupation is greater than the supply for workers in a risky occupation.
     c.   Firms will employ more people or hire people to work more hours as the wage rate increases.
     d.   Equilibrium compensating wage differentials attract more workers from the less risky occupations to the risky ones.
     e.   The lower the hourly wage, the more hours that people are willing and able to work.

Section 3: Market Intervention: Medical Care, Rent Controls, and Agricultural Price Supports

1.   Which of the following caused the demand for health care to increase in recent years?
     a.   The percentage of elderly in the population is greater than before.
     b.   The cost of medical care has increased.
     c.   Government programs enable many people to get medical care without having to pay for it.
     d.   All of the above caused the demand for health care to increase in recent years.
     e.   Only a and c are reasons for the increase in the demand for health care in recent years.

2.   A grant of money given to help produce or purchase a specific good or service is called a
     a.   tariff.
     b.   subsidy.
     c.   price ceiling.
     d.   price floor.
     e.   compensating differential.

3. A price ceiling
   a. is a minimum price.
   b. will cause a shortage if the ceiling is set above the equilibrium price.
   c. will cause a shortage if the ceiling is set below the equilibrium price.
   d. will cause a surplus if the ceiling is set above the equilibrium price.
   e. will cause a surplus if the ceiling is set below the equilibrium price.

4. A price floor
   a. is a maximum price.
   b. will cause a shortage if the floor is set above the equilibrium price.
   c. will cause a shortage if the floor is set below the equilibrium price
   d. will cause a surplus if the floor is set above the equilibrium price.
   e. will cause a surplus if the floor is set below the equilibrium price.

5. Which of the following statements is true?
   a. Governments impose price ceilings because the equilibrium price is perceived as being too high
   b. Governments impose price floors because the equilibrium price is perceived as being too high.
   c. Governments impose price ceilings because the equilibrium price is perceived as being too low.
   d. Price ceilings always result in surpluses.
   e. Price floors always result in shortages.

6. If a price ceiling is set above the equilibrium price,
   a. a shortage will occur.
   b. a surplus will occur.
   c. the demand for the good or service will increase
   d. the supply for the good or service will increase.
   e. the equilibrium price and quantity will prevail.

7. A tax imposed on goods and services purchased from foreign suppliers is called a
   a. tariff.
   b. subsidy.
   c. price ceiling.
   d. price floor.
   e. compensating differential.

PRACTICE QUESTIONS AND PROBLEMS

Section 1: The Market for Fast Foods

1. In the market system, the _____ ultimately determines what is to be produced.

2. The authority of consumers to determine what is produced through their purchases of goods and services is called _____.

3. The _____ business is where restaurant food is delivered to homes.

4. In the 1980s, people preferred to have food delivered to their homes rather than eating in a restaurant. The demand for in-restaurant meals _____ (increased, did not change, decreased), and the demand for delivered food _____ (increased, did not change, decreased).

5. Business firms respond to changes in consumers' tastes because they want to make

    _____.

6. When the demand for a good or service changes, resources move from an activity where their value is relatively _____ to an activity where their value is relatively

    _____.

Section 2: The Labor Market

1. In any labor market, the wage rate and number of jobs depend on the _____ and _____ curves for labor.

2. _____ (Business firms, Households) demand labor.

3. _____ (Business firms, Households) supply labor.

4. The demand for labor slopes _____, showing that the higher the price of labor, the _____ (more, less) labor the firm will demand.

5. The supply of labor slopes _____, showing that the higher the hourly wage, the _____ hours that people are willing to work.

6. Employers must pay _____ to get people to do unpleasant or dangerous jobs.

Section 3: Market Intervention: Medical Care, Rent Controls, and Agricultural Price Supports

1. Health care expenditures have increased so much because the _____ for health care services has increased relative to the _____.

2. _____ and _____ are government programs which pay for medical services.

3. The emergence of Medicare and Medicaid in 1966 caused the _____ (demand, supply) for health care services to _____ (increase, decrease).

4. Because Medicare and Medicaid reduce the cost of purchasing health care, they are examples of _____.

5. _____ are maximum prices.

6. _____ are minimum prices.

7. A price ceiling will cause a shortage only if it is set _____ (above, equal to, below) the equilibrium price.

8. A price floor will cause a surplus only if it is set _____ (above, equal to, below) the equilibrium price.

9. A price ceiling will have no effect if it is set _____ (above, equal to, below) the equilibrium price.

10. Usury laws restricted banks and other lending institutions from charging interest rates higher than some legal maximum. Usury laws create price _____ (ceilings, floors) and may result in _____ (shortages, surpluses).

11. If the U.S. government decided to impose a tariff on imports of televisions into the U.S., you could predict that the tariff would _____ (increase, decrease) the cost of importing televisions, which would _____ (increase, decrease) the _____ (demand, supply) of imported televisions, in turn _____ (increasing, decreasing) the price of imported televisions and _____ (increasing, decreasing) the quantity of televisions imported into the U.S.

12. Use the following graph to answer the following questions. D_1 is the original demand curve.

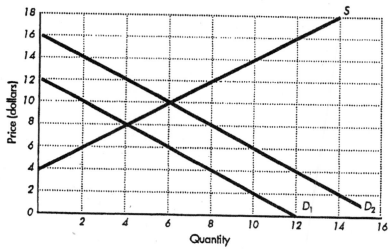

a.   The equilibrium price is _____. The equilibrium quantity is _____ units.

b.   If the floor price was $10, a _____ (surplus, shortage) of _____ units would develop.

c.   If the ceiling price was $6, a _____ (surplus, shortage) of _____ units would develop.

d.   Now suppose consumers' incomes increase, shifting market demand to D_2. The new equilibrium price is _____, and the new equilibrium quantity is _____ units.

THINKING ABOUT AND APPLYING APPLICATIONS OF DEMAND AND SUPPLY

I.   The Tale of the Iguana

The Wall Street Journal ran a story entitled, "Man's New Best Friend: The Scaly Iguana." According to the article, iguanas have become very popular pets in some parts of the United States, with sales rising from 28,000 per year in 1986 to over 500,000 per year now. The movie Jurassic Park is cited as a reason for the new popularity of iguanas.

1. Assuming that the supply of iguanas hasn't changed since 1986, sketch a graph showing what happened in the market for iguanas that explains the increase in sales.

2. Of the six determinants of demand, which one best explains the change in the market for iguanas?

    _____

3. As iguanas became more popular, what do you think happened to the price and quantity sold of iguanas?

    _____

    _____

II.   Price Controls and Medical Care

As the price of health care rises, politicians may consider price controls on certain medical procedures to keep costs down.

1. Would the price controls take the form of a price ceiling or a price floor? _____

2. What do you think would happen in the market for these medical procedures if price controls were adopted? _____

III.   Wooden Bats Versus Metal Bats

The supply of wooden bats is shown as S_w on the following graph. It has a steeper slope than the supply of metal bats, S_m, reflecting the fact that it is easier to produce additional metal bats than additional wooden bats.

1. Assume D_m is the demand for metal bats. Suppose baseball purists are willing to pay more for a "sweet crack" sound than for a dull metallic "ping" when they connect with a fastball. Draw a demand curve for wooden bats and label it D_w.

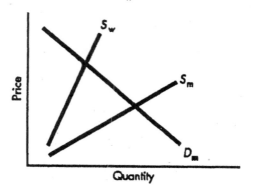

2. What are the consequences for the relative prices of wooden and metal bats?

_____

_____

_____

_____

IV.   Contests and CEO Pay

In many American firms, the pay of the person running the company (the chief executive officer, or CEO) is a hundred times higher than the pay received by most company employees. It's hard to believe that these CEOs are so special that their value to the firm is so much greater than that of regular workers. Does this mean that there's no economic logic behind what companies pay CEOs?

Not necessarily. One way to look at CEO pay is that it's the "prize" for winning a contest among potential CEOs; a high prize not only rewards the current CEO for his or her success but also acts as an incentive to other executives to work harder and more productively, in the hope that someday they will do well enough to "win" and become CEOs themselves.

Let's look at a different kind of contest to see how this idea works. Suppose someone in your town is sponsoring a road race for the ten best runners in town and has decided to offer $10,000 in prizes to the ten runners. The people organizing the race are looking at two different ways to award the $10,000 in prizes:

Method 1:   Pay each runner $1,000 for participating in the race.
Method 2:   Pay the winner $7,000; the second-place finisher $2,000; and the other eight runners $125 for participating.

1. Which method of awarding the prizes will result in all ten runners' working harder to train for the race? Explain your answer.

2. Using your answer to question 1, explain why firms' high CEO salaries may be justified by high productivity.

ANSWERS

QUICK-CHECK QUIZ

Section 1: The Market for Fast Foods

1. c;

2. a;

3. b;

4. d;

5. a;

6. d

If you missed any of these questions, you should go back and review Section 1 in Chapter 3.

Section 2: The Labor Market

1. d;

2. c;

3. b

If you missed any of these questions, you should go back and review Section 2 in Chapter 3.

Section 3: Market Intervention: Medical Care, Rent Controls, and Agricultural Price Supports

1. e;

2. b;

3. c;

4. d;

5. a;

6. e;

7. a

If you missed any of these questions, you should go back and review Section 3 in Chapter 3.

PRACTICE QUESTIONS AND PROBLEMS

Section 1: The Market for Fast Foods

1. consumer

2. consumer sovereignty

3. takeout taxi

4. decreased; increased

5. a profit

6. low; high

Section 2: The Labor Market

1. demand; supply
2. Business firms
3. Households
4. down; less
5. up; more
6. compensating wage differentials

Section 3: Market Intervention: Medical Care, Rent Controls, and Agricultural Price Supports

1. demand; supply
2. Medicare; Medicaid
3. demand; increase
4. subsidies
5. Price ceilings
6. Price floors
7. below
8. above
9. above or equal to
10. ceilings; shortages
11. increase; decrease; supply; increasing; decreasing
12. a. $8; 4:
    b. surplus; 4:
    c. shortage; 4:
    d. $10; 6

THINKING ABOUT AND APPLYING APPLICATIONS OF DEMAND AND SUPPLY

I.   The Tale of the Iguana

1.

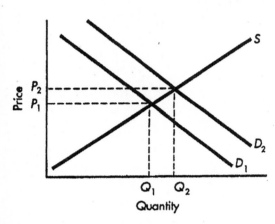

2. change in tastes

3. Both the price and the quantity sold increased.

II.   Price Controls and Medical Care

1. price ceiling

2. Shortages would occur. There would probably be long waits to obtain these procedures,

III.   Wooden Bats Versus Metal Bats

1.

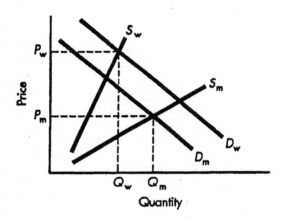

2. If baseball purists prefer wooden bats to metal bats, the demand for wooden bats (D_w) will be to the right of the demand for metal bats (D_m). The price of wooden bats will be higher than the price of metal bats.

IV.   Contests and CEO Pay

1. Method 2. Under Method 1, a runner's performance doesn't affect his or her prize because every runner automatically gets $1,000. In contrast, Method 2 provides a financial incentive for each runner to train hard for the race because his or her prize depends on doing better than the other runners.

2. A high salary is more than a reward for a CEO's value to the firm; it also serves as an incentive for better performance by all the people in the company who want to be CEOs someday. The higher productivity of *all* these people, not just the CEO, is what the CEO's salary is buying.

CHAPTER 4

The Firm and the Consumer

FUNDAMENTAL QUESTIONS

1. How do firms make money?

    Firms get income, or revenue, by selling their product to buyers. To make good decisions, firms must know how their revenue changes when they produce and sell different quantities of output. Total revenue, average revenue, and marginal revenue are all terms that represent how much revenue a firm gets at different quantities of output sold.

    Total revenue is the amount of revenue a firm receives at different quantities. It is calculated by the equation $TR = P \times Q$, where P represents the price of the product, and Q is the quantity sold.

    Average revenue is revenue per unit of output. It is calculated by the equation $AR = TR/Q$. Average revenue is the same as demand.

    Marginal revenue is the additional revenue gained by selling one more unit of the product. It is calculated by the equation $MR = $ change in TR/change in Q

2. What happens to sales when the price of a good or service rises?

    When your favorite clothing store has a sale on jeans, do you go out and buy some? When the bookstore raises the price of required textbooks, do you buy fewer textbooks? We know from our study of demand that people usually respond to price changes by changing the quantity they buy. Most people respond more to changes in the price of jeans than to changes in the price of required textbooks.

    Elasticity gives us a way to measure how much people respond to price changes. The **price elasticity of demand** is the percentage change in quantity demanded of a good divided by the percentage change in price of that good. Although the quantity demanded changes in the opposite direction from the change in price, we usually talk about the price elasticity of demand as a positive number.

    The possible values of the price elasticity of demand are divided into ranges:

    *   We say that demand is **elastic** if the price elasticity of demand is more than one.

    *   We say that demand is **inelastic** if the price elasticity of demand is less than one.

    *   We say that demand is **unit elastic** if the price elasticity of demand is equal to one.

    When your favorite store has a sale on jeans, it sells more jeans but takes in less revenue per pair. Did total revenue increase or decrease because of the sale?

    That depends on the price elasticity of demand. If the demand for jeans is elastic, the percentage change in quantity is bigger than the percentage change in price, so reducing the price of jeans increases total revenue.

But if the demand for jeans is inelastic, the percentage change in quantity is smaller than the percentage change in price, so reducing the price of jeans decreases total revenue. When demand is inelastic, raising the price increases total revenue.

KEY TERMS

total revenue   elastic   perfectly inelastic

average revenue *(AR)*   unit elastic   price discrimination

marginal revenue *(MR)*   inelastic

price elasticity of demand   perfectly elastic

QUICK-CHECK QUIZ

Section 1: Revenue

1. Marginal revenue is
   a. quantity sold multiplied by price.
   b. total revenue divided by the number of units sold.
   c. average revenue multiplied by price.
   d. the additional revenue from selling one more unit of a good.
   e. the additional revenue from selling one more unit of a good times the number of units sold.

2. Average revenue is
   a. quantity sold multiplied by price.
   b. total revenue divided by the number of units sold.
   c. marginal revenue multiplied by price.
   d. the additional revenue from selling one more unit of a good.
   e. the additional revenue from selling one more unit of a good times the number of units sold.

3. Total revenue is
   a. quantity sold multiplied by price.
   b. total revenue divided by the number of units sold.
   c. average revenue multiplied by price.
   d. the additional revenue from selling one more unit of a good.
   e. the additional revenue from selling one more unit of a good times the number of units sold

4. Which of the following is the same as demand?
   a. average revenue
   b. marginal revenue
   c. partial revenue
   d. complete revenue
   e. total revenue

Section 2: How Does a Firm Learn About Its Demand?

1. One day while you are in a shopping mall, someone comes up to you and asks you questions about a product. What is the firm that is paying someone to ask the questions probably trying to get information about?
    a. its supply
    b. its demand
    c. its production costs
    d. the quality of its management
    e. its negative revenue

2. What method for learning about demand for a product can only be used by a firm that has been making the product for a period of time?
    a. shopping mall surveys
    b. telephone surveys
    c. the firm's actual experience
    d. doing a test trial in one or two cities
    e. using focus groups

Section 3: Knowing the Consumer

1. The price elasticity of demand is a measure of the degree to which
    a. consumers alter the prices they pay for a product in response to changes in the quantities they buy of that product.
    b. sellers alter the quantities of a product they offer for sale in response to changes in the price of that product.
    c. consumers alter the quantities of a product they purchase in response to changes in their family income.
    d. consumers alter the quantities of a product they purchase in response to changes in the price of that product.
    e. sellers alter the quantities of a product they offer for sale in response to changes in the incomes of buyers.

2. Which of the following is the equation for price elasticity of demand?

    a. $$e_d = \frac{\text{change in quantity demanded}}{\text{change in price}}$$

    b. $$e_d = \frac{\text{change in price}}{\text{change in quantity demanded}}$$

    c. $$e_d = \frac{\text{percentage change in quantity demanded}}{\text{percentage change in price}}$$

    d. $$e_d = \frac{\text{percentage change in price}}{\text{percentage change in quantity demanded}}$$

    e. $$e_d = \frac{\text{change in price}}{\text{percentage change in quantity demanded}}$$

3. When the price elasticity of demand is greater than 1, demand is
    a. elastic.
    b. unit elastic.
    c. inelastic.
    d. nonelastic.
    e. perfectly inelastic.

4. When the price elasticity of demand is less than 1, demand is
    a. elastic.
    b. unit elastic.
    c. inelastic.
    d. nonelastic.
    e. perfectly elastic.

5. When the price elasticity of demand is equal to 1, demand is
    a. elastic.
    b. unit elastic.
    c. inelastic.
    d. nonelastic.
    e. perfectly inelastic.

6. When elasticity is greater than 1, total revenue increases if price
    a. decreases.
    b. increases.
    c. holds constant.

7. When elasticity is less than 1, total revenue increases if price
    a. decreases.
    b. increases.
    c. holds constant.

8. Charging different customers different prices for the same product is called
    a. foreign exchange exploitation.
    b. labor exploitation.
    c. perfect elasticity.
    d. price discrimination.
    e. pure price competition.

9. A business knows that it has two sets of customers, one of which has a much more elastic demand than the other. If the business uses price discrimination, which set of customers should receive a lower price?
    a. Both sets should receive the same price.
    b. Both sets should receive a higher price.
    c. It doesn't matter to the business which gets a lower price.
    d. The set with the more elastic demand should receive a lower price.
    e. The set with the less elastic demand should receive a lower price.

10. The price elasticity of demand for a product is largest when there
    a. are no good substitutes for the product.
    b. is only one good substitute for the product.
    c. are two or three good substitutes for the product.
    d. are many good substitutes for the product.

11. The price elasticity of demand for a product is largest when the
    a. product constitutes a large portion of the consumer's budget.
    b. product constitutes a small portion of the consumer's budget.
    c. time period under consideration is very short.

12. The price elasticity of demand for a product is largest when the
    a. time period under consideration is long.
    b. time period under consideration is very short.
    c. product constitutes a small portion of the consumer's budget.

PRACTICE QUESTIONS AND PROBLEMS

Section 1: Revenue

1. The equation for calculating total revenue is _____.

2. The equation for calculating average revenue is _____.

3. The equation for calculating marginal revenue is _____.

4. Incremental revenue is another term for _____.

5. Average revenue is the same as _____.

6. Use the following demand curve to calculate total revenue, average revenue, and marginal revenue.

Price	Quantity	Total Revenue	Average Revenue	Marginal Revenue
$10	1	_____	_____	_____
9	2	_____	_____	_____
8	3	_____	_____	_____
7	4			

7. Use the following demand curve to calculate total revenue, average revenue, and marginal revenue.

Price	Quantity	Total Revenue	Average Revenue	Marginal Revenue
$5	1	_____	_____	_____
5	2	_____	_____	_____
5	3	_____	_____	_____
5	4			

How does the relationship between price and marginal revenue differ between problem 6 and problem 7?_____

_____

8. Use the demand curve below to calculate total revenue, average revenue, and marginal revenue. Be careful doing this one—remember the exact definition of marginal revenue.

Price	Quantity	Total Revenue	Average Revenue	Marginal Revenue
$20	100	_____	_____	_____
18	200	_____	_____	_____
16	300	_____	_____	_____
14	400	_____	_____	_____

Section 2: How Does a Firm Learn About Its Demand?

1. Firms that have been in business for a while can use their actual data based on _____ to gain information on demand.

2. List four methods besides experience that firms use to gain information on what consumers say they will do in different circumstances.

   _____

   _____

   _____

   _____

3. What method do firms like Wal-Mart use to gain instantaneous information on customer purchases and prices? _____

Section 3: Knowing the Consumer - Part I

1. The price elasticity of demand measures the degree to which consumers alter their _____ in response to a(n) _____ .

2. The equation used to calculate the price elasticity of demand is

$$e_d = \frac{\text{percentage change in} \underline{\hspace{2cm}}}{\text{percentage change in} \underline{\hspace{2cm}}}$$

3. If e_d is less than 1, demand is _____ .

4. If e_d is greater than 1, demand is _____ .

5. If e_d is equal to 1, demand is _____ .

6. A(n) _____ demand curve shows that consumers can purchase any quantity they want at the prevailing price.

7. A(n) _____ demand curve shows no change in quantity demanded as the price changes.

8. If a 5 percent change in the price of movies causes a 10 percent change in the number of movie tickets sold, e_d equals _____ and demand is _____ (elastic, inelastic, unit elastic).

9. If a 6 percent change in the price of coffee causes a 3 percent change in the quantity of coffee bought, e_d equals _____ and demand is _____ (elastic, inelastic, unit elastic).

10. If a 2 percent change in the price of wine causes a 2 percent change in the number of bottles of wine bought, e_d equals _____ and demand is _____ (elastic, inelastic, unit elastic).

11. If a 5 percent change in the price of heroin causes no change in the amount of heroin bought, e_d equals _____ and demand is _____ (perfectly elastic, perfectly inelastic).

12.

    a. Demand is elastic. The percentage change in _____ (quantity, price) is larger than the percentage change in _____ (quantity, price).

    b. When price decreases, quantity increases and total revenue _____ (increases, decreases).

13.

    a. Demand is inelastic. The percentage change in _____ (quantity, price) is larger than the percentage change in _____ (quantity, price).

    b. When price decreases, quantity increases and total revenue _____ (increases, decreases).

14. Complete the following table.

Demand Elasticity	Price Change	Effect on Total Revenue (Increase, Decrease, Unchanged)
Elastic	Increase	_____
Elastic	Decrease	_____
Inelastic	Increase	_____
Inelastic	Decrease	_____
Unit elastic	Increase	_____
Unit elastic	Decrease	

15. List the three determinants of the price elasticity of demand.

_____

_____

_____

16. A product with _____ (many, few) good substitutes would have a more elastic demand than a product with _____ (many, few) good substitutes.

17. The demand for new cars is likely to be _____ (more, less) elastic than the demand for new Chevrolet cars.

18. The demand for paperback novels is likely to be _____ (more, less) elastic than the demand for required college textbooks.

19. A product that takes a _____ (large, small) portion of a consumer's budget has a more elastic demand than a product that takes a _____ (large, small) portion.

20. When consumers have a _____ (long, short) time to react to price changes, demand is more elastic than when consumers have a _____ (long, short) period of time to react.

Section 3: Knowing the Consumer - Part II

1. Suppose you are the city manager of a small mid-western city. Your city-owned bus system is losing money, and you have to find a way to take in more revenue. Your staff recommends raising bus fares, but bus riders argue that reducing bus fares to attract new riders would increase revenue. You conclude that
    a. your staff thinks that the demand for bus service is elastic, whereas the bus riders think that demand is inelastic.
    b. your staff thinks that the demand for bus service is inelastic, whereas the bus riders think that demand is elastic.
    c. both your staff and the bus riders think that the demand for bus service is elastic.
    d. both your staff and the bus riders think that the demand for bus service is inelastic.
    e. both your staff and the bus riders think that the demand for bus service is unit elastic.

2. Airlines know from experience that vacation travelers have an elastic demand for air travel, whereas business travelers have an inelastic demand for air travel. If an airline wants to increase its total revenue, it should
    a. decrease fares for both business and vacation travelers.
    b. increase fares for both business and vacation travelers.
    c. increase fares for business travelers and decrease fares for vacation travelers.
    d. decrease fares for business travelers and increase fares for vacation travelers.
    e. leave fares the same for both groups.

THINKING ABOUT AND APPLYING THE FIRM AND THE CONSUMER

I.   Taxing Tobacco

According to the law of demand, taxes that increase the price of a product are expected to reduce consumption of the product. Several years ago, California increased its cigarette tax by $.25 a pack; by the next year, cigarette purchases in California had declined by 10 percent. For simplicity, assume that all of this decrease was caused by the price of cigarettes increasing $.25 as a result of the tax increase. Use this information to answer the following questions.

1. Cigarettes back then cost $1 per pack before the tax increase and $1.25 after. The demand elasticity for cigarettes over this price range is _____. Demand for this product is _____ (elastic, inelastic).

2. Use the determinants of demand elasticity discussed in Section 3 of the chapter to explain why you would expect the demand for cigarettes to be inelastic.

    _____

    _____

3. One billion (1,000,000,000) packs of cigarettes were sold in California before the tax increase. After the tax went into effect, _____ packs were sold, and the state earned _____ in tax revenue.

II. Price Discrimination in Airline Fares

Several years ago Northwest Airlines cut fares 35 percent for summer travel. There were some restrictions:

Travel must begin on or after May 27 and be completed by September 15.

The nonrefundable tickets require 14-day advance purchase.

Travelers must stay at their destination over a Saturday night.

People taking a plane trip for a vacation usually can plan their trip far in advance and don't mind spending a weekend at their vacation destination. Business travelers, on the other hand, frequently have to travel without much advance notice and want to be back home on weekends.

1. The main customers for Northwest's discounted tickets will be _____ (business, vacation) travelers.

2. Does Northwest think the demand for airline tickets for vacation travel is elastic, inelastic, or unit elastic? Explain your answer.

_____

_____

_____

3. Based on the restrictions it sets and the effects of those restrictions on business and vacation travelers, Northwest must think that _____ (business, vacation) travelers have a higher price elasticity of demand.

ANSWERS

QUICK-CHECK QUIZ

Section 1: Revenue

1. d;
2. b;
3. a;
4. a

If you missed any of these questions, you should go back and review Section 1 in Chapter 4.

Section 2: How Does a Firm Learn About Its Demand?

1. b;
2. c

If you missed any of these questions, you should go back and review Section 2 in Chapter 4.

Section 3: Knowing the Consumer

1. d;
2. c;

3. a;

4. c;

5. b;

6. a;

7. b;

8. d;

9. d;

10. d;

11. a;

12. a

If you missed any of these questions, you should go back and review Section 3 in Chapter 4.

PRACTICE QUESTIONS AND PROBLEMS

Section 1: Revenue

1. $P \times Q$ (price times quantity)

2. TR/Q (total revenue divided by quantity)

3. change in TR/change in Q

4. marginal revenue

5. demand

6.

Price	Quantity	Total Revenue	Average Revenue	Marginal Revenue
$10	1	$10	$10	$10
9	2	18	9	8
8	3	24	8	6
7	4	28	7	4

(Total revenue = price × quantity; average revenue = total revenue/quantity; marginal revenue = change in total revenue/change in quantity.)

7.

Price	Quantity	Total Revenue	Average Revenue	Marginal Revenue
$5	1	$5	$5	$5
5	2	10	5	5
5	3	15	5	5
5	4	20	5	5

Calculations use the same formulas as problem 6. In problem 6, when price goes down marginal revenue goes down faster. In problem 7, price stays the same, and marginal revenue is the same as the price.

8.

Price	Quantity	Total Revenue	Average Revenue	Marginal Revenue
$20	100	$2,000	$20	$20
18	200	3,600	18	16
16	300	4,800	16	12
14	400	5,600	14	8

(Marginal revenue is the change in total revenue divided by the change in quantity. In this problem, the change in quantity between different prices is 100, not 1.)

Section 2: How Does a Firm Learn About Its Demand?

1. experience

2. surveys;
   opinion polls;
   telemarketing;
   focus groups

3. scanning devices at the check-out register

Section 3: Knowing the Consumer

1. purchases; price

2. quantity demanded; price

3. inelastic

4. elastic

5. unit elastic

6. perfectly elastic

7. perfectly inelastic

8. 2; elastic (Remember the equation for the price elasticity of demand:

$$e_d = \frac{\text{percentage change in quantity demanded}}{\text{percentage change in price}}$$

The change in quantity demanded is 10 percent, and the change in price is 5 percent, so $e_d =$ 10/5 = 2. This is more than 1, so demand must be elastic.)

9. 0.5; inelastic (Refer to the previous equation for the price elasticity of demand. In this problem, the change in quantity demanded is 3 percent, and the change in price is 6 percent, so $e_d = 3/6 =$ 0.5. This is less than 1, so demand must be inelastic.)

10. 1; unit elastic (Refer to the previous equation for the price elasticity of demand. In this problem, the change in quantity demanded is 2 percent, and the change in price is 2 percent, so $e_d = 2/2 = 1$. Therefore, demand must be unit elastic.)

11. 0; perfectly inelastic (Refer to the previous equation for the price elasticity of demand. In this problem, the percentage change in quantity demanded is 0 percent, and the change in price is 5 percent, so $e_d = 0/5 = 0$. Therefore, demand must be perfectly inelastic.)

12.

    a.   quantity; price

    b.   increases

13.

    a.   price; quantity

    b.   decreases

14.

Demand Elasticity	Price Change	Effect on Total Revenue (Increase, Decrease, Unchanged)
Elastic	Increase	Decrease
Elastic	Decrease	Increase
Inelastic	Increase	Increase
Inelastic	Decrease	Decrease
Unit elastic	Increase	Unchanged
Unit elastic	Decrease	Unchanged

1. b (Your staff thinks that increasing the price will increase total revenue; this will happen only if demand is inelastic. The bus riders think that decreasing the price will increase total revenue; this will happen only if demand is elastic.)

2. c (When demand is elastic [vacationers], reducing the price increases total revenue. When demand is inelastic [business travelers], increasing the price increases total revenue.)

15. existence of substitutes;
importance of the product in the consumer's total budget ;
the time period under consideration

16. many; few

17. less (For most people, there are many good substitutes for Chevrolets: Fords, Plymouths, Toyotas, Volkswagens, and so on. The demand for a particular brand of a product is usually more elastic than the demand for the product itself.)

18. more (There are few, if any, good substitutes for required texts, but many other forms of literature, and entertainment in general, are available as substitutes for paperback novels.)

19. large; small

20. long; short

THINKING ABOUT AND APPLYING THE FIRM AND THE CONSUMER

I.   Taxing Tobacco

1. 0.4 (If cigarette prices increased from $1 to $1.25 per pack, this would be a 25 percent increase relative to the average price. Because the quantity demanded decreased only 10 percent when the price increased 25 percent, the price elasticity of demand for cigarettes is 10%/25% = 0.4.); inelastic (Because the price elasticity of demand is less than 1, demand is inelastic.)

2. To people who smoke cigarettes, there are few, if any, good substitutes; many cigarette smokers consider cigarettes a necessity.

3. 900,000,000 (a 10 percent decrease from 1 billion); $225,000,000 (900,000,000 packs × $.25)

II.   Price Discrimination in Airline Fares

1. vacation (Vacation travelers don't mind the restrictions of 14-day advance purchase and a Saturday stayover, but many business travelers do.)

2. elastic; Northwest reduced the price for vacation travelers, so it must think demand is elastic and a price cut would increase revenues.

3. vacation (If Northwest thought that business travelers had a higher price elasticity of demand, it would have cut the price of their tickets.)

CHAPTER 5

Cost and Profit Maximization

FUNDAMENTAL QUESTIONS

1. What is the relationship between costs and output in the short run?

    Let's use a typical business, Joe's Gourmet Hamburgers, as an example. Joe has a small restaurant that makes and sells gourmet-quality hamburgers. It seems pretty obvious that Joe's costs will go up as Joe's output goes up; when Joe wants to produce more hamburgers, he has to hire more workers and buy more hamburger meat, rolls, lettuce, and so on.

    In addition to this simple relationship, there are other relationships between costs and output that apply to most firms in the short run. The **short run** is a period of time just short enough that at least one input can be changed. Joe can quickly hire and train workers, or buy more hamburger meat, but it would take him several months to build a new restaurant. The short run is the time period when Joe can't change the restaurant or its equipment (grill, French fryers, etc.), but he can change the number of people who work for him.

    As Joe thinks about making more hamburgers every hour by adding more workers to the restaurant, total costs will at first increase only slowly. The first few workers Joe hires have lots of room to work and lots of equipment to use, so they can work very efficiently. But as Joe tries to keep making more hamburgers, eventually there will be too many people trying to use the fixed amount of equipment. They'll get in each others' way and not be able to work as efficiently. Total costs will be increasing at a faster and faster rate.

    The **law of diminishing marginal returns** is a formal statement of the pattern described above. The law says that in the short run, as the quantity of variable resources are increased, output initially rises rapidly, then more slowly, and eventually may decline. One implication of this pattern is that the **average total cost (ATC)** curve is U-shaped. Average total cost is the cost of each output unit calculated by the equation TC/Q.

    For Joe's Gourmet Hamburgers, as the number of hamburgers produced per hour increases from zero, at first the cost per hamburger (ATC) decreases. This happens while the increasing number of workers are able to use the equipment more efficiently. But as Joe keeps adding more workers to make more hamburgers per hour, eventually the ATC will start to increase. This increase happens when there becomes too many workers to use the equipment efficiently. The low point on the ATC curve comes when there are just the right number of workers in Joe's restaurant to use the equipment as efficiently as possible.

2. Why is the difference between economic profit and accounting profit important?

    Accountants and bookkeepers are primarily concerned with keeping track of money; that's their job. Economists concentrate on resources rather than money. Both accountants and economists count as costs the resources a firm buys. Economists also include the opportunity cost of the owner's equity capital as part of the cost of producing a product.

    For example, Joe used a large amount of his savings to buy the building and start up his restaurant. Joe's opportunity cost of his capital investment is the interest he would have received if he had kept the money in his savings account. Economists count these forgone savings as a cost; accountants don't.

Both accountants and economists figure profit as total revenue minus total cost. Since economists include the opportunity cost of the owner's equity capital as part of costs, **accounting profit** is always larger than **economic profit**.

When economic profit is zero, economists say that the firm is getting a **normal accounting profit**. **Positive economic profit** means that total revenue is more than all opportunity costs. **Negative economic profit** means that total revenue is less than all opportunity costs.

3. Why is profit maximized when $MR = MC$?

Businesses like Joe's Gourmet Hamburgers want to choose the quantity of output to produce where total revenue exceeds total cost by the largest amount. At that point, economic profits are at their maximum value, and Joe gets as much money as possible from his business. Businesses can find that quantity by comparing marginal revenue (MR) and **marginal cost** (**MC**) and producing the output quantity where $MR = MC$.

KEY TERMS

average total costs (ATC)	**equity**	**zero economic profit**
marginal costs (MC)	**cost of capital**	**normal accounting profit**
short run	**economic profit**	**positive economic profit**
law of diminishing marginal returns	**accounting profit**	**fixed costs**
debt	**negative economic profit**	**variable costs**

QUICK-CHECK QUIZ

Section 1: Costs

1. Average total costs are calculated by the equation
   a. $TC \times Q$.
   b. TC/Q.
   c. Q/TC.
   d. change in TC/change in Q.
   e. change in Q/change in TC.

2. Marginal costs are calculated by the equation
   a. $TC \times Q$.
   b. TC/Q.
   c. Q/TC.
   d. change in TC/change in Q.
   e. change in Q/change in TC.

3. The short run is a period of time
   a. that is shorter than one day.
   b. that is longer than one month.
   c. long enough that all resources can be changed.
   d. short enough that at least one resource is fixed
   e. short enough that all resources are fixed.

4.   According to the law of diminishing marginal returns, as successive units of a variable resource are added to some fixed resources, the additional output will
   a.   initially rise but will eventually decline.
   b.   initially decline but will eventually rise.
   c.   continually rise.
   d.   continually decline.
   e.   remain constant.

5.   The law of diminishing marginal returns results in average-total-cost and marginal-cost curves that are
   a.   horizontal straight lines.
   b.   vertical straight lines.
   c.   U-shaped.
   d.   M-shaped.
   e.   diagonal straight lines.

Section 2: Maximizing Profit

1.   The primary objective of business firms is to
   a.   sell as much as possible.
   b.   keep their total costs to the minimum.
   c.   keep their marginal costs to the minimum.
   d.   maximize profit.
   e.   pay their employees more than other workers

2.   Economic profit is the
   a.   difference between the value of output and the full costs of inputs.
   b.   sum of the value of output and the full costs of inputs.
   c.   highest value of output.
   d.   highest value of input costs.
   e.   difference between profits and taxes.

3.   Funds owed to lenders by borrowers are called
   a.   debt.
   b.   equality.
   c.   eventuality.
   d.   equity.
   e.   debits.

4.   The value of a firm less debt is called
   a.   debit.
   b.   equality.
   c.   eventuality.
   d.   equity.
   e.   debits.

5.   Businesses can acquire capital through
   a.   debt only.
   b.   equity only.
   c.   either debt or equity, but not both.
   d.   debt, equity, or both.
   e.   neither debt nor equity.

6. The factor that makes accounting profit different from economic profit is
    a. opportunity cost of debt capital.
    b. opportunity cost of equity capital.
    c. opportunity cost of labor.
    d. opportunity cost of land.
    e. all opportunity costs.

7. A firm is getting normal accounting profit when
    a. revenue just pays all opportunity costs.
    b. it has a zero economic profit.
    c. revenue just pays the cost of capital.
    d. all of the above are true.
    e. only a and b are true.

Section 3: The Profit-Maximizing Rule: *MR = MC*

1. A firm can increase its profit by producing another unit of output when
    a. total revenue is more than total cost.
    b. total revenue is less than total cost.
    c. total revenue is equal to total cost.
    d. marginal revenue is more than marginal cost.
    e. marginal revenue is less than marginal cost.

2. A firm would decrease its profit if it produced another unit of output when
    a. total revenue is more than total cost.
    b. total revenue is less than total cost.
    c. total revenue is equal to total cost.
    d. marginal revenue is more than marginal cost.
    e. marginal revenue is less than marginal cost.

3. Costs that don't change as output changes are
    a. flexible costs.
    b. inflexible costs.
    c. specified costs.
    d. fixed costs.
    e. variable costs.

4. Costs that change as output changes are
    a. flexible costs.
    b. inflexible costs.
    c. specified costs.
    d. fixed costs.
    e. variable costs.

5. The profit-maximizing rule for a firm is to set the price and sell the quantity where
    a. $MC = ATC$.
    b. $MR = MC$.
    c. $AR = ATC$.
    d. $TR = TC$.
    e. $MR = ATC$.

PRACTICE QUESTIONS AND PROBLEMS

Section 1: Costs

1. You calculate average total costs (*ATC*) by using this equation:

    _____

2. You calculate marginal costs (*MC*) by using this equation:

    _____

3. The short run is a period of time just short enough that _____ of the resources is

    _____.

4. State the name of the law that says, "As successive units of a variable resource are added to the fixed resources, the additional output will initially rise but will eventually decline."

    _____

5. Diminishing marginal returns happen in any type of business firm because the efficiency of variable resources depends on the _____ of the _____.

6. Use the following total cost table for Joe's Gourmet Hamburgers to calculate Joe's *ATC* and *MC*, then plot the *TC*, *ATC*, and *MC* curves on the graph.

Burgers	TC	ATC	MC
0	$05.50	$_____	$_____
1	9.00	_____	_____
2	10.00	_____	_____
3	10.50	_____	_____
4	11.50	_____	_____
5	13.00	_____	_____
6	15.00	_____	_____
7	17.50	_____	_____
8	20.50	_____	_____
9	24.00	_____	_____
10	28.00	_____	_____

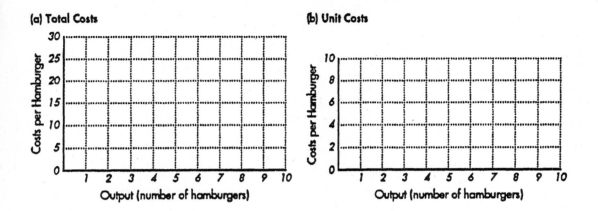

(a) Total Costs   (b) Unit Costs

7. The *ATC* and *MC* curves are shaped like the letter _____.

Section 2: Maximizing Profits

1. Business firms try to maximize _____, which is also known as _____.

2. Capital can be acquired through either _____ or _____.

3. Funds owed to lenders by borrowers are called _____.

4. The value of a firm less its debt is called _____.

5. The cost of debt is the _____ that is paid on the debt.

6. The cost of equity is the _____ that the owners or investors could have gotten if they had put their money into some other investment.

7. Accounting profit = _____ – costs of inputs: _____, _____, and _____.

8. Economic profit = accounting profit – _____.

9. Economic profit is always _____ (larger, smaller) than accounting profit.

10. If accounting profit is more than the cost of equity capital, the firm is receiving _____ (negative, positive, zero) economic profits.

11. If accounting profit is less than the cost of equity capital, the firm is receiving _____ (negative, positive, zero) economic profits.

12. If accounting profit is equal to the cost of equity capital, the firm is receiving _____ (negative, positive, zero) economic profits.

13. When a firm is receiving zero economic profit, it is getting a _____ accounting profit.

14.

   a. If Joe's Gourmet Hamburgers and other similar restaurants are currently getting a _____ (negative, positive, zero) economic profit, other people are likely to start up similar restaurants.

   b. If Joe's Gourmet Hamburgers and other similar restaurants are currently getting a _____ (negative, positive, zero) economic profit, other people are *not* likely to want to start up similar restaurants.

15. Last year, the accountant for Joe's Gourmet Hamburgers gave Joe the following information:

Revenues:	$200,000
Labor costs:	140,000
Land costs:	10,000
Debt costs:	20,000
Equity costs:	50,000

    a. Joe's accounting profit was _____ .

    b. Joe's economic profit was _____ .

    c. Joe received a _____ (negative, positive, zero) economic profit.

    d. Based on Joe's results, other people are _____ (likely, unlikely) to start up new restaurants like Joe's.

    e. How much more revenue does Joe need to get a normal profit (assuming his costs don't change)? _____

Section 3: The Profit-Maximizing Rule: *MR = MC*

1. If the marginal revenue from selling another unit of output is _____ (more, less) than the marginal cost, the firm should produce another unit.

2. If the marginal revenue from selling another unit of output is _____ (more, less) than the marginal cost, the firm should not produce another unit.

3. The profit-maximizing rule is to set the price and produce the quantity of output where _____ .

4. Sally Smith is a world-famous artist who carves exquisite models of birds out of rare, expensive woods. Sally knows that if she carves only one bird per month, her customers will pay a high price for it because of its rarity. If she makes more birds per month, people will only be willing to pay lower prices. Moreover, when she carves more birds per month, her hands get very sore and she has to spend more money having them massaged.

a. The following table lists the price Sally can charge for different numbers of birds sold per month and her total costs of making different numbers of birds per month. Calculate Sally's total revenue, marginal revenue, marginal cost, and profit for each output level.

Q	P	TR	TC	MR	MC	Profit
0	—	$ 0	$ 500	—	—	
1	$2,000		700			
2	1,800		1,100			
3	1,600		1,700			
4	1,400		2,500			
5	1,200		3,500			
6	1,000		4,700			

b. Sally's profit is at its maximum at an output level of _____ bird(s).

c. Sally's marginal revenue equals her marginal cost at an output level of _____ bird(s).

d. On the following *graph a,* plot Sally's profit at each output level. On the following *graph b,* plot Sally's marginal cost and marginal revenue. As you can see, profit is maximized at the output level where $MR = MC$ (4 birds).

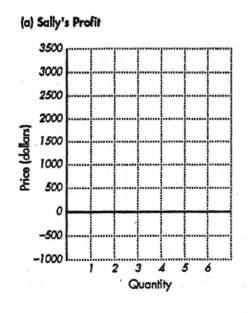

(a) Sally's Profit

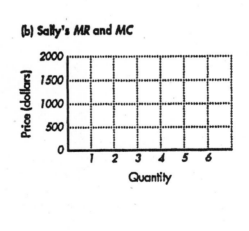

(b) Sally's MR and MC

THINKING ABOUT AND APPLYING COSTS AND PROFIT MAXIMIZATION

Profit Maximization and Pollution Reduction

The ideas of profit maximization and of comparing marginal revenue and marginal cost to find the profit-maximizing output level can be useful even for organizations that aren't involved in profit maximization. All organizations need to find the most effective ways of reaching their goals.

Suppose you are the head of the Environmental Protection Agency (EPA), and you have to decide how much, if any, pollution a particular water treatment plant should be allowed to produce. Right now, the plant produces 4 tons of pollutants per day. The plant is owned by the federal government, so any cleanup costs will be paid for through taxes. Let's assume that the EPA knows what the benefits and cost (in dollars) are from reducing pollution by various amounts. Using the benefits and costs in the following table, find the amount of pollution reduction that gives people the biggest "profit." Profit in this case is the net value people get from pollution reduction: the total benefits minus the total costs.

Pollution Improvement: Tons Reduced per Day	Marginal Benefits	Marginal Costs
1	$10 million	$ 1 million
2	5 million	4 million
3	2 million	10 million
4	1 million	30 million

1. The plant should reduce pollution by _____ tons per day.

2. Explain why you chose this amount.

_____

_____

_____

ANSWERS

QUICK-CHECK QUIZ

Section 1: Costs

1. b; 2. d; 3. d; 4. a; 5. c.

If you missed any of these questions, you should go back and review Section 1 in Chapter 5.

Section 2: Maximizing Profit

1. d; 2. a; 3. a; 4. d; 5. d; 6. b; 7. e

If you missed any of these questions, you should go back and review Section 2 in Chapter 5.

Section 3: The Profit-Maximizing Rule: MR = MC

1. d; 2. e; 3. d; 4. e; 5. b

If you missed any of these questions, you should go back and review Section 3 in Chapter 5.

PRACTICE QUESTIONS AND PROBLEMS

Section 1: Costs

1. total costs/quantity of output

2. change in total costs/change in quantity of output

3. at least one; fixed

4. law of diminishing marginal returns

5. quantity; fixed resources

6.

Burgers	TC	ATC	MC
0	$ 5.50		
1	9.00	$9.00	$3.50
2	10.00	5.00	1.00
3	10.50	3.50	.50
4	11.50	2.88	1.00
5	13.00	2.60	1.50
6	15.00	2.50	2.00
7	17.50	2.50	2.50
8	20.50	2.56	3.00
9	24.00	2.67	3.50
10	28.00	2.80	4.00

$ATC = TC/Q$

MC = change in TC/change in Q

(a) Total Costs

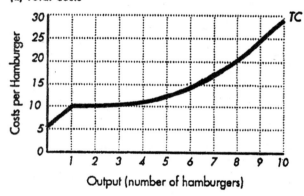

(b) Unit Costs

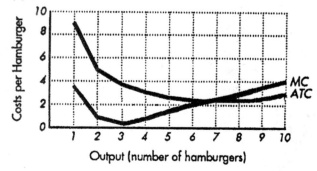

7. U

Section 2: Maximizing Profit

1. added value; economic profit

2. debt; equity

3. debt

4. equity

5. interest

6. alternative returns

7. revenue; land; labor; debt capital

8. opportunity cost of equity capital

9. smaller

10. positive

11. negative

12. zero

13. normal

14. a. positive

    b. negative; zero

15. a. $30,000 ($200,000 – [140,000 + 10,000 + 20,000])

    b. –$20,000 ($30,000 accounting profit – $50,000 cost of equity)

    c. negative

    d. unlikely (Joe's negative economic profit means other people could make more money investing in other areas of the economy.)

    e. $20,000 (A normal profit means a zero economic profit.)

Section 3: The Profit-Maximizing Rule: MR = MC

1. more

2. less

3. $MR = MC$

4. a.

Q	P	TR	TC	MR	MC	Profit
0	—	$ 0	$ 500	—	—	$ −500
1	$2,000	2,000	700	$2,000	$ 200	1,300
2	1,800	3,600	1,100	1,600	400	2,500
3	1,600	4,800	1,700	1,200	600	3,100
4	1,400	5,600	2,500	800	800	3,100
5	1,200	6,000	3,500	400	1,000	2,500
6	1,000	6,000	4,700	0	1,200	1,300

$(TR = P \times Q$

(*MR* is the change in *TR* from selling one more bird per month.)

(*MC* is the change in *TC* from making one more bird per month.)

(Profit = *TR* − *TC*)

b. Both 3 birds and 4 birds give Sally $3,100 profit per month.

c. 4 (*MR* = *MC* = $800 at 4 birds per month.)

d.

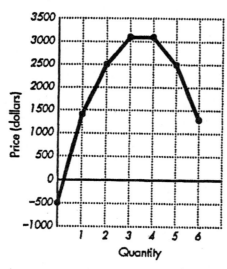

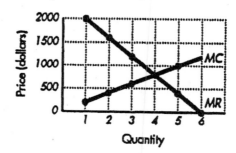

THINKING ABOUT AND APPLYING COSTS AND PROFIT MAXIMIZATION

Profit Maximization and Pollution Reduction

1. 2

2. For the first 1-ton reduction, people gain $10 million in benefits at a cost of $1 million; the "profit" is $9 million from the first 1-ton reduction.

   The second 1-ton reduction gives us $5 million in benefits at a cost of $4 million; we gain an additional $1 million profit from the second 1-ton reduction. After reducing pollution by 2 tons, we have total benefits of $15 million ($10 million + $5 million), and total costs of $5 million ($1 million + $4 million), for a total net gain or profit of $10 million.

   If we made the third 1-ton reduction, we would gain $2 million in benefits at a cost of $10 million; we'd "lose" $8 million on the third 1-ton reduction. If we reduced pollution by a total of 3 tons, our total benefits would be $17 million ($10 million + $5 million + $2 million), and our total costs would be $15 million ($1 million + $4 million + $10 million), for a total net gain of $2 million. By the criterion specified for this example, we would be better off with only 2 tons of pollution reduction; we would get more value from spending $10 million on other things than on the third 1-ton reduction of pollution.

   (Although making decisions about pollution reduction is much more complex than this simple example, the problem does illustrate the basic concepts involved, including some of the economic principles we've been studying in the last few chapters.)

CHAPTER 6

Competition and Market Structures

FUNDAMENTAL QUESTIONS

1. What is a market structure, and what can it tell us about how a firm will behave?

   A market structure is a model of the firm's environment: how the firm interacts with its customers, its suppliers, and its competitors. For analyzing how markets operate, economists divide the world into four types of market structures: **perfect competition, monopoly, monopolistic competition,** and **oligopoly.** The four market structures are based on different combinations of three factors: how many sellers are competing in the market, how easy or difficult it is for new competitors to enter the market, and whether the product being produced is differentiated or not.

   Perfect competition: This market structure has a very large number of small firms, entry is easy, and all firms produce identical products, so buyers do not care at all which firm they buy from. Farm products like wheat or corn are examples of perfectly competitive markets.

   Monopoly: This market structure has only one seller, and there are barriers to entry that prevent other firms from entering the market. Your local water system is an example of a monopoly.

   Monopolistic competition: Like perfect competition, this market structure has lots of small sellers, and entry is easy; the difference is that in monopolistic competition, the product is differentiated, with each seller producing their own brand of the product. The market for novels is a good example of monopolistic competition: lots of different authors, easy entry, and each novel is different from the others.

   Oligopoly: This market structure has only a few sellers, and entry into the market is difficult but not impossible. Oligopolies can produce identical products (steel, for example) or differentiated products (fast-food hamburgers).

2. Do all firms maximize profit when MR = MC?

   Yes. All business firms, regardless of the market structure they are selling in, will receive the maximum possible economic profit by producing the quantity of output where marginal revenue is equal to marginal cost (MR = MC).

   In market structures where an individual firm has some control over its price (monopoly, monopolistic competition, and oligopoly), the firm should set its price at the level where buyers will choose to buy the quantity the firm wants to sell. The firm finds this price by looking at its demand curve at the profit-maximizing quantity.

3. Is it possible to earn positive economic profit in the long run?

   Firms need to create barriers to entry to keep economic profits in the **long run**. A firm like Joe's Gourmet Hamburgers can use a variety of methods to build barriers to entry. Advertising could convince consumers that Joe's hamburgers are better than other hamburgers. If there are **economies of scale** in making and selling hamburgers, and Joe's economies of scale were much larger than other competitors', Joe would have a cost advantage over other competitors and could sell his hamburgers at a lower price and still make economic profits.

4. What are the benefits of competition?

Competition benefits both consumers and society in general by maximizing the sum of **consumer surplus** and **producer surplus.** Consumer surplus is the difference between what consumers would be willing and able to pay for a product (the value they get from the product) and the amount they actually have to pay for the product—it is a bonus to consumers provided by the market system. Producer surplus is the difference between the price producers would be willing and able to accept for making a product (their costs) and the amount they actually receive for the product—it is another bonus provided by the market system.

When entry into markets is not restricted and firms actively compete with each other, the total of consumer surplus and producer surplus is higher than when entry and competition are restricted. Restricted entry can increase producer surplus at the expense of reducing consumer surplus, but restricted entry also causes a **deadweight loss**—the total of consumer and producer surplus gets smaller.

5. Why does it matter whether there are barriers to entry?

When Joe first opened his restaurant, nobody else in his town made gourmet hamburgers. Gourmet hamburgers turned out to be very popular, and Joe could charge a high price for them and make a very nice economic profit (for Joe).

Pretty soon, other restaurant owners noticed Joe's high profits and started planning to open other restaurants in competition with Joe. Remember from our study of demand and supply that an increase in the number of sellers causes the price to go down. If new competitors opened restaurants to compete with Joe, his economic profits would eventually disappear.

If Joe could create some barrier that prevented other people from opening competing restaurants, Joe could keep on getting economic profits into the future. If Joe could prevent entry, he would also cause a deadweight loss.

KEY TERMS

consumer surplus	economies of scale	monopoly
producer surplus	diseconomies of scale	monopolistic competition
deadweight loss	perfect competition	oligopoly
sunk cost		

QUICK-CHECK QUIZ

Section 1: Characteristics of the Market Structures

1. Which of the market characteristics below are *not* used to define market structures?
    a. the number of firms in the market
    b. the ease of entry into the market by new competitors
    c. the percentage of the firm's income that is paid in taxes
    d. the type of product produced (identical or differentiated)
    e. All of the above characteristics are used to define market structures.

2. Which of the following is *not* one of the market structures defined in the chapter?
   a. perfect competition
   b. monopolistic competition
   c. monopoly
   d. oligopoly
   e. oligopolistic competition

3. In which of the following market structures does only one firm supply the product and entry is not possible?
   a. perfect competition
   b. monopolistic competition
   c. monopoly
   d. oligopoly
   e. None of these market structures match the definition.

4. In which of the following market structures do many firms supply an identical product and entry is easy?
   a. perfect competition
   b. monopolistic competition
   c. monopoly
   d. oligopoly
   e. None of these market structures match the definition.

5. In which of the following market structures do many firms supply a differentiated product and entry is easy?
   a. perfect competition
   b. monopolistic competition
   c. monopoly
   d. oligopoly
   e. None of these market structures match the definition.

6. In which of the following market structures do a few firms supply the product?
   a. perfect competition
   b. monopolistic competition
   c. monopoly
   d. oligopoly
   e. None of these market structures match the definition.

7. In which of the following market structures does a firm face a horizontal demand curve?
   a. perfect competition
   b. monopolistic competition
   c. monopoly
   d. oligopoly
   e. None of these market structures match the definition.

8. In which of the following market structures does a firm face a downward-sloping demand curve?
   a. perfect competition
   b. monopolistic competition
   c. monopoly
   d. oligopoly
   e. All of the above *except* perfect competition.

9. Regardless of market structure, a firm maximizes its profits by producing the quantity of output where
    a. P = MR.
    b. MR = MC.
    c. D = MR.
    d. P = MC.
    e. MC = D.

Section 2: Firm Behavior in the Long Run

1. Which of the following can only occur in the long run?
    a. the entry of new firms into the market
    b. the exit of existing firms from the market
    c. a change in the number of workers the firm employs
    d. Choices a, b, and c ALL occur only in the long run; they cannot happen in the short run.
    e. Choices a and b occur only in the long run; c can be a short-run change.

2. Which of the following statements is true of perfect competition in the long run?
    a. Firms can receive economic profits.
    b. Firms receive only a normal profit.
    c. Firms can face economic losses.
    d. Firms cannot enter the market.
    e. Firms cannot exit the market.

3. When the owner of a firm is getting zero economic profit,
    a. the owner should exit that market in the short run.
    b. the owner should exit that market in the long run.
    c. the owner cannot make any more money by exiting the market and doing something else with her resources.
    d. the owner is not receiving any income from owning the firm.
    e. the owner is getting rich.

4. In which market structures do firms receive just a normal profit in the long run?
    a. monopoly and perfect competition
    b. monopolistic competition and perfect competition
    c. monopoly and monopolistic competition
    d. monopoly and oligopoly
    e. monopolistic competition and oligopoly

5. What is the most important determinant of whether or not firms receive economic profits in the long run?
    a. how easy it is for new firms to enter the market
    b. the size of the firms in a market
    c. the size of the market overall
    d. the amount of taxes firm owners pay
    e. the amount of taxes the firms' customers pay

Section 3: The Benefits of Competition

1. The difference between what buyers would be willing to pay and what they have to pay to purchase some item is called
    a. excess consumption.
    b. excess production.
    c. consumer surplus.
    d. producer surplus.
    e. surplus value.

2. The difference between what sellers would require to supply some item and the price they actually receive is called
    a. excess consumption.
    b. excess production.
    c. consumer surplus.
    d. producer surplus.
    e. surplus value.

3. The total benefits that come from an exchange in a market are
    a. producer surplus minus consumer surplus.
    b. producer surplus plus consumer surplus.
    c. consumer surplus minus producer surplus.
    d. only producer surplus.
    e. only consumer surplus.

4. Consumer surplus will be higher when
    a. consumers dislike a product.
    b. consumers like a product.
    c. entry is free than when entry is restricted.
    d. entry is restricted than when entry is free.
    e. producing the product has a lower cost.

5. Producer surplus will be higher when
    a. consumers dislike a product.
    b. consumers like a product.
    c. entry is free than when entry is restricted.
    d. entry is restricted than when entry is free.
    e. producing the product has a lower cost.

6. The loss in benefits that comes from restricting entry is called
    a. highline loss.
    b. deadweight loss.
    c. efficient loss.
    d. producer loss.
    e. market restraint.

7. Barriers to entry are designed to
    a. encourage entry by new firms.
    b. reduce current firm's profits.
    c. discourage entry by new firms.
    d. reduce taxes.
    e. reduce employment.

8. Entry by new firms drives
    a. accounting profits to their maximum.
    b. accounting profits to zero.
    c. accounting profits to their minimum.
    d. economics profits to their maximum.
    e. economic profits to zero.

9. Which of the following is *not* a barrier to entry that a firm intentionally creates?
    a. product differentiation
    b. brand name
    c. economies of scale
    d. unique resources
    e. reputation

10. Costs that cannot be recouped are called
    a. nonmeasurable costs.
    b. sunk costs.
    c. shattered costs.
    d. variable costs.
    e. couped costs.

11. When a firm successfully differentiates its product from its competitors, the price elasticity of its demand is
    a. decreased.
    b. increased.
    c. brought to zero.
    d. brought to infinity.
    e. brought to negative infinity.

12. The time period in which all resources are variable is called the
    a. short run.
    b. extended period.
    c. medium run.
    d. long run.
    e. extensive period.

13. Economies of scale means that
    a. two scales are cheaper than one.
    b. per-unit costs increase as the size of the firm increases in the long run.
    c. per-unit costs decrease as the size of the firm increases in the long run.
    d. total costs increase as the size of the firm increases in the long run.
    e. total costs decrease as the size of the firm increases in the long run.

14. Diseconomies of scale means that
    a. two scales are cheaper than one.
    b. per-unit costs increase as the size of the firm increases in the long run.
    c. per-unit costs decrease as the size of the firm increases in the long run.
    d. total costs increase as the size of the firm increases in the long run.
    e. total costs decrease as the size of the firm increases in the long run.

15. If there are economies of scale, then
    a. a larger firm can produce a product at a lower cost than a small firm.
    b. a larger firm can produce a product at a higher cost than a small firm.
    c. a larger firm can produce a product at the same cost as a small firm.
    d. small firms make more profits than large firms.
    e. small firms make the same profits as large firms.

PRACTICE QUESTIONS AND PROBLEMS

Section 1: Characteristics of the Market Structures

1. The four market structures are _____ , _____ , _____ , and
   _____ .

2. _____ competition is the market structure in which _____ (many, few, one)
   firms are producing a(n) _____ (identical, differentiated) product and entry is
   _____ (easy, difficult, impossible).

3. _____ competition is the market structure in which _____ (many, few, one)
   firms are producing a(n) _____ (identical, differentiated) product and entry is
   _____ (easy, difficult, impossible).

4. _____ is the market structure in which there is one firm and entry is _____
   (easy, difficult, impossible).

5. _____ is the market structure in which there are few firms and entry is _____
   (easy, difficult, impossible).

6. A firm in a monopoly market has a demand curve that is _____ (horizontal,
   downward-sloping).

7. A firm in an oligopoly market has a demand curve that is _____ (horizontal,
   downward-sloping).

8. A firm in a perfectly competitive market has a demand curve that is _____ (horizontal,
   downward-sloping).

9. A firm in a monopolistic competition market has a demand curve that is _____
   (horizontal, downward-sloping).

Section 2: Firm Behavior in the Long Run

1. In the short run, new firms _____ (do, do not) have time to enter a market. In the long
   run, new firms _____ (do, do not) have time to enter a market.

2. The existing firms in a perfectly competitive market are currently receiving economic profits.
   In the long run, firms will _____ (enter, exit) the market, driving the market price
   _____ (up, down) and economic profits _____ (up, down). This will continue
   until firms are receiving _____ profits.

3. The existing firms in a perfectly competitive market are currently receiving economic losses. In
   the long run, firms will _____ (enter, exit) the market, driving the market price
   _____ (up, down) and economic profits _____ (up, down). This will continue
   until firms are receiving _____ profits.

4. In monopolistic competition, firms receive _____ (economic profits, economic losses, normal profits) in the long run.

5. In a monopoly or an oligopoly, firms usually receive _____ (economic profits, economic losses, normal profits) in the long run, unless _____ occurs.

Section 3: The Benefits of Competition

1. Consumer surplus is a bonus of the market system that goes to _____.

2. Consumer surplus is the difference between what consumers are _____ to pay for a product and what they _____ to pay.

3. Producer surplus is a bonus of the market system that goes to _____.

4. Producer surplus is the difference between what _____ are willing to accept for a product and what they actually _____.

5. If entry into a market is restricted, consumer surplus will become _____ (larger, smaller).

6. Restrictions on entry lead to some _____ loss.

7. The following graph shows a market with free entry, with price and quantity determined by where demand and supply cross. Mark the area of consumer surplus with horizontal lines, and mark the area of producer surplus with vertical lines.

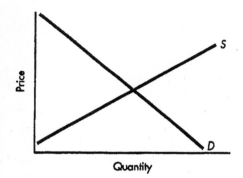

8. The following graph shows a market with entry so restricted that there is only one supplier. On this graph, show the quantity that the one supplier will produce and the price it will charge. Mark the area of consumer surplus with horizontal lines, and mark the area of producer surplus with vertical lines. Mark the deadweight loss with diagonal lines.

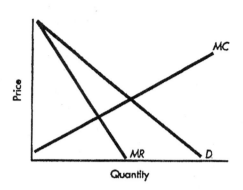

9. Compare the graphs in questions 7 and 8.

    a. Is consumer surplus larger with free entry or restricted entry? _____

    b. Is producer surplus larger with free entry or restricted entry? _____

    c. Is the sum of consumer surplus and producer surplus larger with free entry or restricted entry? _____

10. If a business wants to maintain positive economic profits over a long time period, it has to have _____.

11. A firm will have a _____ (lower, higher) price elasticity of demand if customers believe its product is better than its competitors' products, compared to its price elasticity of demand if customers believe its product is the same as its competitors' products.

12. The process of convincing customers that your product is better than your competitors' products is called _____.

13. Costs that a firm cannot recover are called _____ costs.

14. List three ways that a firm can create barriers to entry.

    _____

    _____

    _____

15. Aluminum is extracted from a mineral called bauxite. Before World War II, the Aluminum Company of America owned a lot of bauxite deposits and tried to buy new deposits of bauxite as they were discovered. Use the concepts in this section to explain why Alcoa bought all that bauxite.

    _____

    _____

    _____

16. In the long run _____ resources are variable, while in the short run only _____ resources are variable.

17. In the long run, the law of _____ does not apply.

18. Economies of scale exist when average costs _____ (increase, decrease, remain the same) as the size of the firm increases.

19. Diseconomies of scale exist when average costs _____ (increase, decrease, remain the same) as the size of the firm increases.

20. Explain why economies of scale can be a barrier to entry.

_____

_____

_____

THINKING ABOUT AND APPLYING COMPETITION

Is Advertising Profitable?

Joe's Gourmet Hamburgers is thinking about using advertising to differentiate its burgers from all the other burgers in town. An advertising agency has developed a campaign that will add $5 per hour to Joe's costs. The agency also estimated the increases in demand it expects Joe's Gourmet Hamburgers to get from the campaign.

1. The following table shows Joe's Gourmet Hamburgers current demand and costs.

Joe's Gourmet Hamburgers: Current Demand and Costs

Quantity Sold/Hour	ATC	MC	P	MR
1	$26.50	$12.50	$12.00	$12.00
2	16.25	6.00	11.00	10.00
3	11.50	2.00	10.00	8.00
4	9.25	2.50	9.00	6.00
5	8.00	3.00	8.00	4.00
6	6.79	3.50	7.00	2.00
7	7.25	4.00	6.00	0
8	6.50	4.50	5.00	−2.00

a. Joe's current profit-maximizing quantity is _____ hamburgers.

b. His current profit-maximizing price is _____.

c. At this quantity and price, Joe's economic profit would be _____.

2. The following table shows the agency's estimates of Joe's demand and costs after the advertising campaign.

Joe's Gourmet Hamburgers: With Advertising Campaign

Quantity Sold/Hour	ATC	MC	P	MR
1	$31.50	$12.50	$15.00	$15.00
2	18.75	6.00	13.75	12.50
3	13.17	2.00	12.50	10.00
4	10.50	2.50	11.25	7.50
5	9.00	3.00	10.00	5.00
6	8.08	3.50	8.75	2.50
7	7.50	4.00	7.50	0
8	7.13	4.50	6.25	−2.50

a. Joe's profit-maximizing quantity here is _____ hamburgers.

b. His profit-maximizing price is _____.

c. At this quantity and price, Joe's economic profit would be _____.

ANSWERS

QUICK-CHECK QUIZ

Section 1: Characteristics of the Market Structures

1. c;
2. e;
3. c;
4. a;
5. b;
6. d;
7. a;
8. e;
9. b

If you missed any of these questions, you should go back and review Section 1 in Chapter 6.

Section 2: Firm Behavior in the Long Run

1. e;
2. b;
3. c;
4. b;
5. a

If you missed any of these questions, you should go back and review Section 2 in Chapter 6.

Section 3: The Benefits of Competition

1. c;
2. d;
3. b;
4. c;
5. d;
6. b;
7. c;
8. e;
9. c;
10. b;
11. a;
12. d;

13. c;

14. b;

15. a

If you missed any of these questions, you should go back and review Section 3 in Chapter 6.

PRACTICE QUESTIONS AND PROBLEMS

Section 1: Characteristics of the Market Structures

1.   perfect competition; monopoly; monopolistic competition; oligopoly

2.   Perfect; many; identical; easy

3.   Monopolistic; many; differentiated; easy

4.   Monopoly; impossible

5.   Oligopoly; difficult

6.   downward-sloping

7.   downward-sloping

8.   horizontal

9.   downward-sloping

Section 2: Firm Behavior in the Long Run

1.   do not; do

2.   enter; down; down; normal

3.   exit; up; up; normal

4.   normal profits

5.   economic profits; entry

Section 3: The Benefits of Competition

1.   consumers

2.   willing; have

3.   sellers or producers

4.   sellers; receive

5.   smaller

6.   deadweight

7.

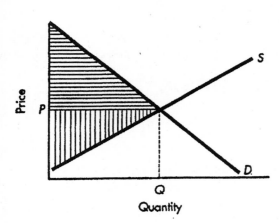

8.

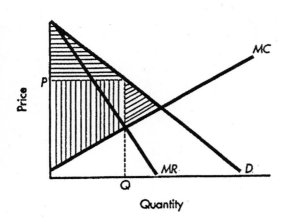

9.

   a. free entry

   b. restricted entry

   c. free entry

10. barriers to entry

11. lower

12. product differentiation

13. sunk

14. product differentiation; guarantees; unique resources

15. Owning all the bauxite in the world gave Alcoa control of a unique resource that was necessary to produce aluminum. Without access to bauxite, other firms could not enter the market for new aluminum.

16. all; some

17. diminishing marginal returns

18. decrease

19. increase

20. A new firm entering the market cannot start out small and then grow larger; to compete with existing large firms, a new firm has to start out large enough to gain all the economies of scale.

THINKING ABOUT AND APPLYING COMPETITION

Is Advertising Profitable?

1.

    a.   5 (The first 5 hamburgers have $MR > MC$. The sixth hamburger's MR is $2, less than its MC of $3.50, so it is not worth making and selling.)

    b. $8 (This is the price at which consumers will buy 5 hamburgers.)

    c.   zero ($P = ATC$)

2.

    a.   5 (The first 5 hamburgers have $MR > MC$. The sixth hamburger's MR is $2.50, less than its MC of $3.50, so it is not worth making and selling.)

    b. $10 (This is the price at which consumers will buy 5 hamburgers.)

    c. $5 [profit per hamburger = $10 ($P$) − $9 ($ATC$) = $1; $1 profit per hamburger × 5 hamburgers = $5]

CHAPTER 7

Competition, Cooperation, and the Government

FUNDAMENTAL QUESTIONS

1. Why might a firm not charge everyone the same price for the same product?

   We've been looking at firms using the $MR = MC$ rule to choose their output quantity and price; a pricing strategy is a way to apply this rule in more complex situations. So far, we've been assuming that firms charge the same price to all their customers. In some real-world markets, firms use price discrimination to charge different customers different prices.

   Also, in some real-world markets, firms are interdependent. That is, the actions of one firm have a noticeable effect on other firms, and these other firms are likely to react. Interdependence makes it more difficult for firms to choose a profit-maximizing pricing strate

2. What is the difference in rivalry between firms that are interdependent and those that are not?

   When firms are interdependent, the decisions of any one firm have a significant effect on their rivals. These rivals are then likely to react to the initial decision. Trying to figure how your rivals will react makes it much harder to determine a firm's profit-maximizing decisions.

   For example, think about what would happen in the market for pizza if Pizza Hut cut its prices for pizzas. Pizza Hut's rivals, like Domino's, Godfather's, Papa John's, and others, would lose customers to Pizza Hut—something they would not like. They could react by matching Pizza Hut's price cuts, or in other ways like offering free soda pop or bread sticks. Pizza Hut would have to figure out how its rivals would react before it can decide whether cutting prices would increase Pizza Hut's profits or not.

3. Why and under what conditions do firms cooperate rather than compete?

   Firms often cooperate with other competitors in their market. Cooperation frequently enables firms to retain economic profits that would be lost if the firms actively competed with each other. Cooperation can take many forms, from formal cartels where sellers get together and jointly set prices and divide markets, to informal collusion or price leadership. Some actions that don't seem to be cooperative, such as **cost-plus pricing** and **most-favored-customer (MFC)** arrangements, can help reduce competition.

4. Why does the government intervene in the affairs of business?

   Although competitive markets work well for consumers, many real-world markets are not very competitive. Firms in these markets may cooperate with each other to increase their profits by raising prices. In these cases, the government may interfere with the decisions of firms by making the firms act in ways that are more competitive. Sometimes, the government may intervene in markets to provide benefits to special interest groups.

KEY TERMS

business firm	prisoner's dilemma	monopolization of a market
sole proprietorship	cartel	regulation
partnership	facilitating practices	natural monopolies
corporation	cost-plus markup pricing	social regulation
dumping	most-favored customer (MFC)	rent or benefit seeking
dominant strategy	antitrust laws	

QUICK-CHECK QUIZ

Section 1: Price Strategies for Independent Firms

1. The general term for an organization in which resources are combined to produce an output is a
    a. seller.
    b. business firm.
    c. revenue generator.
    d. sole partnership.
    e. corporate entity.

2. A firm where there is only one owner is called a
    a. sole proprietorship.
    b. partner firm.
    c. corporation.
    d. combined firm.
    e. partnership.

3. A firm where the owners are shareholders is called a
    a. sole proprietorship.
    b. partner firm.
    c. corporation.
    d. combined firm.
    e. partnership.

4. A firm where there are several owners is called a
    a. sole proprietorship.
    b. partner firm.
    c. corporation.
    d. combined firm.
    e. partnership.

5.   A firm where the owners are not responsible for the debts of the firm is called a
   a.   sole proprietorship.
   b.   partner firm.
   c.   corporation.
   d.   combined firm.
   e.   partnership.

6.   Price discrimination means
   a.   making careful decisions about price.
   b.   selling different products to people with different skin colors.
   c.   charging different customers different prices for the same product.
   d.   refusing to serve certain groups of people.
   e.   providing different customers with the same product.

7.   Price discrimination is worthwhile only when
   a.   different people have different price elasticities of demand.
   b.   different people live in different places.
   c.   business firms don't maximize profits.
   d.   business firms have the same costs.
   e.   different people like different colors of the product.

8.   Which of the following is an example of peak-load pricing?
   a.   selling a red sports car for a higher price than the same car painted blue
   b.   selling a computer with specific software already installed
   c.   charging more for water during the summer, when people use lots of water on their lawns
   d.   giving shoppers who buy Crest toothpaste a 50-cents-off coupon on Colgate toothpaste
   e.   giving a buyer of a new car ten $50 bills when the deal is closed

9.   Which of the following is an example of discount coupons?
   a.   selling a red sports car for a higher price than the same car painted blue
   b.   selling a computer with specific software already installed
   c.   charging more for water during the summer, when people use lots of water on their lawns
   d.   giving shoppers who buy Crest toothpaste a 50-cents-off coupon on Colgate toothpaste
   e.   giving a buyer of a new car ten $50 bills when the deal is closed

10.   Which of the following is an example of bundling?
   a.   selling a red sports car for a higher price than the same car painted blue
   b.   selling a computer with specific software already installed
   c.   charging more for water during the summer, when people use lots of water on their lawns
   d.   giving shoppers who buy Crest toothpaste a 50-cents-off coupon on Colgate toothpaste
   e.   giving a buyer of a new car ten $50 bills when the deal is closed

11.   Which of the following is an example of rebates?
   a.   selling a red sports car for a higher price than the same car painted blue
   b.   selling a computer with specific software already installed
   c.   charging more for water during the summer, when people use lots of water on their lawns
   d.   giving shoppers who buy Crest toothpaste a 50-cents-off coupon on Colgate toothpaste
   e.   giving a buyer of a new car ten $50 bills when the deal is closed

Section 2: Interdependence

1. In markets with interdependent firms, one firm's actions will affect
    a. other firms' demand curves.
    b. other firms' marginal revenue curves.
    c. other firms' profits.
    d. all of the above.
    e. none of the above.

2. A kinked demand curve occurs when
    a. other firms follow price cuts but not price increases.
    b. other firms follow price increases but not price cuts.
    c. price leadership is operating.
    d. economic profits exist for all firms in a market.
    e. economic profits exist for only some firms in a market.

3. A firm has a dominant strategy when which alternative strategy is better
    a. depends on the choices rivals make.
    b. doesn't depend on the choices rivals make.
    c. is affected by government policies.
    d. is affected by cartel policies.
    e. depends on the choices the firm itself makes.

4. A situation where the best outcome is not selected because firms' actions depend on other firms' actions is called a
    a. definitive situation.
    b. poisoner's dilemma.
    c. static monopoly.
    d. prisoner's dilemma.
    e. flexible monopoly.

5. A cartel is a(n)
    a. firm that sells cars by telephone.
    b. firm that sells cars on the Internet.
    c. organization of sellers that dictates the quantities produced by each seller.
    d. organization of buyers that controls the prices charged by sellers.
    e. market where one firm sets its price and other firms follow.

6. Actions that lead to cooperation among rivals are called
    a. cooperative supplements.
    b. facilitating practices.
    c. factional agreements.
    d. defusing competition.
    e. positive expectations.

Section 3: Government and Firms

1. Laws that make rules defining acceptable competitive behavior are called
    a. competition laws.
    b. pro bono laws.
    c. antitrust laws.
    d. antimonopoly laws.
    e. regulations.

2. Monopolization of a market can be illegal when
    a. the monopoly is gained unfairly.
    b. consumers receive benefits from the monopoly.
    c. the monopolist benefits from economies of scale.
    d. the monopolist makes political contributions.
    e. the government grants the monopoly.

3. To economists, regulation means the
    a. control of a firm by its stockholders.
    b. use of accounting rules to prepare financial statements.
    c. control of some aspect of business by government.
    d. control of some aspect of government by business.
    e. determination of prices by demand and supply.

4. Social regulation refers to government regulation of
    a. prices.
    b. health, safety, and environmental policies.
    c. employment practices.
    d. all of the above.
    e. only b and c above.

5. Natural monopoly is caused by
    a. diseconomies of scale.
    b. economies of scale.
    c. predatory behavior.
    d. collusion among firms.
    e. social regulation.

6. Rent or benefit seeking activities use resources to gain benefits from
    a. consumers.
    b. a firm's owners.
    c. government.
    d. rival firms.
    e. partners.

PRACTICE QUESTIONS AND PROBLEMS

Section 1: Price Strategies for Independent Firms

1. A _____ is a business owned by two or more individuals who share both the profits of the business and the responsibility for the business's debts.

2. A _____ is a business owned by shareholders who are not responsible for the business's debts.

3. A _____ is a business owned by one person.

4. In the United States, the most common form of business organization is the _____.

5. In the United States, the form of business organization that generates the most revenues and profits is the _____.

6. The practice of charging different customers different prices for the same good or service is called _____.

7. _____ means that a firm is selling its product for a lower price in a foreign country than it is charging in its own country.

8. All pricing strategies are based on the profit-maximization equation _____.

9. The purpose of price discrimination is to allow a firm to get part of buyers' _____.

Section 2: Interdependence

1. Interdependence means that firms have to consider the actions of _____ in making their decisions about price and quantity.

2. A firm faces a kinked demand curve when its rival firms _____ price cuts, but _____ price increases.

3. A strategy that produces better results no matter what strategy a rival firm follows is a(n) _____ strategy.

4. An organization of independent firms whose purpose is to control and limit production and increase prices and profits is a(n) _____.

5. Cartels are generally _____ (legal, illegal) in the u.s.

6. Briefly describe how a price-leadership arrangement works.

    _____

    _____

    _____

7. Briefly explain how cost-plus markup pricing and most-favored-customer agreements facilitate cooperation among rival firms.

    _____

    _____

    _____

8. Joe's and Moe's are two competing gas stations in town. Both are considering adding a video game parlor to their stations. The payoff matrix below shows the expected daily profits for each gas station:

		Joe's Station	
		Adds Video Games	**Doesn't Add Video Games**
Moe's Station	**Adds Video Games**	Joe's $200	Joe's $100
		Moe's $500	Moe's $300
	Doesn't Add Video Games	Joe's $250	Joe's $180
		Moe's $350	Moe's $400

Video Games	Moe's $350	Moe's $400

a. Does Joe have a dominant strategy? If yes, what is it?

_____

_____

_____

b. Does Moe have a dominant strategy? If yes, what is it?

_____

_____

c. If you were Joe, would you add video games, not add video games, or wait to see what Moe does? Explain your answer.

_____

_____

_____

d. If you were Moe, would you add video games, not add video games, or wait to see what Joe does? Explain your answer.

_____

_____

_____

Section 3: Government and Firms

1. Laws designed to increase competition are called _____ laws.

2. Antitrust laws are enforced by two government agencies: _____ and _____ .

3. Antitrust laws focus primarily on _____ (large, small) businesses.

4. The prescription of prices by government is called _____; the prescribing of health, safety, environmental, and employment policies is called _____ .

5. In the U.S. at present, regulation is used primarily to control the prices charged by _____ .

6. Natural monopolies can result from large _____ .

7. During the last few decades, _____ (regulation, social regulation) has been out of favor, but _____ (regulation, social regulation) has grown

THINKING ABOUT AND APPLYING COMPETITION, COOPERATION, AND THE GOVERNMENT

Cartel Behavior

The key difference between oligopoly and other market structures is that oligopolists are interdependent: the decisions of one affect others. In many situations, interdependence creates conflicting incentives both to cooperate with others and to "cheat" on one's cooperation.

You can see how this happens in oligopolies by looking at the choices faced by a member of a cartel such as OPEC. Let's make you the oil minister of Scheherazade, a hypothetical small member of OPEC. You are responsible for managing your country's oil output and price, and your objective is to maximize your country's total revenues from oil. (Your marginal cost of producing more oil is so low that you don't have to pay any attention to costs.)

Last week, the OPEC countries met and agreed to charge $25 per barrel for oil. Scheherazade was given an output quota of 300,000 barrels per day. The following graph shows your current position and possible options. D_1 is the demand curve for your oil if the rest of OPEC ignores any price changes you make, and D_2 is your demand curve if the rest of OPEC matches any price changes. Like the kinked demand curve model, the other members of OPEC will ignore any price increases you make but will match any price cuts they know about. Use this information to answer the questions.

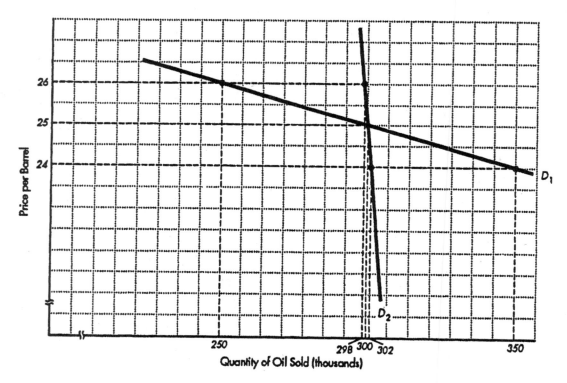

1. At $25 per barrel, Scheherazade takes in _____ from selling 300,000 barrels.

2. If you could get the rest of OPEC to go along with raising its price to $26 per barrel, Scheherazade would take in _____ .

3. Unfortunately, the rest of OPEC thinks that $25 is the best price and will not go along with a higher price. If only Scheherazade raises its price to $26, it will take in _____ .

4. Because raising your price individually will not increase your revenues, you can try cutting the price to $24. If the rest of OPEC matches your price cut, Scheherazade will take in
    _____.

5. Late one night, the buyer for Euro-Oil, a large oil refiner, knocks quietly on your door. She offers to buy 350,000 barrels of oil a day from Scheherazade if you cut the price to $24 and keep the price cut a secret. Would this deal be profitable for Scheherazade? Explain your answer.

    _____

    _____

    _____

ANSWERS

QUICK-CHECK QUIZ

Section 1: Price Strategies for Independent Firms

1. b;
2. a;
3. c;
4. e;
5. c;
6. c;
7. a;
8. c;
9. d;
10. b;
11. e

If you missed any of these questions, you should go back and review Section 1 in Chapter 7.

Section 2: Interdependence

1. d;
2. a;
3. b;
4. d;
5. c;
6. b

If you missed any of these questions, you should go back and review Section 2 in Chapter 7.

Section 3: Government and Firms

1. c;
2. a;
3. c;
4. e;
5. b;
6. c

If you missed any of these questions, you should go back and review Section 3 in Chapter 7.

PRACTICE QUESTIONS AND PROBLEMS

Section 1: Price Strategies for Independent Firms

1. partnership

2. corporation

3. sole proprietorship

4. sole proprietorship

5. corporation

6. price discrimination

7. Dumping

8. $MR = MC$

9. consumer surplus

Section 2: Interdependence

1. other firms

2. follow; don't follow

3. dominant

4. cartel

5. illegal

6. One firm determines the price, and all other firms follow along and match any price changes.

7. Cost-plus markup pricing leads to the same or very similar pricing behavior among rival firms. Firms with the same production costs figure their prices by adding the same profit margin to their costs, so that their prices come out the same without any need for collusion. Most-favored-customer agreements discourage price cutting by requiring a firm to cut its price to the price of all firms with most-favored-customer agreements rather than use selective price cuts to attract new customers from other firms.

8.

a. Yes. Joe has a dominant strategy: add video games. If Moe adds video games, Joe is better off if he adds video games ($200 compared to $100); if Moe doesn't add video games, Joe is still better off if he adds video games ($250 compared to $180).

b. No. Moe doesn't have a dominant strategy. If Joe adds video games, Moe is better off to add them too ($500 compared to $350), but if Joe doesn't add video games, Moe is better off ($400 compared to $300) not adding video games himself.

c. Because Joe has a dominant strategy in adding video games, he should go ahead and act.

d. Moe doesn't have a dominant strategy, so his decision is more complex than Joe's. Waiting to see what Joe does would be a reasonable decision, although Moe also could justify going ahead and adding video games now because he expects that Joe will choose to add video games. (Adding games is Joe's best choice.)

Section 3: Government and Firms

1. antitrust

2. Department of Justice; Federal Trade Commission

3. large

4. regulation; social regulation

5. natural monopolies

6. economies of scale

7. regulation; social regulation

THINKING ABOUT AND APPLYING COMPETITION, COOPERATION, AND THE GOVERNMENT

Cartel Behavior

1. $7,500,000 ($25 × 300,000)

2. $7,748,000 ($26 × 298,000)

3. $6,500,000 ($26 × 250,000)

4. $7,248,000 ($24 × 302,000)

5. Yes. Scheherazade will take in $8,400,000 ($24 × 350,000), so it will be quite profitable. What makes it profitable is keeping it secret so that the rest of OPEC does not match your price. Secret cheating on cartel agreements is usually profitable for any member of the cartel as long as the other members of the cartel do not find out about the cheating and match the price cut immediately.

CHAPTER 8

Social Issues

FUNDAMENTAL QUESTIONS

1. What does it mean to say "incentives matter"?

    One of the fundamental principles of economics is that people respond predictably to incentives. If the cost of buying something or taking some action increases, people will buy or do less; if the cost of buying something or taking some action decreases, people will buy or do more. This principle applies not just to purchases in the mall, but also to government policies, environmental issues, and even illegal activities. Many times, governments could do a more effective job if they remembered this principle.

2. What is the primary economic problem with the environment?

    Economists agree that perfectly competitive markets are usually economically efficient: they produce the right amount of output and allocate the right amount of resources to alternative uses. Market failure is the failure of the market system to make economically efficient decisions. In the real world, resource markets sometimes fail to produce the economically efficient output or fail to allocate resources efficiently because of externalities and poorly defined property rights.

    There are two types' of natural resources. **Nonrenewable natural resources**, like oil and natural gas, can be used only once and cannot be replaced. **Renewable resources**, like trees and animals, can replenish themselves.

    Since the amount of a nonrenewable resource is fixed, the more that is used in the present, the less that is available in the future. As the price for the resource increases, more is extracted now, leaving less for the future. As more is extracted, the supply for the future shifts up, because costs increase as producers must extract resources from less and less accessible places. Since the price of the resource will likely be higher in the future, the resource owner must decide whether to extract the resource today or save it for the future. The supply and demand for nonrenewable resources limit the rate at which the nonrenewable resources are consumed.

    Renewable resources are not fixed in quantity; however, they cannot be consumed too rapidly, or they won't be able to reproduce themselves. The role of the market for renewable resources is to determine a price at which the quantity of the resource used is just sufficient to enable the resource to renew itself at a rate that best satisfies society's wants.

    The lack of property rights is a major problem in global environmental problems. Nobody owns the air that blows from the United States into Canada. If U.S. power plant emissions cause acid rain in Canada, there is no market or government mechanism that allows the Canadians to restrict the behavior of U.S. firms, unless the Canadian government can convince the U.S. government to intervene. Solving global pollution problems requires governments to cooperate, sometimes in ways that aren't beneficial to their own interests.

3. Does the war on drugs make economic sense?

    The government's objective is to reduce the use of drugs and the crime associated with drug use. However, current measures concentrate on reducing the supply of drugs by increasing the costs. This policy reduces the number of suppliers and increases the barriers to entry, thereby ensuring that the remaining suppliers control the market and earn positive economic profits.

    Instead of focusing on reducing the supply, it might be more effective to focus on decreasing demand. The demand for illegal drugs by hard core addicts is very price inelastic, while the demand for illegal drugs by experimental users is price elastic. Any policy designed to decrease drug use must take both types of markets into account.

4. Does discrimination make economic sense?

    Discrimination is the practice of treating people differently based on a characteristic having nothing to do with that market. In the labor market, discrimination occurs when some factor not related to the individual's value to the firm affects the wage rate someone receives.

    In a freely functioning labor market, discrimination should not exist; there is a profit to be made in *not* discriminating. Of course, discrimination does exist. One source of labor market discrimination is employers' personal prejudice. Hiring people on the basis of personal prejudice adds to employers' costs and is not compatible with free markets. A second source, statistical discrimination, is a way of dealing with a lack of information: employers wrongly perceive that all members of a group have characteristics that make them less productive.

5. Does a minimum wage make economic sense?

    A **minimum wage** is a government-imposed price floor defining the least that someone can be paid. A minimum wage creates unemployment among those who have the least value to a firm, namely teenagers and low-skilled workers. It also adversely affects firms who must now hire fewer workers and pay them more.

6. Why are incomes not equally distributed?

    In a market system, income is derived from the ownership of resources: people with more resources, or with more highly valued resources, receive higher incomes. Doctors are more highly paid than ditch diggers; people who have accumulated lots of capital receive more interest than people without any savings. In the United States, the top 20 percent of the population earns over 44 percent of the total national income, and the bottom 20 percent of the population earns less than 5 percent of the national income.

    A **Lorenz curve** shows the degree to which income is distributed equally (or unequally) within a society. If all incomes are the same, the Lorenz curve is a straight line; the more unequally distributed incomes are, the more bowed the Lorenz curve becomes. Lorenz curves provide an easy way to compare **income distributions** across countries or within the same country at different times.

7. What does it mean to be in poverty?

Poverty can be measured in two ways. Lorenz curves look at poverty in relative terms: What share of the national income do the poorest people get? Poverty also can be looked at in absolute terms: What per capita income is necessary to meet basic human needs? The official U.S. poverty statistics gathered by the federal government use an absolute standard to set the minimum income level ($17,960 in 2001) that avoids poverty, based on the cost of a nutritionally adequate diet. Using this standard, over 14 percent of the U.S. population—over 36 million people—live in poverty.

The incidence of poverty is distributed unevenly across groups within the United States. Age is one factor here. Younger and older people make up most of the poverty group. The percentage of families headed by a female that are below the poverty line is much higher than that of families headed by a male; black and Hispanic families have larger percentages below the poverty line than do white families.

KEY TERMS

renewable natural resources	**positive externality**	**income distribution**
nonrenewable natural resources	**private property right**	**Lorenz curve**
private costs	**discrimination**	**poverty**
negative externality	**statistically discriminating**	
social cost	**minimum wage**	

QUICK-CHECK QUIZ

Section 1: The Environment

1. Which of the following is a renewable resource?
    a. coal
    b. the rain forest
    c. uranium
    d. oil
    e. natural gas

2. Externalities occur when
    a. someone outside a business makes decisions that affect the business.
    b. an activity creates costs or benefits that are borne by parties not directly involved in the activity
    c. taxes affect the amount of a good produced.
    d. subsidies affect the amount of a good produced.
    e. private benefits equal social benefits.

3. When private costs are less than social costs,
    a. an externality exists.
    b. resources are not being used in their highest-valued activity.
    c. a market is producing too much of a good.
    d. all of the above are true.
    e. only a and c are true.

4. Which of the following is *not* one of the policies followed by the U.S. government in attempting to improve the environment?
    a. public ownership of polluting firms
    b. assigning pollution rights
    c. regulations
    d. emissions standards
    e. assignment of private property rights

5. Which of the following statements is false?
    a. The cost of extracting a nonrenewable resource increases as the amount of the resource in existence falls.
    b. A problem with renewable resources is that they may be consumed too rapidly to replenish themselves.
    c. If private costs exceed social costs, too little of a good or service will be produced.
    d. Lack of property rights for a renewable resource results in overharvesting.
    e. The assignment of pollution rights by the EP A has resulted in increased pollution.

Section 2: Illicit Drugs

1. Which of the following statements is false?
    a. The demand for illicit drugs by hard-core users is price inelastic.
    b. When drug dealers price discriminate, they give a price break to their best customers—the hard core users.
    c. Drug cartels dictate the prices and quantities of illicit drugs sold in their territories.
    d. The government's war on drugs raises the costs of providing illicit drugs.
    e. The market for designer drugs is characterized by easy entry.

2. Which of the following statements is true?
    a. Suppliers of illicit drugs would like to see these drugs legalized because their costs would decrease.
    b. The markets for cocaine and heroin have barriers to entry.
    c. If illicit drugs were legalized, the drug cartels would make higher profits.
    d. The government's policy of eliminating drug "factories" and confiscating supplies addresses the differences between addicts and experimental users.
    e. Designer drugs are extremely difficult to manufacture.

Section 3: Discrimination

1. When factors not related to a person or group's job performance affect the workers' value in the labor market
    a. compensating wage differentials do not exist.
    b. discrimination is occurring.
    c. the supply of labor is backward bending.
    d. labor force participation is high.
    e. labor force participation is low.

2. Statistical discrimination can occur when
    a. wages are based on an individual worker's actual value to the firm.
    b. employers base wage decisions on personal prejudice.
    c. employers with imperfect information about people's productivity rely on incorrect assumptions to set wages.
    d. the immigration of unskilled people lowers the wages for all unskilled workers.
    e. an employer has a taste for or against a certain group.

Section 4: Minimum Wages

1. Which of the following groups tend *not* to suffer unemployment as a result of minimum wage laws?
    a. teenagers
    b. minorities
    c. women
    d. union workers
    e. unskilled workers

2. Which of the following statements about minimum wage laws is false?
    a. Minimum wage laws require that certain jobs pay no less than a prescribed minimum wage.
    b. Minimum wage laws can cause unemployment.
    c. An increase in the minimum wage law tends to reduce teenage employment.
    d. Minimum wage laws are price floors set above the equilibrium wage.
    e. All of these statements are true.

Section 5: Income Inequality and Poverty - part I

1. A graph that shows the degree to which income is distributed unequally within a society is called a(n)
    a. Lorenz curve.
    b. in-kind curve.
    c. poverty line.
    d. poverty ratio plot.
    e. absolute income standard.

Section 5: Income Inequality and Poverty - part II

Use the following graph to answer question 2.

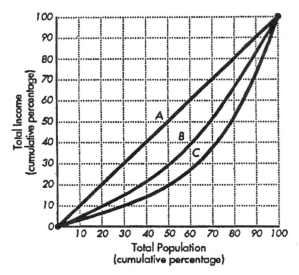

1.   Which of the following statements about these Lorenz curves is correct?
    a.   Line *A* shows the most unequally distributed income.
    b.   Line *C* shows a more equal income distribution than line *B* does.
    c.   Line *A* shows a perfectly equal distribution.
    d.   All of the above are correct.
    e.   Only a and b are correct.

Section 5: Income Inequality and Poverty - part III

1.   Relative to developed nations, less developed nations have
    a.   the same income distribution.
    b.   a more unequal income distribution.
    c.   a more equal income distribution.
    d.   an almost perfectly equal income distribution.
    e.   an almost perfectly unequal income distribution.

2.   Of the people currently below the poverty line, what percentage are expected to still be below the poverty line in ten years?
    a.   about 5 percent
    b.   about 15 percent
    c.   about 30 percent
    d.   about 50 percent
    e.   about 75 percent

PRACTICE QUESTIONS AND PROBLEMS

Section 1: The Environment

1.   _____ resources, like trees, plants, and animals can replenish themselves.

2.   _____ resources can be used only once and cannot be replaced.

3. Costs borne solely by the individuals involved in a transaction are called _____ costs.

4. A(n) _____ occurs when a cost or benefit of an activity is borne by parties not directly involved in the activity.

5. When social costs are higher than private costs, the market produces _____ (too much, not enough) of the product.

6. _____ is the right to claim ownership of an item.

7. When private property rights are ill-defined, _____ (too much, too little) of a resource is consumed.

8. Environmental problems may occur because of _____ or _____.

9. When positive externalities exist, _____ (too much, too little) of a good is consumed or produced.

Section 2: Illicit Drugs

1. The demand for illicit drugs by hard-core users is price _____ (elastic, inelastic).

2. Experimental users pay a _____ (higher, lower) price for illegal drugs than do hard core addicts.

3. The market for designer drugs _____ (is, is not) characterized by ease of entry.

4. Legalizing drugs would _____ (increase, decrease) the costs of production and _____ (increase, decrease) the profits made by drug cartels.

5. The U.S. anti-drug effort consists of trying to reduce the _____ (supply of, demand for) illegal drugs.

6. The market for heroin and cocaine is _____ (easy, difficult) to enter.

Section 3: Discrimination

1. _____ is the practice of treating people differently in a market based on characteristics having nothing to do with that market.

2. Discrimination based on personal prejudice is usually _____ (costly, profitable) for a firm.

3. _____ discrimination can occur when employers use indicators of group performance that do not accurately reflect the value to the firm of individual workers.

4. When entry is _____ (easy, difficult), having higher costs due to discrimination may drive a firm out of the market.

5. Studies have shown most discrimination takes place in _____, _____, and _____ because they have few competitors.

Section 4: Minimum Wages

1. In a competitive market, a minimum wage set above the equilibrium wage creates a labor _____.

2. The minimum wage in the United States is currently $_____ per hour.

3. Which groups are likely to suffer unemployment as a result of increases in the minimum wage law? _____

4. An increase in the minimum wage is likely to _____ (increase, decrease) teenage employment.

5. The minimum wage is a price _____ (ceiling, floor).

Section 5: Income Inequality and Poverty

1. The _____ curve shows the amount of income inequality within a society.

2. The following table gives income distribution data for the United States and Mexico for the late 1980s. On the graph below, draw the Lorenz curves for the two countries. The country with the more equal income distribution is _____.

	Lowest 20%	Second 20%	Third 20%	Fourth 20%	Highest 20%
Mexico	3	7	12	20	58
United States	5	12	18	25	40

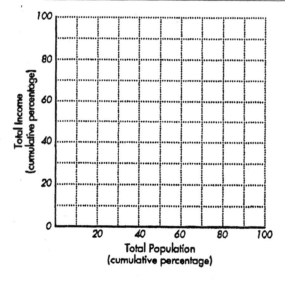

3. The poverty line for the U.S. said that a family of four was in poverty if its income was less than $_____.

4. Poverty _____ (increases, decreases) when the economy enters a recession and _____ (increases, decreases) when the economy is growing strongly.

5. The poor are primarily those without _____.

6. In terms of age, the highest incidence of poverty is for _____.

7. Income is determined by who owns _____.

THINKING ABOUT AND APPLYING SOCIAL ISSUES

I.   International Cooperation on Pollution Cleanup

Although across-border pollution problems can cause political problems, there have been instances where countries have cooperated in cleaning up pollution. One case was described in *The Wall Street Journal*:

> [Officials have] used a state law classifying lead slag as a hazardous waste to negotiate toxic-waste cleanups south of the border [in Mexico]. In the deal ... a privately-owned Dallas lead recycler said it will pay $2.5 million ... [for] improperly transporting lead waste from its Los Angeles smelter to Mexico.

Of the $2.5 million fine, $2 million was going to be spent to clean up the toxic waste, and $300,000 was going to a foundation that provides medical care for border-area residents. The Mexican government planned to use the lead recovered from the cleanup, valued at $100,000 to $200,000, to help pay the back wages to workers at the plant.

What characteristics of this agreement made it worthwhile for the United States and Mexico to cooperate in cleaning up the polluted site in Mexico? *(Hint:* Why do people choose to engage in voluntary trade?)

_____

_____

_____

II.   Comparable Worth and High School Teachers

Labor markets in the United States frequently have resulted in wage patterns that seem discriminatory; minorities and women, on average, are paid substantially less than white males. One approach (known as *comparable worth*) to making wage patterns more equal is to disregard the market forces of demand and supply and to set wages for jobs based on job characteristics. Using this approach, people who hold jobs that take place in the same sort of environment, that require the same level of responsibility, and that require the same amount of education should receive the same rate of pay.

The job market for high school teachers in most of the United States has worked this way for many years. In most high schools, teachers with the same education and years of experience are paid the same salary, regardless of the subject area they teach. This fits the comparable worth idea: the working conditions and demands on English teachers are the same as for math teachers. But ignoring demand and supply has some economic effects worth looking at.

1. Suppose U.S. high schools decide to improve the training of skilled workers by requiring students to take more math classes. The following graphs show the demand and supply (D_1 and S_1) for math teachers and English teachers before adding math classes, with both math and English teachers earning $30,000, and a new demand curve (D_2) for math teachers after adding more math classes. Mark on *graph a* the old and new equilibrium salary and number of math teachers.

(a) Market for Math Teachers

(b) Market for English Teachers

a.   The market equilibrium salary for math teachers now is _____.

b.   Using the ideas in this chapter and the last, explain why the salary has to go up to attract new math teachers.

_____

_____

_____

2. If the schools maintain equal salaries for all teachers, English teachers also will receive a salary of $35,000. Mark on *graph b* the quantity demanded and quantity supplied of English teachers when the salary is $35,000. Explain what will happen in the market for English teachers if their salaries are raised to $35,000.

_____

_____

_____

3. One of the most useful characteristics of a market economy is that price changes signal changes in the relative scarcity of different products and resources and encourage people to respond to those changes. Can you think of any ways that labor markets, by setting salaries through comparable worth, can do the same thing, without math teachers' receiving higher salaries than English teachers?

_____

_____

_____

III.   Discrimination and Minimum Wage Laws

Walter Williams, an economist and columnist, was quoted in *The Wall Street Journal* as saying, "The brunt of the minimum wage law is borne by low-skilled workers ... particularly black teenagers." In this chapter, we've found that discrimination in competitive labor markets is usually costly to employers, and minimum wage laws can create a labor surplus in competitive labor markets. Use these two ideas to explain the logic behind Williams' comment. *(Hint:* Think about the effects of a surplus on the costs of discriminating.)

_____

_____

_____

IV.   Welfare, Workfare, and Incentives to Work

In a story called "Problem of the Poor," *New York Newsday* stated:

> Liberal critics and welfare-rights groups point to [New York's] high poverty rate—60 percent above the national average—citing inadequate welfare benefits, a lack of public housing and other holes in the safety net. Yet New York has provided some of the most generous welfare benefits in the country, both in terms of the amount of benefits offered and the number of people covered ... The level of cash benefits in the basic welfare program is 50 percent above that of the median state in the United States.

The article also points out that about 16 percent of the people in New York City receive cash payments from public assistance programs, compared to less than 8 percent for the United States as a whole.

1.   Use what you've learned in this chapter and previous chapters about the supply of labor to explain why generous welfare programs in New York City might increase the number of people living in poverty in New York.

_____

_____

_____

2.   How would a workfare program change incentives? Do you think workfare is a good idea or a bad idea? Why?

_____

_____

_____

V.   Oil Wells and Interest Rates

Let's suppose you own a small oil well that produces one barrel of oil per day if you run the pump. If you don't run the pump, the oil stays in the ground and you can produce it later. Running the pump costs you $1 for every barrel you pump; you don't have any other costs to consider.

1. Your oil today sells for $21 per barrel. If the interest rate is 10 percent per year, and you expect oil to sell for $24 per barrel next year, are you better off pumping and selling a barrel of oil today or leaving it in the ground for next year? Explain your answer.

    _____

    _____

    _____

2. If the interest rate is 10 percent, what is the minimum price next year that will convince you to wait until next year to sell your oil?

    _____

3. If the interest rate is 5 percent, what is the minimum price next year that will convince you to wait until next year to sell your oil?

    _____

ANSWERS

QUICK-CHECK QUIZ

Section 1: The Environment

1. b;
2. b;
3. d;
4. a;
5. e

If you missed any of these questions, you should go back and review Section 1 in Chapter 8.

Section 2: Illicit Drugs

1. b;
2. b

If you missed either of these questions, you should go back and review Section 2 in Chapter 8.

Section 3: Discrimination

1. b;
2. c

If you missed either of these questions, you should go back and review Section 3 in Chapter 8.

Section 4: Minimum Wages

1. d;
2. e

If you missed either of these questions, you should go back and review Section 4 in Chapter 8.

Section 5: Income Inequality and Poverty - part I

1. a;

Section 5: Income Inequality and Poverty - part II

1. c;

Section 5: Income Inequality and Poverty - part III

1. b;
2. d

If you missed any of these questions, you should go back and review Section 5 In Chapter 8.

PRACTICE QUESTIONS AND PROBLEMS

Section 1: The Environment

1. Renewable

2. Nonrenewable

3. private

4. externality

5. too much

6. A private property right

7. too much

8. externalities; a lack of private property rights

9. too little

Section 2: Illicit Drugs

1. inelastic

2. lower

3. is

4. decrease; decrease

5. supply of

6. difficult

Section 3: Discrimination

1. Discrimination

2. costly

3. Statistical

4. easy

5. government agencies; firms that do business with government agencies; regulated monopolies

Section 4: Minimum Wages

1. surplus

2. $5.15

3. low-skilled workers, particularly women, teenagers and minorities

4. decrease

5. floor

Section 5: Income Inequality and Poverty

1. Lorenz

2. the United States

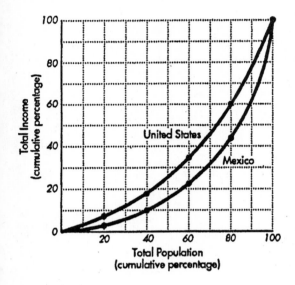

3. $17,960

4. increases; decreases

5. a job

6. young people—those under 18 years old

7. resources

THINKING ABOUT AND APPLYING SOCIAL ISSUES

I.   International Cooperation on Pollution Cleanup

Both sides benefit from the agreement. Mexico gets a cleaner environment plus some money from
the recovered lead. The United States gets $300,000 to help provide medical care.

II.   Comparable Worth and High School Teachers

1.

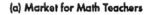

(a) Market for Math Teachers

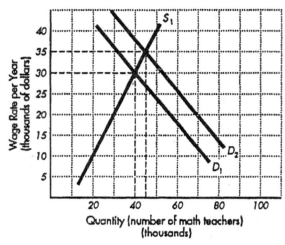

a. $35,000

b.   The salary has to increase to pay the costs of acquiring the human capital needed to be a math teacher and to compete with other occupations for people with mathematical training and ability. At the current salary, a shortage exists.

2.   There will be a surplus in the market for English teachers as the salary increase attracts more people into that occupation; at the same time, schools may hire fewer English teachers at the higher salary.

(b) Market for English Teachers

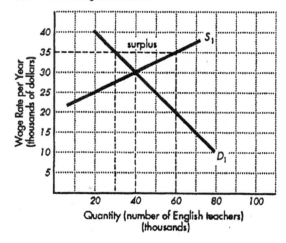

3.   There does not seem to be any way to do it. Either you keep salaries equal, or you respond to changes. You can't do both.

III.   Discrimination and Minimum Wage Laws

As we saw in this chapter, discriminatory hiring in competitive labor markets is usually costly to employers because it reduces supply and raises wages. When there is a surplus in the labor market, employers do not have to raise wages to attract new employees—there already is a pool of unemployed people looking for jobs. Employers can discriminate against some members of this pool (black teenagers, for example) and still be able to get as many employees as they want to hire at the minimum wage.

IV.   Welfare, Workfare, and Incentives to Work

1. Welfare programs raise the opportunity cost of working. Not only do you have to give up leisure to work, but you also have to give up welfare benefits. The more generous the welfare benefits, the higher the opportunity costs of working. When those costs are too high to make working worthwhile, people are better off staying on welfare.

2. Workfare removes the choice of not working and staying on welfare. It reduces the opportunity cost of working by making nonworkers ineligible for welfare benefits. Whether you think it's a good idea or not depends on your values.

3. Welfare programs raise the opportunity cost of working. Not only do you have to give up leisure to work, but you also have to give up welfare benefits. The more generous the welfare benefits, the higher the opportunity costs of working. When those costs are too high to make working worthwhile, people are better off staying on welfare.

4. Workfare removes the choice of not working and staying on welfare. It reduces the opportunity cost of working by making nonworkers ineligible for welfare benefits. Whether you think it's a good idea or not depends on your values.

V.   Oil Wells and Interest Rates

1. You should leave it for next year. If you pump the oil now, you gain $20 now—the $21 price minus the $1 cost for pumping. If you save the $20 until next year at 10 percent interest, next year you will have $22 ($20 + $2 interest). If you wait until next year to produce the oil, you will have $23 next year ($24 price – $1 cost). $23 is more than $22.

2. $23. (After you subtract your $1 cost, you would get $22 next year, the same amount you would get by producing this year and saving the money for a year.)

3. $22. (After you subtract your $1 cost, you would get $21 next year, the same amount you would get by producing this year and saving the money for a year.)

CHAPTER 9

An Overview of the National and International Economics

FUNDAMENTAL QUESTIONS

1. What is a household, and what is household income and spending?

   A household consists of one or more persons who occupy a unit of housing. Household income is the income earned by the members of the household. Household spending is called **consumption** and consists of spending on housing, transportation, food, entertainment and other goods and services.

2. What is a business firm, and what is business spending?

   A business firm is a business organization controlled by a single management. Business firms can be organized as sole proprietorships, partnerships, or corporations. Business spending by firms is called **investment** and consists of expenditures for machines, tools and buildings that are used in producing goods and services.

3. How does the international sector affect the economy?

   The nations of the world can be divided into two categories: industrial countries and developing countries. The economies of industrial nations are highly interdependent. As business conditions change in one country, business firms shift resources among countries so that economic conditions in one country spread to other countries.

   The international trade of the United States occurs primarily with its neighbors Canada and Mexico. **Exports** are products the United States sells to foreign countries. **Imports** are products it buys from other countries along with the major industrial powers. The U.S. tends to import agricultural products and minerals from developing countries. Developing countries buy mostly manufactured goods from the United States.

4. What does government do?

   The economic role of government can be divided into two categories: microeconomic policy and macroeconomic policy. Microeconomic policy deals with providing public goods, like police and military protection, correcting problems like pollution, and promoting competition. Macroeconomic policy is divided into two categories: fiscal policy and monetary policy. **Monetary policy** is directed toward control of money and credit, and **fiscal policy** is directed toward government spending and taxation.

5. How do the three private sectors—households, businesses, and the international sector- interact in the economy?

   Households own the factors of production and sell them to firms in return for income. Business firms combine the factors of production into goods and services and sell them to households and the international sector in exchange for revenue. The international sector buys and sells goods and services to business firms. The **circular flow diagram** illustrates these relationships.

6. How does the government interact with the other sectors of the economy?

   Households sell resources to the government—which uses those resources to produce government services—in return for income. Business firms sell the goods and services they produce to the government for revenue. Taxes are the income the government receives from households and business firms. In reality, the government may interact directly with foreign consumers and businesses, but most government activity with the international sector occurs when the government uses business firms as intermediaries.

KEY TERMS

Household	trade surplus	transfer payments
Consumption	trade deficit	budget surplus
multinational business	net exports	budget deficit
Investment	monetary policy	private sector
Imports	Federal Reserve	public sector
Exports	fiscal policy	circular flow diagram

QUICK-CHECK QUIZ

Section I: Households

1. Householders _____ years old make up the largest number of households.
   a. 15 to 24
   b. 25 to 34
   c. 35 to 44
   d. 45 to 54
   e. 55 to 64

2. Householders _____ years old have the largest median annual income.
   a. 15 to 24
   b. 25 to 34
   c. 35 to 44
   d. 45 to 54
   e. 55 to 64

3. The largest percentage of households consists of _____ person(s).
   a. one
   b. two
   c. three
   d. four
   e. five

4. Household spending, or consumption, is the _____ component of total spending in the economy.
   a. largest
   b. second largest
   c. third largest
   d. fourth largest
   e. smallest

5. Which of the following is <u>not</u> a component of household spending?
    a. capital goods
    b. housing
    c. transportation
    d. food
    e. entertainment

Section 2: Business Firms

1. In _____ the owner(s) of the business is(are) responsible for all the debts incurred by the business and may have to pay those debts from his/her(their) personal wealth.
    a. a sole proprietorship
    b. a partnership
    c. a corporation
    d. sole proprietorships and partnerships
    e. sole proprietorships, partnerships, and corporations

2. _____ are the most common form of business organization, but _____ account for the largest share of total revenues.
    a. Sole proprietorships; partnerships
    b. Sole proprietorships; corporations
    c. Partnerships; corporations
    d. Corporations; sole proprietorships
    e. Partnerships; sole proprietorships

3. *Investment* as used in the text is
    a. a financial transaction, like buying bonds or stock.
    b. business spending on capital goods.
    c. equal to about one-half of household spending.
    d. a relatively stable form of spending.
    e. All of the above describe *investment*.

Section 3: The International Sector

1. The United States tends to import primary products such as agricultural produce and minerals from _____ countries.
    a. low-income
    b. medium-income
    c. high-income
    d. industrial
    e. developing

2. U.S. trade is concentrated with
    a. major industrial powers.
    b. developing countries.
    c. Canada and Mexico.
    d. oil exporters.
    e. a and c

3. A trade surplus occurs when
   a. net exports are positive.
   b. net exports are negative.
   c. a country buys more from other countries than it sells to other countries.
   d. imports exceed exports.
   e. industrial countries sell to less-developed countries.

4. Low-income countries are concentrated heavily in
   a. Central America.
   b. South America.
   c. North America.
   d. Africa.
   e. Western Europe.

5. Which of the following statements is false?
   a. Imports are products that a country buys from another country.
   b. Exports are products that a country sells to another country.
   c. Net exports equal exports minus imports.
   d. Net exports equal imports minus exports.
   e. A trade surplus is the same as positive net exports.

Section 4: Overview of the United States Government

1. Combined government spending on goods and services is larger than _____ but smaller than _____.
   a. consumption; net exports
   b. consumption; investment
   c. net exports; investment
   d. investment; net exports
   e. investment; consumption

2. A budget deficit
   a. exists when federal revenues exceed federal spending.
   b. last occurred in the United States in 1969.
   c. occurs when federal spending exceeds federal revenues.
   d. has no effect on consumption and investment.
   e. has no effect on economic relationships with other countries.

3. Which of the following is a macroeconomic function of government?
   a. provision of military protection
   b. promotion of competition
   c. determining the level of government spending and taxation
   d. provision of police protection
   e. correction of pollution problems

4. The _____ is(are) responsible for fiscal policy, and the _____ is(are) responsible for monetary policy.
   a. Federal Reserve; Congress
   b. Federal Reserve; Congress and the president
   c. Congress; Federal Reserve
   d. Congress and the president; Federal Reserve
   e. Congress; Federal Reserve and the president

5.   Which agency enforces the legal setting of business?
    a.   The Office of Management and Budget
    b.   The Treasury
    c.   The Justice Department
    d.   The Council of Economic Advisors
    e.   The Treasury Department

Section 5: Linking the Sectors

1.   Which of the following statements is false?
    a.   Households sell the factors of production in exchange for money payments.
    b.   Firms buy the factors of production from households.
    c.   The value of output must equal the value of income.
    d.   The value of input must equal the value of household income.
    e.   Money that is saved by households reenters the economy in the form of investment spending.

2.   _____ own(s) the factors of production.
    a.   Corporations
    b.   Partnerships
    c.   The international sector
    d.   State and local governments
    e.   Households

3.   Which of the following is not considered one of the private sectors?
    a.   Households
    b.   Businesses
    c.   International Sector
    d.   Government

PRACTICE QUESTIONS AND PROBLEMS

Section 1: Households

1.   A(n) _____ consists of one or more persons who occupy a unit of housing.

2.   Household spending is called _____.

3.   Householders between _____ and _____ years old have the largest median incomes.

4.   A household is most likely to consist of _____ persons.

5.   _____ percent of all households are two-person households.

Section 2: Business Firms

1.   A(n) _____ is a business organization controlled by a single management.

2.   A(n) _____ is a business owned by one person.

3.   A(n) _____ is a business owned by two or more individuals who share both the profits of the business and the responsibility for the firm's losses.

4.   A(n) _____ is a legal entity owned by shareholders whose liability for the firm's losses is limited to the value of the stock they own.

5. A(n) _____ business is a firm that owns and operates producing units in foreign countries.

6. In the United States, the most common form of business organization is the _____.

7. _____ is the expenditure by business firms for capital goods.

8. _____ account for the largest percentage of business revenue.

Section 3: The International Sector

1. The _____ is an international organization that makes loans to developing countries.

2. Low-income economies are heavily concentrated in _____ _____

3. Products that a country buys from another country are called _____.

4. Products that a country sells to another country are called _____.

5. The United States trades the most with _____ , _____ and the major industrial powers.

6. A trade _____ exists when exports exceed imports

7. A trade _____ exists when imports exceed exports.

8. _____ equal exports minus imports.

9. _____ net exports signal a trade surplus; _____ net exports signal a trade deficit.

10. The World Bank groups countries according to _____.

Section 4: Overview of the United States Government

1. List three microeconomic functions of government.

    _____

    _____

    _____

2. Macroeconomic policy attempts to control the economy through _____ and _____ policy.

3. The _____ is the central bank of the United States.

4. Monetary policy is directed toward control of _____ and_____.

5. _____ involve taking money from taxpayers with higher incomes and transferring this income to those lower incomes.

Section 5: Linking the Sectors

1. The circular flow diagram shows that the value of _____ is equal to income.

2. _____ own the factors of production.

3. The _____ is a model showing the flow of output and income from one sector of the economy to another.

THINKING ABOUT AND APPLYING AN OVERVIEW OF THE NATIONAL AND INTERNATIONAL ECONOMIES

The Circular Flow Diagram

Use the diagram below to see if you understand how the three sectors of the economy are linked together. In the blanks below, fill in the appropriate labels. Money flows are represented by broken lines. Flows of physical goods and services are represented by solid lines.

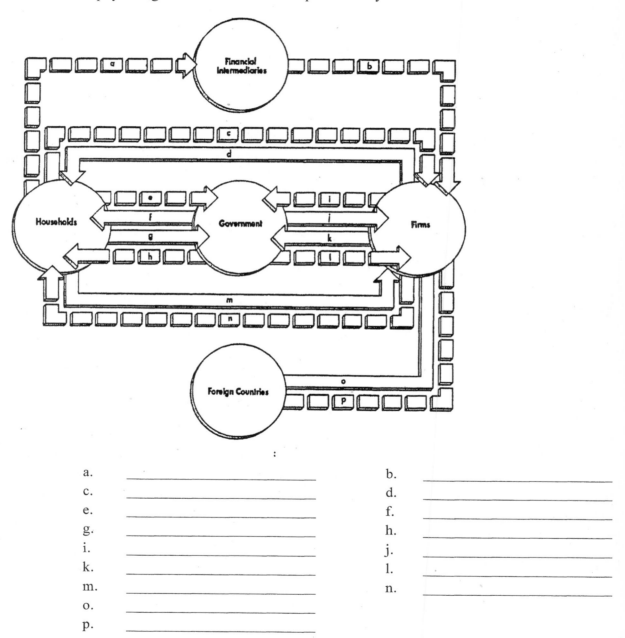

a. _____   b. _____

c. _____   d. _____

e. _____   f. _____

g. _____   h. _____

i. _____   j. _____

k. _____   l. _____

m. _____   n. _____

o. _____

p. _____

ANSWERS

QUICK-CHECK QUIZ

Section 1: Households

1. c;

2. d;

3. b;

4. a;

5. a

If you missed any of these questions, you should go back and review Section 1 in Chapter 9.

Section 2: Business Firms

1. d;

2. b;

3. b

If you missed any of these questions, you should go back and review Section 2 in Chapter 9.

Section 3: The International Sector

1. e;

2. e;

3. a;

4. d;

5. d

If you missed any of these questions, you should go back and review Section 3 in Chapter 9.

Section 4: Overview of the United States Government

1. e;

2. c;

3. c;

4. d;

5. c

If you missed any of these questions, you should go back and review Section 4 in Chapter 9.

Section 5: Linking the Sectors

1. d;

2. e;

3. d

If you missed either of these questions, you should go back and review Section 5 in Chapter 9.

PRACTICE QUESTIONS AND PROBLEMS

Section 1: Households

1. household or company or enterprise

2. consumption or consumer spending

3. 45; 54

4. two

5. thirty-three

Section 2: Business Firms

1. business firm

2. sole proprietorship

3. partnership

4. corporation

5. multinational

6. sole proprietorship

7. Investment

8. Corporations

Section 3: The International Sector

1. World Bank

2. Africa

3. imports

4. exports

5. Canada

6. surplus

7. deficit

8. Net exports

9. Positive; negative

10. per capita income

Section 4: Overview of the United States Government

1. provision of police protection;
    provision of military protection;
    correction of a problem such as pollution

2. fiscal; monetary

3. Federal Reserve

4. money; credit

5. transfer payments

Section 5: Linking the Sectors

1. output

2. Households

3. circular flow diagram

THINKING ABOUT AND APPLYING AN OVERVIEW OF THE NATIONAL AND INTERNATIONAL ECONOMIES

The Circular Flow Diagram

a. saving

b. investment

c. payments for goods and services

d. goods and services

e. taxes

f. government services

g. resource services

h. payments for resource services

i. taxes

j. government services

k. goods and services

l. payments for goods and services

m. resource services

n. payments for resource services

o. net exports

p. payments for net exports

CHAPTER 10

Macroeconomic Measures

FUNDAMENTAL QUESTIONS

1. How is the total output of an economy measured?

    Suppose you read an article in the financial section of today's newspaper in which the president argues that the Federal Reserve should lower interest rates because of recent slow growth in the economy. How did the president know that the economy was growing slowly?

    We want to be able to compare the condition of the economy across different points in time and also against the economies of other countries. How can we tell whether the economy is better or worse than before? If we are producing more goods and services than before, the economy is growing. In order to combine dissimilar items like apples and oranges, economists use the market value of goods and services. The **gross domestic product (GDP)** is the market value of all final goods and services produced in a year in a country. We use final goods and services to avoid double-counting. If a tire is to be sold directly to a consumer, the value of the tire is included in the GDP. But, if the tire is sold as part of an automobile, its value is already included in the value of the automobile, so we do not count it separately.

2. What is the difference between nominal and real GDP?

    Nominal GDP measures output in terms of its current dollar value. A rise in nominal GDP can be from an increase in physical goods and services, a rise in prices, or both. **Real GDP** measures output in constant prices. Real GDP can only increase if the production of physical goods and services increases. Real GDP is thus a better indicator of economic activity than nominal GDP.

3. What is the purpose of a price index?

    A **price index** measures the level of average prices and shows how prices, on average, have changed. If a pair of running shoes costs $75 this year, then 10 pairs of running shoes have a market value of $750. If the same shoes cost $80 next year, then 10 pairs have a market value of $800. The nominal value has increased, but we still have only 10 pairs of running shoes. A price index adjusts nominal values for price changes.

4. How is money traded internationally?

    People trade one currency for another in **foreign exchange markets**. It is not necessary for large traders to go to a specific place to conduct such transactions. Traders call a bank that deals in foreign currency and ask the bank to convert some of their dollars to the currency they want. The amount of foreign currency exchanged for dollars depends on the exchange rate—the price of one country's money in terms of another.

5. How do nations record their transactions with the rest of the world?

The record of a nation's transactions with the rest of the world is called its **balance of payments**. The balance of payments is divided into two categories: the current account and the capital account. The **current account** is the sum of the balances for merchandise, services, investment income, and unilateral transfers. The **capital account** records the transactions necessary to move these into and out of the country. The net balance in the balance of payments must be zero, so a deficit (or surplus) in the current account must be offset by a surplus (or deficit) in the capital account. A country becomes a larger net debtor (or smaller net creditor) if it shows a deficit in its current account (or surplus in its capital account).

KEY TERMS

national income accounting	gross investment	consumer price index (CPI)
gross domestic product (GDP)	net investment	cost of living adjustment (COLA)
intermediate good	national income (NI)	producer price index (PPI)
value added	personal income (PI)	foreign exchange
inventory	disposable personal income (DPI)	foreign exchange market
capital consumption allowance	nominal GDP	balance of payments
depreciation	real GDP	double-entry bookkeeping
indirect business tax	price index	current account
gross national product (GNP)	base year	balance of trade
net national product (NNP	GDP price index	capital account

QUICK CHECK QUIZ

Section 1: Measures of Output and Income

1. Gross domestic product is the
   a. market value of all goods and services produced in the United States in a year.
   b. market value of all final goods and services produced in a year.
   c. market value of all final goods and services produced in a year within a country's borders
   d. market value of all final goods and services sold in a year.
   e. total number of final goods and services produced in a year by domestic resources.

2. GDP *as expenditures* can be expressed as
   a. $C + I + G + X$.
   b. wages + interest + rent + profits − net factor income from abroad + capital consumption allowance + indirect business taxes.
   c. the sum of the values added at each stage of production.
   d. NI + indirect business taxes.
   e. NI + capital consumption allowance.

3.   Which of the following is incorrect?
      a.   PI = DPI – personal taxes
      b.   GDP = GNP – net factor income from abroad
      c.   DPI = PI – personal taxes
      d.   NI = NNP – indirect business taxes
      e.   NNP = GNP – capital consumption allowance

4.   Unplanned inventory is
      a.   a cushion above expected sales.
      b.   gross investment – capital consumption allowance.
      c.   the difference between the value of the output and the value of the intermediate goods
            used in the production of that output.
      d.   unsold goods that the firm had expected to be able to sell when it placed the order.
      e.   the market value of the goods and services produced by a firm in one year.

5.   The largest component of total expenditures is
      a.   consumption.
      b.   investment.
      c.   government spending.
      d.   net exports.
      e.   rent.

6.   To get disposable personal income from GNP, we must subtract all of the following *except*
      a.   indirect business taxes.
      b.   net factor income from abroad.
      c.   capital consumption allowance.
      d.   income earned but not received.
      e.   personal taxes.

7.   To get NNP from GNP, we subtract
      a.   capital consumption allowance.
      b.   net factor income from abroad.
      c.   capital consumption allowance and indirect business taxes.
      d.   capital consumption allowance, indirect business taxes, and personal taxes.
      e.   capital consumption allowance, indirect business taxes, net transfer payments, and
            personal taxes.

8.   National income equals
      a.   GNP – capital consumption allowance.
      b.   GNP – net factor income from abroad.
      c.   GNP – capital consumption allowance – indirect business taxes.
      d.   NNP – indirect business taxes.
      e.   Both c and d above are correct.

9.   Which of the following is counted in the GDP?
      a.   the value of homemaker services
      b.   estimated illegal drug transactions
      c.   the value of oil used in the production of gasoline
      d.   estimated in-kind wages
      e.   the sale of a used automatic dishwasher

Section 2: Nominal and Real Measures

1. Nominal GDP
    a. is real GDP divided by the price level.
    b. measures output in constant prices.
    c. decreases when the price level increases.
    d. measures output in terms of its current dollar value.
    e. is real GDP divided by the consumer price index.

2. The producer price index (PPI)
    a. is the price index given by the ratio of nominal GDP to real GDP.
    b. measures the average price of consumer goods and services that a typical household purchases.
    c. measures average prices received by producers.
    d. was originally known as the COLA.
    e. is used to get real GDP from nominal GDP.

3. The real GDP
    a. is calculated by multiplying the GDP price index by nominal GDP.
    b. measures the average level of prices in the economy and shows, on average, how prices have changed.
    c. measures output in constant prices.
    d. is calculated by dividing nominal GDP by the CPI.
    e. is calculated by dividing nominal GDP by the PPI.

4. A price index equal to 90 in a given year
    a. indicates that prices were lower than prices in the base year.
    b. indicates that the year in question was a year previous to the base year.
    c. indicates that prices were 10 percent higher than prices in the base year.
    d. is inaccurate—price indexes cannot be lower than 100.
    e. indicates that real GDP was lower than GDP in the base year.

5. Social security payments are tied to the
    a. GDP price index.
    b. CPI.
    c. PPI.
    d. wholesale price index.
    e. nominal GDP.

Section 3: Flows of Income and Expenditures

1. Total expenditures on final goods and services
    a. equal NNP.
    b. equal the total value of goods and services produced
    c. equal total income from selling goods and services.
    d. Items b and c above are correct.
    e. All of the above are correct.

Section 4: The Foreign Exchange Market Part I

1. The foreign exchange market, like the New York Stock Exchange, is located in a specific building in New York City. _____ (true or false?)

2. Most foreign exchange transactions involve the movement of currency. _____ (true or false?)

3. As a country's currency depreciates, international demand for its products _____ (rises, falls), all other things being equal.

Section 4: The Foreign Exchange Market Part II

1. If one U.S.dollar sells for 90.00 yen, then the price of the Japanese yen in terms of dollars is
    a. $.01111.
    b. $.1111.
    c. $1.1111.
    d. $90.00.
    e. $.90.

2. Suppose that a cassette recorder costs 226.44 Norwegian krone and that the current exchange rate between the U.S. dollar and the Norwegian krone is $.1590. What is the price of the cassette recorder in U.S. dollars?
    a. $1,424.15
    b. $36.00
    c. $181.15
    d. $283.05
    e. $212.99

3. Suppose that the exchange rate between the U.S. dollar and the Australian dollar is $.7985 (1A$ = $.7985). If the exchange rate tomorrow is $.7975, then the Australian dollar has _____ against the U.S. dollar. Australian goods will be _____ in the United States
    a. appreciated; more expensive
    b. appreciated; less expensive
    c. depreciated; more expensive
    d. depreciated; less expensive
    e. depreciated; the same price as before

4. If an Austrian schilling is equivalent to $.088677 U.S. dollars, then $1 is equal to _____ schillings, and an opal ring costing 1,700 schillings would have a U.S. dollar value of _____.
    a. 11.28; $19,170.70
    b. 11.28; $150.75
    c. .09; $19,170.70
    d. .09; $150.76
    e. 1; $1.700

5. If the U.S. dollar drops to 1.1485 euros from 1.1598 euros, then the dollar has
   a. appreciated against the euro, and the prices of European cars will increase in the United States.
   b. appreciated against the euro, and the prices of European cars will decrease in the United States
   c. depreciated against the euro, and the prices of European cars will increase in the United States.
   d. depreciated against the euro, and the prices of European cars will decrease in the United States
   e. depreciated against the euro, and the prices of American cars will increase in Europe.

6. The great majority of transactions in the foreign exchange market involve
   a. foreign coins.
   b. foreign paper money.
   c. bank deposits denominated in foreign currency.
   d. foreign currency.
   e. items b and c above.

Section 5: The Balance of Payments

1. Which of the following is *not* included in the current account?
   a. merchandise balances
   b. service balances
   c. unilateral transfer accounts
   d. investment income
   e. All of the above are included in the current account.

2. If a Japanese investor bought the Epic Center office building in Wichita, Kansas, the transaction would be recorded as a _____ in the _____ account.
   a. credit; current
   b. debit; current
   c. credit; investment income
   d. credit; capital
   e. debit; capital

3. Before the 1980s, the United States traditionally had what kind of balance in its investment income account because of its large investments in the rest of the world?
   a. deficit
   b. surplus

4. Trade involving financial assets and international investment is recorded in the _____ account.
   a. current
   b. merchandise
   c. capital
   d. services
   e. investment income

5. If export goods exceed import goods, the (merchandise, services, unilateral transfers) account will show a (deficit, surplus).
    a. merchandise; deficit
    b. merchandise; surplus
    c. services; deficit
    d. services; surplus
    e. unilateral transfers; surplus

6. Which account contains all of the activities involving goods and services?
    a. merchandise
    b. services
    c. unilateral transfers
    d. current
    e. capital

7. In the terminology of the balance of payments, *capital* refers to all of the following *except*
    a. bank deposits.
    b. purchases of stocks.
    c. purchases of bonds
    d. loans.
    e. purchases of equipment.

8. A country with a deficit in its current account
    a. exports more goods and services than it imports.
    b. is running a deficit in its capital account.
    c. is a net lender to the rest of the world.
    d. is a net borrower from the rest of the world.
    e. is running a surplus in its merchandise account.

9. The net balance in the balance of payments
    a. is positive if a country is a net creditor to the rest of the world.
    b. is negative if a country imports more goods and services than it exports.
    c. is negative if the country is a net debtor to the rest of the world.
    d. is positive if a country exports more goods and services than it imports.
    e. must be zero.

10. The United States
    a. has always run a surplus in its merchandise account.
    b. typically runs a surplus in its unilateral transfers account.
    c. typically runs a deficit in its services account.
    d. was an international creditor from the end of World War I until the mid-1980s.
    e. had large capital account deficits in the 1980s.

PRACTICE QUESTIONS AND PROBLEMS

Section 1: Measures of Output and Income - part I

1. Gross domestic product is the _____ value of all goods _____ and services produced in a year within a country's borders.

2. _____ are goods that are used in the production of a final product.

3. _____ is the difference between the value of output and the value of the intermediate goods used in the production of that output.

4. _____ is, a firm's stock of unsold goods.

5. The estimated value of capital goods used up or worn out in a year plus the value of accidental damage to capital goods is called _____ or depreciation.

6. Excise taxes and sales taxes are forms of _____.

7. List the three factors of production and the name of the payments each factor receives. What additional three items must be figured in to find gross domestic product?

_____

_____

_____

8. GNP minus net factor income from abroad yields _____.

9. A lei maker buys flowers from a nursery for $125. She makes 50 leis from the flowers and sells each lei for $3.99. What is the value added for the lei maker? _____.

10. A Kansas farmer sells wheat to a craftsperson to make into decorative ornaments. The farmer sells his wheat to the craftsperson for $300. The craftsperson adds labor, valued at $200, and some ribbons, valued at $50, and produces 110 ornaments. What is the final market value of each ornament? _____.

11. Unplanned inventory _____ (is, is not) included in the GDP.

12. Government spending on goods and services _____ (is, is not) the largest component of GDP as expenditures.

13. Write the formulas for the following:

Gross domestic product as expenditures (GDP):

Gross domestic product as income (GDP):

Gross national product (GNP):

Net national product (NNP):

National income (NI):

Personal income (PI):

Disposable personal income (DPI):

14. Use the following information to calculate GDP, GNP, NNP, and NI. All figures are in billions of dollars.

Capital consumption allowance	328	Wages and salaries	1,803
Corporate profits	124	Personal taxes	398
Rents	6	Indirect business taxes	273
Interest	264	Proprietor's income	248
Net factor income from abroad	43		

GDP _____

GNP _____

NNP _____

NI _____

Section 2: Nominal and Real Measures

1. The following table shows nominal GDP and the implicit GDP deflator for 3 years. Use this information to calculate the real GDP and to answer the following questions.

Year	Nominal GDP	Implicit GDP Deflator	Real GDP
1	206	98	_____
2	216	100	_____
3	228	115	_____

   a. Which year is the base year? _____.

   b. Prices in year 3 were _____ (higher, lower) than prices in the base year.

   c. During year 3, nominal GDP _____ (increased, did not change, decreased)

2. An increase in the _____ index can indicate a coming change in the CPI.

3. Why isn't nominal GDP a good measure of the strength or weakness of the economy? What measure would be better?

_____

_____

_____

4. If the price index in the current year is 212, then prices have _____ (increased, not changed, decreased) by _____ percent from the base year.

Section 3: Flows of Income and Expenditures

1. Fill in the following diagram with the terms listed below. Dollar flows are represented by
    broken lines. The flow of physical goods and services is represented by solid lines.

    investment
    payments for goods and services
    taxes
    resource services
    net exports

    saving
    goods and services
    government services
    payments for resource services
    payments for net exports

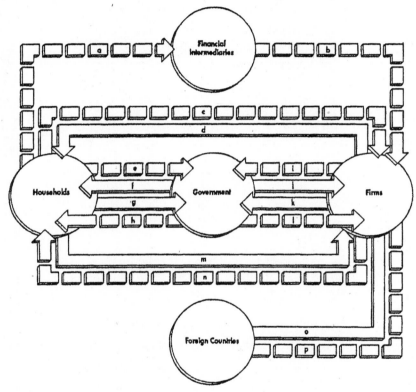

Section 4: The Foreign Exchange Market

1. _____ is another expression for foreign money.

2. A global market in which people trade one currency for another is called a(n) _____ .

3. A(n) _____ is the price of one country's money in terms of another.

4. A rise in the value of currency is called _____, and a decrease in the value of a
    currency is called _____ .

5.   What is the price of one U.S. dollar given the following exchange rates?

   a.   1 Canadian dollar = $.86610

   b.   1 Swiss franc = $.70597

   c.   1 Euro = $.8707

   d.   11 Japanese yen = $.00677

   e.   1 British pound = $1.8155

6.   A 35mm camera manufactured in the United States costs $150. Using the exchange rates listed in the following table, what would the camera cost in each of the following countries?

Country	U.S. Dollar Equivalent	Currency per U.S. Dollar
Euro area (euro)	.8707	1.1485
Greece (drachma)	.006196	161.40
Netherlands (guilder)	.5379	1.8590
Pakistan (rupee)	.0463	21.61
Philippines (peso)	.04413	22.66

   a.   Euro area

   b.   Greece

   c.   Netherlands

   d.   Pakistan

   e.   Philippines

7.   Suppose the dollar ended at 1.4165 Swiss francs today, well above yesterday's 1.4045 francs.

   a.   The dollar has _____ (appreciated, depreciated) against the franc.

   b.   Swiss goods are now _____ (more expensive, cheaper) in the United States.

   c.   As a result of the change in exchange rates, U.S. exports to Switzerland will _____ (increase, decrease), all other things being equal.

8.   You read in the paper that the Finnish markka is expected to depreciate against the dollar, Therefore, the price of a Finnish sweater sold in the United States will _____ (increase, decrease) and the price of U.S. blue jeans sold in Finland will _____ (increase, decrease).

Section 5: The Balance of Payments

1.   The _____ is a record of a country's trade in goods, services, and financial assets with the rest of the world.

2.   _____ record activities that bring payments into a country, and _____ record activities that involve payments to the rest of the world.

3.   _____ means that for every transaction there is a credit entry and a debit entry.

4.   When exports exceed imports, the merchandise account shows a _____.

5.   The balance on the _____ account is frequently referred to as the balance of trade.

6. A net _____ owes more to the rest of the world than it is owed.

7. The sum of the balances in the merchandise, services, investment income, and unilateral transfers accounts is called the _____ account.

8. Use the following table to calculate the current account, capital account, and statistical discrepancy for the mythical country of Dimmenland.

Account	Credit	Debit	Net Balance
Merchandise	412.68	212.89	199.79
Services	142.52	108.37	34.15
Investment income	114.24	91.12	23.12
Unilateral transfers			−100.32
Current account			_____
Capital account	170.36	322.36	_____
Statistical discrepancy			_____

9. Refer to problem 8. Dimmenland is running a _____ (deficit, surplus) in its current account and a _____ (deficit, surplus) in its capital account. Dimmenland is becoming a greater net _____ (debtor, creditor) to the rest of the world.

10. Net exports is the sum of the merchandise and services balances. Refer to problem 8. Calculate Dimmenland's net exports. If consumption = $2,490, investment = $58.48, and government spending = $540.12, what is Dimmenland's GDP? _____

THINKING ABOUT AND APPLYING MACROECONOMIC MEASURES

I.   Difficulties in Measuring GDP

GDP is used to measure economic performance and to determine whether the overall standard of living is improving or declining. But does GDP really measure the total output of the economy? Decide if each item listed below is counted as part of GDP. If the item is *not* counted but is productive activity, indicate whether its omission overstates or understates GDP.

1. cocaine sold by Colombians to U.S. consumers

2. your parents' service to the family doing housework

3. a college textbook published this year

4. the fee for your cat's yearly rabies vaccine

5. intermediate goods

6. $10 paid for a 3-year-old infant car seat purchased at a garage sale

7. your teacher's salary this year

8. this year's rental income from an office building

9. the services of a homeowner painting his or her own house

10. pollution produced as a result of steel production

II.   The Expenditures Approach for Calculating GDP

1. Use the information below to calculate GDP, GNP, NNP, NI, PI, and DPI. All figures are in billions of dollars.

Net factor income from abroad: 112

Income earned but not received: 110

Personal taxes: 198

Government purchases of goods and services: 396

Capital consumption allowance: 684

Personal consumption expenditures: 1,326

Imports: 800

Gross private domestic investment: 296

Income received but not earned: 225

Exports: 670

Indirect business taxes: 515

GDP   _____

GNP   _____

NNP   _____

NI   _____

PI   _____

DPI   _____

III.   Understanding Price Indexes

Suppose the economy of Strandasville produces only four goods: trolls, pizza, desk chairs, and sweaters. The following tables show the dollar value of output for three different years.

Year	Number of Trolls	Price per Troll	Number of Pizzas	Price per Pizza
1	1,000	$5	8,000	$6.60
2	1,000	$6	8,000	$6.60
3	4,000	$7	10,000	$6.80

Year	Number of Desk Chairs	Price per Chair	Number of Sweaters	Price per Sweater
1	3,000	$20	5,000	$20
2	3,000	$25	5,000	$18
3	3,500	$25	4,900	$15

1. Calculate the total dollar value of output for year 1, year 2, and year 3.

2. The dollar value of output in year 2 is higher than the dollar value of output in year 1

    a. entirely because of price changes.

    b. entirely because of output changes.

    c. because of both price and output changes.

3. The dollar value of output in year 3 is higher than the dollar value of output in year

    a. entirely because of price changes.

    b. entirely because of output changes.

    c. because of both price and output changes.

IV. Reconciling GDP as Income and GDP as Expenditures

Martin Rabblerouser is trying to calculate the GDP for an obscure Latin American country, but has gotten his accounts all mixed up. Use the information below to calculate

1. GDP as expenditures _____

    _____

2. GDP as income   _____

    _____

Income received but not earned: 133

Net factor income from abroad: 50

Personal consumption expenditures: 2,466

Rent: 15

Capital consumption allowance: 396

Imports: 25

Indirect business taxes: 331

Personal taxes: 452

Income earned but not received: 45

Government spending: 691

Wages: 2,200

Gross investment: 457

Profits: 454

Interest: 284

Exports: 11

Your answers to (1) and (2) should match

3. Now use your answer from (1) and (2) and the information above to calculate GNP, NNP, NI, PI, and DPI.

GNP   _____

NNP   _____

NI   _____

PI   _____

DPI   _____

V.   The Balance of Payments as an Indicator

A surplus in the merchandise account means that a nation is exporting more goods than it is importing. This is often interpreted as a sign that a nation's producers can produce at a lower cost than their foreign counterparts. A trade deficit may indicate that a nation's producers are less efficient than their foreign counterparts.

Interpret these statements in terms of what you have read about the United States as the world's largest debtor nation. Can you explain why many analysts viewed the U.S. balance of payments accounts with concern in the mid-1990s?

_____

_____

_____

VI.   The Balance of Payments and Exchange Rates

If U.S. residents lend and invest less in foreign countries than foreigners lend and invest in the United States, the capital account will be in surplus. If U.S. purchases of foreign stocks and bonds exceed foreign purchases of U.S. stocks and bonds, then more funds are leaving the country than entering it, and the capital account will be in deficit. Pretend that you are willing to sell your stereo system to a French resident. Would you prefer to be paid in U.S. dollars or French francs? Since you can't easily spend francs in this country, you would prefer to be paid in U.S. dollars. So if the French buy more U.S. goods and services, they will need dollars to pay for them, and the dollar will appreciate against the franc. Similarly, if U.S. investors demand more French bonds and stocks, the franc will appreciate.

What impact will a capital account surplus have on a domestic currency? If U.S. federal budget deficits continue, what will be the impact on the dollar?

_____

_____

_____

VII. The Current Account

Martin Rabblerouser has gotten his accounts all jumbled again. Please place these accounts under their proper heading.

travel and tourism   merchandise   investment income
unilateral transfers   insurance premiums   services
royalties   transportation costs

Current Account

1. _____

2. _____

3. _____

    a. _____

    b. _____

    c. _____

    d. _____

4. _____

VIII. Japan's Trade Surplus

In the mid-90s, The *Wall Street Journal* reported that U.S. and Japanese negotiators would meet in Washington to discuss a "framework accord" aimed at opening Japanese markets.

> "Mr. Bentsen [Treasury Secretary] and other U.S. officials increasingly blame Japan for much of what ails the world's economy. Mr. Bentsen said Japan's huge trade surplus hurts world growth, and he continued his call on Japan to step up government spending or cut taxes to strengthen its economy . . . ."

From what you know about the balance of payments, is Mr. Bentsen referring to a surplus in Japan's current account or in its capital account? Is Japan a net lender to or a net borrower from the rest of the world?

_____

_____

_____

ANSWERS

QUICK-CHECK QUIZ

Section 1: Measures of Output and Income

1. c;

2. a;

3. a;

4. d;

5. a;

6. b;

7. a;

8. e;

9. d

If you missed any of these questions, you should go back and review Section 1 of Chapter 10.

Section 2: Nominal and Real Measures

1. d;

2. c;

3. c;

4. a;

5. b

If you missed any of these questions, you should go back and review Section 2 of Chapter 10.

Section 3: Flows of Income and Expenditures

1. d.

    If you missed this question, you should go back and review Section 3 of Chapter 10.

Section 4: The Foreign Exchange Market

1. false;

2. false;

3. rises;

1. a;

2. b;

3. d;

4. b;

5. c;

6. c

If you missed any of these questions, you should go back and review Section 4 of Chapter 10.

Section 5: The Balance of Payments

1. e;

2. d;

3. b;

4. c;

5. b;

6. d;

7. e;

8. d;

9. e;

10. d

If you missed any of these questions, you should

PRACTICE QUESTIONS AND PRO

Section 1: Measures of Output an

1. market; final

2. Intermediate goods

3. Value added

4. Inventory

5. capital consumption allowance

6. indirect business taxes

7. real property; rent: labor: wages and profits: capital: interest

    To get GDP, you must add capital consumption allowance and indirect business taxes, and subtract net factor income from abroad.

8. gross domestic product

9. $74.50 (The lei maker gets $3.99 for each of her 50 leis, for a total of$199.50. Since her cost for the flowers was $125, her value added is $199.50 – $125 = $74.50.)

10. $5 (The total of the values added is $300 + $200 + $50 = $550. The 110 ornaments are worth $550, or $5 each.)

11. is

12. is not (Consumption is the largest expenditure component.)

Chapter 10: Macroeconomi

154

13. GDP(as expenditures) =

GDP (as income) =
business taxes + c

GNP = GDP +

NNP = GNF

NI = NN

PI =

$C + I + G + X$

ages + rent + interest + profits − net factor income from abroad + indirect
pital consumption allowance

et factor income from abroad

− capital consumption allowance

P − indirect business taxes

NI + income received but not earned − income earned but not received

PI = PI − personal taxes

. GDP = wages + rent + interest + profits (corporate profits + proprietor's income) − net factor
income from abroad + indirect business taxes + capital consumption allowance = 1,803 + 6 +
264 + (124 + 248) − 43 + 328 + 273 = 3,003

GNP = GDP + net factor income from abroad = 3,003 + 43 = 3,046

NNP = GNP − capital consumption allowance = 3,046 − 328 = 2,718

NI = NNP − indirect business taxes = 2,718 − 273 = 2,445

Section 2: Nominal and Real Measures

1.

Year	Real GDP
1	206/98 × 100 = 210.20
2	216 (this is the base year)
3	228/115 × 100= 198.26

  a. Year 2. (You can tell because the price index is 100 for that year.)

  b. higher

  c. increased; decreased

2. producer price

3. Increases in nominal GDP can come about from a rise in prices, an increase in output, or both.
To know if the economy is performing better than before, we need to know if output has
increased. Real GDP is a better measure, since it rises only when output has increased.

4. increased; 112

Section 3: Flows of Income and Expenditures
1.

line a—saving

line b—investment

line c—payments for goods and services

line d—goods and services

line e—taxes

line f—government services

line g—resource services

line h—payment for resource services

line i—taxes

line j—government services

line k—goods and services

line l—payments for goods and services

line m—resource services

line n—payments for resource services

line o—net exports

line p—payment for net exports

Section 4: The Foreign Exchange Market
1. Foreign exchange
2. foreign exchange market
3. exchange rate
4. appreciation; depreciation
5.

    a. $1/.86610 = C\$I.154601$

    b. $1/.70597 = SF1.4164907$

    c. $1/.8707 = € 1.1485$

    d. $1/.00677 = ¥147.71048$

    e. $1/1.8155 = £.5508124$

6.

   a. $\$150 \times €\,1.1485/\$ = €\,172.275$

   b. $\$150 \times DrI61.40/\$ = Dr24{,}21\ 0$

   c. $\$150 \times FL1.8590/\$ = FL278.85$

   d. $\$150 \times RS21.61/\$ = RS3{,}241.5$

   e. $\$150 \times 22.66\ pesos/\$ = 3{,}399\ pesos$

7.

   a. appreciated

   b. cheaper

   c. decrease

8. decrease; increase

Section 5: The Balance of Payments

1. balance of payments

2. Credits; debits

3. Double-entry bookkeeping

4. surplus

5. merchandise

6. debtor

7. current

8. current account = 156.74 (merchandise balance + services balances + investment income + unilateral transfers = 199.79 + 34.15 + 23.12 − 100.32 = 156.74)

   capital account = −152 (capital credits − capital debits = 170.36 − 322.36 = −152)
   statistical discrepancy = 4.74 (current account + capital account + statistical discrepancy = 0, 156.74 + (−152) + statistical discrepancy = 0)

9. surplus; deficit; creditor

10. 3,322.54 (net exports = merchandise balance + services balance = 199.79 + 34.15 = 233.94, GDP = $C + I + G + X$ = 2,490 + 58.48 + 540.12 + 233.94 = 3,322.54)

THINKING ABOUT AND APPLYING MACROECONOMIC MEASURES

I.   Difficulties in Measuring GDP

1. The Colombians' sale of cocaine to U.S. consumers is an illegal activity and therefore not represented in the GDP. If the resources used to produce cocaine are domestically owned and production occurred this year, then this activity should be included in the GDP. Its omission would understate the GDP.

2. This activity does not involve a market transaction and therefore is not included in the GDP. It is productive activity, however, and its omission understates the GDP.

3. A college textbook published this year would be included in the GDP.

4. The fee for your cat's yearly rabies vaccine would be included in the GDP.

5. Intermediate goods are not counted in the GDP. To do so would be double-counting.

6. A 3-year-old car seat was not produced this year. It is not and should not be counted in the GDP.

7. Your teacher's salary this year is for productive activity and is included in the GDP.

8. This year's rental income from an office building represents productive activity-the use of the space over a period of time. It is included in the GDP.

9. The services of a homeowner painting his or her own house would not be included in the GDP, since no market transaction is involved. However, it does represent productive activity and should be included. GDP is understated by its omission.

10. Some economists feel that the production of "bads" such as pollution should be included in GDP if we are to get a true picture of economic well-being. Production of "bads" such as pollution is not currently included in GDP. Inclusion of "bads" would lower the GDP.

II.   The Expenditures Approach for Calculating GDP

1. GDP = $C+I+G+X$ = 1,326 + 296 + 396 + (670 – 800)= 1,888

    GNP = GDP + net factor income from abroad = 1,888 + 112 = 2,000

    NNP = GNP – capital consumption allowance = 2,000 – 684 = 1,316

    NI = NNP – indirect business taxes = 1,316 – 515 = 801

    PI = NI – income earned but not received + income received but not earned
        = 801 – 110 + 225 = 916

    DPI = PI – personal taxes = 916 – 198 = 718

III.   Understanding Price Indexes

1. The dollar value of output for year 1 is 1,000(5) + 8,000(6) + 3,000(20) + 5,000(20) = 213,000.
    For year 2 the value is 1,000(6) + 8,000(6.6) + 3,000(25) + 5,000(18) = 223,800.
    For year 3 the value is 4,000(7) + 10,000(6.8) + 3,500(25) + 4,900(15) = 257,000.

2. a

3. c

IV.   Reconciling GDP as Income and GDP as Expenditures

1. GDP (as expenditures)   = $C + I + G + X$
    = $2,466 + 457 + 691 + (11 - 25) = 3,600$

2. GDP (as income) =   wages + rent + interest + profits – net factor income from abroad + indirect business taxes + capital consumption allowance

    = $2,200 + (-15) + 284 + 454 - 50 + 331 + 396 = 3,600$

3. GNP   =   GDP + net factor income from abroad = $3,600 + 50 = 3,650$

    NNP   =   GNP – capital consumption allowance = $3,650 - 396 = 3,254$

    NI   =   NNP – indirect business taxes = $3,254 - 331 = 2,923$

    PI   =   NI + income received but not earned – income earned but not received
    = $2,923 + 133 - 45 = 3,011$

    DPI   =   PI – personal taxes = $3,011 - 452 = 2,559$

V.   The Balance of Payments as an Indicator

A merchandise deficit may indicate that domestic producers have higher costs than their foreign competitors. Many analysts viewed the mid-1990s current account deficit as a sign that U.S. manufacturers had lost their competitive edge.

VI.   The Balance of Payments and Exchange Rates

A capital account surplus means that there are more foreign purchases of U.S. stocks and bonds than U.S. purchases of foreign stocks and bonds. Foreign purchasers therefore need to acquire U.S. dollars, so the dollar will appreciate. U.S. federal budget deficits may signal higher domestic interest rates. Foreign investors will be attracted to the high U.S. interest rates, and the dollar will appreciate.

VII.   The Current Account

Current Account

1. merchandise

2. unilateral transfers

3. services

    a.   travel and tourism

    b.   royalties

    c.   insurance premiums

    d.   transportation costs

4. investment income

VIII. Japan's Trade Surplus

Mr. Bentsen refers to a surplus in Japan's current account, meaning that Japan exported more goods and services than it imported. Japan is a net lender to the rest of the world.

CHAPTER 11

Unemployment, Inflation, and Business Cycles

FUNDAMENTAL QUESTIONS

1. What is a business cycle?

   Business cycles are recurring patterns of ups and downs in real GDP. A typical cycle has four stages: expansion, peak, contraction, and trough. During an economic expansion (boom), output, employment, incomes, and prices all rise. A peak is reached, after which economic activity declines. During the contraction (**recession**) phase, output, employment, and income all drop. If the contraction is severe enough, prices may also decline. The trough marks the end of a contraction and the beginning of a new expansion.

2. How is the unemployment rate defined and measured?

   The **unemployment rate** is the percentage of the labor force that is not working. Economists do not include the entire population in the labor force; it is of little consequence, for example, that a newborn baby is unemployed. To be in the U.S. labor force, an individual must be working or actively seeking work.

   Some types of unemployment have more impact on the economy than others. *Frictional unemployment* occurs when previously employed workers change jobs or new workers seek their first jobs. *Seasonal unemployment* is a product of regular, recurring changes in the hiring needs of certain industries. Both these types of unemployment tend to be short-term. Structural unemployment, on the other hand, results from fundamental changes in the structure of the economy and can be long-term. Structurally unemployed persons can't find *any* job they can do. Likewise, *cyclically unemployed* persons who are out of work because the economy is in a recession may be unemployed for a long time.

3. What is the cost of unemployed resources?

   The cost of unemployed resources is lost output. **Potential real GDP** is the level of output that can be produced if all non labor resources are fully utilized and unemployment is at its natural rate- that is, if the economy is producing the level of output it can realistically produce. To measure lost output, one subtracts the actual real GDP from potential real GDP. The resulting figure indicates the *GDP gap*—the cost of unemployed resources.

   Economists do not advocate a zero unemployment rate. Some unemployment is necessary so workers may be channeled to their most productive employment as their skills change. Economists use the term **natural rate of unemployment** to describe the unemployment rate that would exist in the absence of cyclical unemployment. It describes the labor market when the economy is producing what it realistically can produce. Estimates of the natural rate of unemployment vary from 4 percent to around 7 percent.

4. What is inflation?

   Inflation is a sustained rise in the average level of prices. This does not mean that *all* prices will rise. Some may rise and some may fall, but inflation occurs when the *average* level of prices rises.

5. Why is inflation a problem?

    Inflation is not a problem if prices and incomes rise at the same rate. But if incomes rise more slowly than prices, households will not be able to buy as many goods and services as they did before. Unanticipated inflation redistributes income away from those who receive fixed incomes toward those who make fixed expenditures. Suppose that your mother agrees to lend you $1,000 for school and that prices unexpectedly double between the time you receive the money and the time you repay your mother. Your mother has lost half of her purchasing power; the $1,000 that you paid back can only buy what $500 bought at the time she lent you the money. Your mother, like other creditors, has lost purchasing power to inflation.

KEY TERMS

business cycle	unemployment rate	nominal interest rate
recession	discouraged workers	real interest rate
depression	underemployment	demand-pull inflation
leading indicator	potential real GDP	cost-push inflation
coincident indicator	natural rate of unemployment	hyperinflation
lagging indicator	inflation	

QUICK-CHECK QUIZ

Section 1: Business Cycles

1. All of the following are leading economic indicators except
    a. the average workweek.
    b. unemployment claims.
    c. new plant and equipment orders.
    d. the prime interest rate.
    e. All of the above are leading indicators.

2. All of the following change at the same time real output changes *except*
    a. inventories to sales ratio.
    b. personal income.
    c. payroll employment.
    d. industrial production.
    e. manufacturing and trade sales.

3. Which of the following does *not* change its value until after the value of real GDP has changed?
    a. outstanding commercial loans
    b. the prime interest rate
    c. the labor cost per unit of output
    d. unemployment duration
    e. All of the above are lagging indicators.

4.   In correct sequence, the four stages of the business cycle are
      a.   peak, boom, expansion, and contraction.
      b.   peak, contraction, trough, and expansion.
      c.   recession, expansion, peak, and boom.
      d.   contraction, trough, boom, and expansion.
      e.   recession, contraction, peak, and boom.

5.   Which of the following statements is true?
      a.   Leading indicators are infallible predictors of future changes in real GDP.
      b.   Business fluctuations are called business cycles because they tend to follow regular and predictable patterns.
      c.   Real GDP has risen over the long term.
      d.   According to the NBER, there have been eight recessions since 1929.
      e.   The average time workers are unemployed is a coincident indicator.

6.   Which of the following statements is false?
      a.   Consumer expectations are a leading indicator.
      b.   The inventories to sales ratio is a lagging indicator.
      c.   Manufacturing and trade sales are a coincident indicator.
      d.   The money supply is a coincident indicator.
      e.   Delivery times of goods are a leading indicator.

Section 2: Unemployment

1.   To arrive at the number in the U.S. labor force, we subtract all of the following from the number of all U.S. residents *except*
      a.   residents under 16 years old.
      b.   institutionalized adults.
      c.   adults who are not looking for work.
      d.   unemployed adults.
      e.   All of the above must be subtracted from the number of U.S. residents to arrive at the number in the labor force.

2.   Which of the following cause(s) the unemployment rate to be overstated?
      a.   discouraged workers
      b.   underground economic activities
      c.   part-time employment
      d.   underemployment
      e.   students who are not looking for work

3.   A graduating college basketball star who has one month off before reporting to his new NBA team is an example of
      a.   frictional unemployment.
      b.   structural unemployment.
      c.   cyclical unemployment.
      d.   technological unemployment.
      e.   a rich, employed person.

4. Unemployed migrant workers are examples of
    a. frictional unemployment.
    b. seasonal unemployment.
    c. structural unemployment.
    d. discouraged workers.
    e. cyclical unemployment.

5. A person who finds that her skills are no longer needed because she has been replaced by a machine is an example of
    a. frictional unemployment.
    b. seasonal unemployment.
    c. cyclical unemployment.
    d. search unemployment.
    e. structural unemployment.

6. A steelworker who has been laid off during a recession is an example of
    a. frictional unemployment.
    b. seasonal unemployment.
    c. cyclical unemployment.
    d. search unemployment.
    e. structural unemployment.

7. Job training and counseling are policy measures used to fight primarily
    a. frictional unemployment.
    b. seasonal unemployment.
    c. cyclical unemployment.
    d. structural unemployment.
    e. both a and d.

8. Which of the following statements is false?
    a. The GDP gap widens during recessions and narrows during expansions.
    b. The natural rate of unemployment varies over time and across countries.
    c. Men have higher unemployment rates than women because women move out of the labor force to have children.
    d. Teenagers have the highest unemployment rates in the economy.
    e. Nonwhites have higher unemployment rates than whites.

Section 3: Inflation

1. If a college professor's income has increased by 3 percent at the same time that prices have risen by 5 percent, the professor's real income has
    a. decreased by 2 percent.
    b. increased by 2 percent.
    c. Increased by 7 percent.
    d. decreased by 7 percent.
    e. not changed.

2. Which of the following groups benefits from unexpectedly high inflation?
    a. creditors
    b. retirees on fixed incomes
    c. debtors
    d. workers whose salaries are tied to the CPI
    e. suppliers who have contracted to supply a fixed amount of their product for a fixed price

3. Which of the following could be a cause of demand-pull inflation?
    a. war in the Middle East, which can increase oil prices
    b. drought in the Midwest, which can cause crop failures
    c. suppliers who increase their profit margins by raising prices faster than their costs increase
    d. increased government spending in the absence of increased taxes
    e. labor unions, which can force wage increases that are not justified by increases in productivity

4. Which of the following statements is true?
    a. The higher the price level, the higher the purchasing power of money.
    b. Demand-pull inflation can be a result of increased production costs.
    c. High rates of inflation are generally caused by rapid growth of the money supply.
    d. Unexpectedly high inflation redistributes income away from those who make fixed dollar payments toward those who receive fixed dollar payments.
    e. The real interest rate increases as the rate of inflation increases.

5. A lender who does not expect any change in the price level is willing to make a mortgage loan at a 10 percent rate of interest.   If that same lender anticipates a future inflation rate of 5 percent, she will charge the borrower
    a. 5 percent interest.
    b. 10 percent interest.
    c. 15 percent interest.
    d. 2 percent interest.
    e. 1/2 percent interest.

PRACTICE QUESTIONS AND PROBLEMS

Section 1: Business Cycles

1. The recurring pattern of real GDP rising and then falling is called a(n) _____.

2. When real GDP is growing, the economy is in the _____ phase, or boom period, of the business cycle.

3. The _____ marks the end of a contraction and the start of a new business cycle.

4. The _____ marks the end of the expansion phase of a business cycle.

5. Real GDP falls during the contraction, or _____ phase of the business cycle.

6. The _____ has the responsibility of officially dating recessions in the United States.

7. A(n) _____ is a prolonged period of severe economic contraction.

8. _____ change before real GDP changes.

9. _____ are economic variables that tend to change at the same time real output changes.

10. Variables that do not change their value until after the value of real GDP has changed are called _____.

Section 2: Unemployment

1. The _____ is the percentage of the labor force that is not working.

2. _____ have given up looking for work because they believe that no one will hire them.

3. The employment of workers in tasks that do not fully utilize their productive potential is called _____.

4. _____ unemployment is a product of business-cycle fluctuations.

5. _____ unemployment is a product of regular, recurring changes in the hiring needs of certain industries over the months or seasons of the year.

6. _____ unemployment is a product of short-term movements of workers between jobs and of first-time job seekers.

7. _____ unemployment is a product of technological change and other changes in the structure of the economy.

8. The level of output produced when non labor resources are fully utilized and unemployment is at its natural rate is called _____.

9. The _____ is the unemployment rate that would exist in the absence of cyclical unemployment.

10. Potential real GDP minus actual real GDP equals the _____.

11. The existence of _____ and _____ causes the official unemployment rate in the United States to be understated.

12. The existence of the underground economy causes the official unemployment rate in the United States to be _____.

13. Economists measure the cost of unemployment in terms of _____.

Section 3: Inflation

1. _____ is a sustained rise in the average level of prices.

2. The higher the price level, the _____ the purchasing power of the dollar.

3. The observed rate of interest in the market is called the _____ rate of interest.

4. The nominal interest rate minus the rate of inflation equals the _____ interest rate.

5. Unexpectedly high inflation hurts _____ and benefits _____ because it lowers real interest rates.

6. _____ inflation is the result of increased spending that is not offset by increases in the supply of goods and services.

7. Increases in prices caused by increases in production costs characterize _____ inflation.

8. A very high rate of inflation is called a(n) _____.

9. _____-push pressures are created by suppliers who want to increase their profit margins by raising prices faster than their costs increase.

10. _____-push pressures are created by labor unions and workers who are able to increase their wages faster than their productivity.

THINKING ABOUT AND APPLYING UNEMPLOYMENT, INFLATION, AND BUSINESS CYCLES

I. Economic Indicators

A clumsy economist has dropped his basket of the following economic indicators, and now they are all jumbled together. Try to use economic reasoning to sort them out in the table that follows.

- Labor cost per unit of output
- Money supply
- Stock prices
- Prime interest rate
- Payroll employment
- Average workweek
- Outstanding commercial loans
- Interest rate spread
- New plant and equipment orders
- Unemployment duration
- Unemployment claims
- Manufacturing and trade sales
- New building permits
- Personal income
- Consumer credit to personal income ratio
- Manufacturers' new orders
- Inventories to sales ratio
- Delivery time of goods
- Industrial production
- Consumer expectations
- Inflation rate for services

Leading Indicators	Coincident Indicators	Lagging Indicators
_____	_____	_____
_____	_____	_____
_____		_____
_____		_____
_____		

_____

_____

_____

II.   Unemployment Rates and Discouraged Workers

1. The tiny country of Lanastan has a civilian labor force of 40,000, of whom 38,000 are employed. There are _____ unemployed persons in Lanastan, and the unemployment rate is _____ percent.

2. Five hundred of the unemployed people become discouraged and quit looking for a job. Now the official unemployment rate in Lanastan _____ is percent. These discouraged workers have _____ the unemployment rate.

III.   Inflation and the Elderly

Thanks to the late congressman Claude Pepper, most of us immediately think of elderly people living on fixed incomes when we think of people who are hurt by unexpected inflation. Social security payments are now indexed to the CPI, but elderly people still say they are hurt by unexpected inflation: the inflation adjustment does not cover the rising prices of things they must buy. What do elderly people buy that is inadequately represented by the CPI?

_____

_____

_____

IV.   In or Out of the Labor Force?

The Department of Labor defines the labor force as all u.s. residents minus residents under 16 years old minus institutionalized adults minus adults who are not looking for work. A person is seeking work if he or she is available to work, has looked for work in the past four weeks, is waiting for a recall after being laid off, or is starting a job within 30 days.

Place an "X" next to those who would be considered part of the labor force.

_____   Per Olsen is a Norwegian citizen who is looking for a job in the United States. He plans to move to the U.S. to marry his American sweetheart.

_____   Carl Wolcutt is a retired police chief who has recently been offered a position as head of his state's police academy. Mr. Wolcutt is happily raising beagles and has turned down the job.

_____   Blake Stephans has just been laid off from his quality-control job at Boeing. He is waiting for a recall, but the company has just announced it will lay off even more workers.

_____   Thomas Buttking is a recent college graduate who quit his part-time job but is taking the summer off before searching for a "real" job.

_____   Joe Shocker, a pitcher on Wichita State University's baseball team, has been selected in the first round of the draft and expects to join the Mets after he finishes playing in the College World Series. In the meantime he will enjoy the sights and sounds of beautiful downtown Omaha.

V.   Illustrating the Business Cycle

The horizontal axis measures time and the vertical axis measures economic activity. Label the points on the diagram with the appropriate phases of the business cycle.

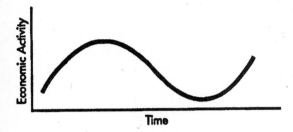

VI.   Economic Reporting

Assume you a reporter for *The Wall Street Journal.* Respond to the following developments. You should bear in mind whether the indicator in question leads, lags, or moves with the economy.

1. The Commerce Department has just released its index of leading indicators, which rose only 0.1 percent in April after dropping 1 percent the previous month. What can you tell your readers about the probable growth of the economy?

_____

_____

_____

2. The Commerce Department reported that new plant and equipment orders were flat in April after a 3.7 percent decline in March. What does this news imply about the economy?

_____

_____

_____

3. Stock prices rose in April, up 4.8 percent from March.

_____

_____

_____

4. The Commerce Department originally reported that the economy grew at a 1.8 percent annual rate in the first quarter. What measure was released? The figures were revised after the U.S. trade deficit increased sharply in March. Would your estimate of economic growth be revised upward or downward as a result of the trade figures?

_____

_____

_____

ANSWERS

QUICK-CHECK QUIZ

Section 1: Business Cycles

1. d;

2. a;

3. e;

4. b;

5. c;

6. d

If you missed any of these questions, you should go back and review Section 1 of Chapter 11.

Section 2: Unemployment

1. d;

2. b;

3. a;

4. b;

5. e;

6. c;

7. e;

8. c

If you missed any of these questions, you should go back and review Section 2 of Chapter 11.

Section 3: Inflation

1. a;

2. c;

3. d;

4. c;

5. c

If you missed any of these questions, you should go back and review Section 3 of Chapter 11.

PRACTICE QUESTIONS AND PROBLEMS

Section 1: Business Cycles

1. business cycle

2. expansion

3. trough

4. peak
5. recession
6. NBER (National Bureau of Economic Research)
7. depression
8. Leading indicators
9. Coincident indicators
10. lagging indicators

Section 2: Unemployment

1. unemployment rate
2. Discouraged workers
3. underemployment
4. Cyclical
5. Seasonal
6. Frictional (or search)
7. Structural
8. potential real GDP
9. natural rate of unemployment
10. GDP gap
11. discouraged workers; underemployment
12. overstated
13. lost output (or the GDP gap)

Section 3: Inflation

1. Inflation
2. lower
3. nominal
4. real
5. creditors; debtors
6. Demand-pull
7. cost-push
8. hyperinflation
9. Profit
10. Wage

THINKING ABOUT AND APPLYING UNEMPLOYMENT, INFLATION, AND BUSINESS CYCLES

I. Economic Indicators

Leading Indicators	Coincident Indicators	Lagging Indicators
Money supply	Payroll employment	Labor cost per unit of output
Stock prices	Manufacturing and trade sales	Prime interest rate
Average workweek	Personal income	Outstanding commercial loans
Interest rate spread	Industrial production	Unemployment duration
New plant and equipment orders		Consumer credit to personal
Unemployment claims		income ratio
New building permits		Inventories to sales ratio
Manufacturers' new orders		Inflation rate for services
Delivery time of goods		
Consumer expectations		

II. Unemployment Rates and Discouraged Workers

1. 2,000; 5

   (To find the number of unemployed persons, we subtract the number employed from the number in the labor force: $40,000 - 38,000 = 2,000$. The unemployment rate is the number unemployed divided by the labor force: $2,000/40,000 = .05$, or 5 percent.)

2. 3.8; understated

   (If 500 unemployed people drop out of the labor force, the labor force becomes $40,000 - 500 = 39,500$. We still have 38,000 employed, so the number of "unemployed" people is $39,500 - 38,000 = 1,500$. The official unemployment rate becomes $1,500/39,500 = .03789746$, or about 3.8 percent. Thus the existence of discouraged workers understates the true unemployment rate.)

III. Inflation and the Elderly

Elderly people spend a greater proportion of their incomes on health-care costs than the "typical" family represented in the CPI market basket. Since health-care costs have been rising faster than the CPI, increases in social security payments linked to the CPI do not keep up with increases in health-care costs.

IV. In or Out of the Labor Force?

Mr. Olsen is not in the U.S. labor force since he is not a U.S. resident.

Mr. Wolcutt is not looking for work and therefore would not be considered part of the labor force.

X Mr. Stephans was laid off and is waiting for a recall, so he is part of the labor force.

Thomas Buttking is not looking for work and therefore would not be considered part of the labor force.

X Joe Shocker will start a new job within 30 days, so he is part of the labor force.

V.   Illustrating the Business Cycle

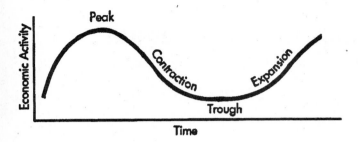

VI.   Economic Reporting

1. A one-time increase in the index of leading indicators does not signal an expansion. Economists look for several consecutive months of a new direction in the leading indicators before forecasting a change in output. When these figures came out, most economists said the new numbers did not really suggest anything new.

2. New plant and equipment orders are a leading indicator. One would expect orders for new plant and equipment to increase when the economy enters an expansion. By themselves, the previous decline and subsequent flat performance suggest that the economy may be in a rut, but there is not enough evidence to tell.

3. Stock prices are a leading indicator. By itself, a big increase might indicate that the economy is picking up, but several months of increase are needed to establish a pattern.

4. The GDP is the main measure of the economy's performance. The increase in the trade deficit indicates that net exports decreased. Since $GDP = C + I + G + X$; the GDP would be revised downward.

CHAPTER 12

Macroeconomic Equilibrium: Aggregate Demand and Supply

FUNDAMENTAL QUESTIONS

1. What is aggregate demand?

   Aggregate demand is the relation between aggregate expenditures and the price level. The downward slope of the **aggregate demand curve** is due to the wealth effect, the interest rate effect, and the international trade effect.

2. What causes the aggregate demand curve to shift?

   Anything that affects consumption, investment, government spending, or net exports will cause the aggregate demand curve to shift: changes in income, wealth, demographics, expectations, taxes, the interest rate, technology, the cost of capital goods, capacity utilization, foreign income and price levels, exchange rates, and government policies.

3. What is aggregate supply?

   The **aggregate supply curve** shows the quantity of national output (or income) produced at different price levels. It has an upward slope because higher prices, all other things being equal, mean higher profits which induce producers to offer more output for sale.

4. Why does the short-run aggregate supply curve become steeper as real GDP increases?

   As the level of real GDP increases, more and more sectors of the economy approach capacity. In order to lure resources from other uses, firms must offer higher and higher resource payments. Prices must rise higher and higher to induce increases in output. Finally, no more output can be produced and existing output must be "rationed" to those who are willing to pay the highest prices.

5. Why is the long-run aggregate supply curve vertical?

   The **long-run aggregate supply curve** is vertical because, in the long run, there is no relationship between changes in the price level and changes in output. The economy has made all of its adjustments, and no further output can be produced with existing resources and technology. In particular, higher prices cannot induce more output.

6. What causes the aggregate supply curve to shift?

   The aggregate supply curve shifts if resource prices, technology, or expectations change.

7. What determines the equilibrium price level and real GDP?

   The equilibrium price level and real GDP are determined by the intersection of aggregate demand and aggregate supply.

KEY TERMS

wealth effect

interest rate effect

international trade effect

aggregate demand curve

aggregate supply curve

long-run aggregate supply curve *(LRAS)*

QUICK-CHECK QUIZ

Section 1: Aggregate Demand, Aggregate Supply, and Business Cycles

1. If aggregate demand increases,
   a. the equilibrium price and the level of real GDP will increase.
   b. the equilibrium price will increase, but the level of real GDP will decrease.
   c. the equilibrium price and the level of real GDP will decrease.
   d. the equilibrium price will decrease, but the level of real GDP will increase.
   e. unemployment will increase.

2. If aggregate supply increases,
   a. the equilibrium price and the level of real GDP will increase.
   b. the equilibrium price will increase, but the level of real GDP will decrease.
   c. the equilibrium price and the level of real GDP will decrease.
   d. the equilibrium price will decrease, but the level of real GDP will increase.
   e. demand-pull inflation will result.

3. Demand-pull inflation results from
   a. an increase in aggregate demand.
   b. a decrease in aggregate demand.
   c. an increase in aggregate supply.
   d. a decrease in aggregate supply.
   e. the price level rising because of higher production costs.

4. Cost-push inflation results from
   a. an increase in aggregate demand.
   b. a decrease in aggregate demand.
   c. an increase in aggregate supply.
   d. a decrease in aggregate supply.
   e. the price level rising because of increasing demand for output.

5. Which of the following would cause an increase in both the equilibrium price level and the equilibrium level of real GDP?
   a. an increase in aggregate demand
   b. a decrease in aggregate demand
   c. an increase in aggregate supply
   d. a decrease in aggregate supply
   e. a decrease in aggregate demand accompanied by an increase in aggregate supply

Section 2: Factors That Influence Aggregate Demand

1. Which of the following does *not* affect consumption?
    a. income
    b. wealth
    c. expectations
    d. the cost of capital goods
    e. taxation

2. Which of the following is *not* a determinant of investment?
    a. the interest rate
    b. profit expectations
    c. disposable income
    d. the cost of capital goods
    e. capacity utilization

3. Which of the following will increase investment?
    a. an increase in the rate of capacity utilization
    b. an increase in interest rates
    c. an increase in disposable income
    d. an increase in the cost of capital goods
    e. a decrease in expected profits

4. Which of the following will *not* decrease investment?
    a. an increase in the cost of capital goods
    b. an improvement in technology
    c. an increase in interest rates
    d. unfavorable changes in tax policy
    e. rumors that the government will nationalize firms

5. Which of the following will increase consumption?
    a. a decrease in disposable income
    b. an increase in wealth
    c. gloomy expectations about the economy
    d. a decrease in population
    e. an increase in expected profits

6. Which of the following does the text cite as a determinant of government spending?
    a. population
    b. disposable income
    c. interest rates
    d. taxes
    e. The text does not cite any of these as determinants of government policy; it assumes that government authorities set government spending at whatever level they choose.

7. Which of the following is *not* a determinant of exports?
    a. foreign income
    b. domestic disposable income
    c. tastes
    d. government trade restrictions .
    e. exchange rates

8. Which of the following will *not* cause an increase in exports?
   a. an increase in foreign incomes
   b. domestic currency depreciation
   c. a favorable change in tastes
   d. domestic currency appreciation
   e. a lowering of trade restrictions

9. Which of the following does *not* affect aggregate demand?
   a. consumption
   b. production costs
   c. investment
   d. government spending
   e. net exports

Section 3: The Aggregate Demand Curve

1. Which of the following will increase aggregate demand?
   a. a decrease in wealth
   b. an increase in interest rates
   c. a decrease in foreign incomes
   d. appreciation of the domestic currency
   e. an increase in foreign price levels

2. Which of the following will *not* decrease aggregate demand?
   a. expectations that the economy is heading toward a recession
   b. depreciation of the domestic currency
   c. a fall in foreign incomes
   d. an increase in the cost of capital goods
   e. excess capacity in manufacturing

3. Which of the following will increase aggregate demand?
   a. an increase in taxes
   b. an increase in the proportion of middle-age households
   c. an increase in government spending
   d. a decrease in taxes
   e. items c and d above

4. Which of the following is a reason for the aggregate demand curve to slope downward?
   a. the substitution effect
   b. the income effect
   c. the interest rate effect
   d. the expectations effect
   e. the foreign price level effect

5. When prices increase, people and businesses need _____ money. They _____ bonds, causing interest rates to _____ and aggregate expenditures to _____.
   a. more; buy; fall; rise
   b. more; sell; fall; rise
   c. more; buy; rise; fall
   d. more; sell; rise; fall
   e. less; buy; fall; rise

6. When the price level falls, domestic goods become _____ for foreigners.   Net exports _____, and aggregate expenditures _____.   This is called the _____ effect.
    a. cheaper; rise; rise; international trade
    b. cheaper; fall; fall; international trade
    c. cheaper; rise; fall; international trade
    d. more expensive; fall; fall; international trade
    e. cheaper; rise; rise; wealth

7. Which of the following does *not* cause aggregate demand to have a negative slope?
    a. wealth effect
    b. substitution effect
    c. international trade effect
    d. interest rate effect
    e. All of the above cause aggregate demand to have a negative slope.

8. When the price level falls, the value of household and business assets _____. Households and firms spend _____, the aggregate expenditures _____. This is called the _____ effect.
    a. increases; more; rise; income
    b. increases; more; rise; wealth
    c. decreases; less; fall; income
    d. decreases; less; fall; wealth
    e. decreases; more; rise; wealth

9. Which of the following do *not* cause aggregate demand to shift?
    a. changes in expectations
    b. changes in the price level
    c. changes in foreign incomes
    d. changes in foreign prices
    e. changes in government policy

Section 4: Aggregate Supply

1. The aggregate supply curve illustrates a _____ relationship between the quantity of national output and different price levels. This relationship is explained by the effect of _____.
    a. negative; changing prices on profits
    b. positive; changing prices on profits
    c. negative; relative price changes
    d. positive; negative price changes
    e. positive; changes in interest rates

2. Which of the following will cause aggregate supply to shift?
    a. changes in the domestic price level
    b. changes in real GDP
    c. changes in foreign incomes
    d. changes in resource prices
    e. changes in national output

3. If a change in technology reduces costs, we move from _____ to _____ on the graph below.
    a. point *A;* point *B*
    b. point *B;* point *C*
    c. point *A;* point *C*
    d. AS_1; AS_2
    e. AS_1; AS_3

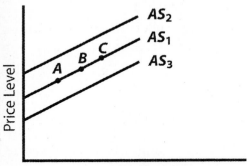

4. The long-run aggregate supply curve is
    a. upward-sloping, because of the effect of higher prices on profits.
    b. horizontal, reflecting excess capacity in all parts of the economy.
    c. upward-sloping, reflecting excess capacity in some parts of the economy.
    d. horizontal, because there is no relationship between the price level and national income in the long run.
    e. vertical, because there is no relationship between the price level and national income in the long run.

5. Which of the following statements is false?
    a. The long-run aggregate supply curve can shift to the right if new technologies are developed.
    b. The long-run aggregate supply curve can shift to the left if the quality of the factors of production decreases.
    c. The long-run aggregate supply curve is fixed at potential output and cannot shift.
    d. An increase in long-run aggregate supply will decrease the equilibrium price level.
    e. A decrease in long-run aggregate supply will decrease the equilibrium level of real GDP.

6. The slope of the aggregate supply curve is explained by
    a. relative price changes.
    b. the effect of changing prices on profits.
    c. the wealth effect.
    d. the interest rate effect.
    e. the international trade effect.

7. Which of the following will increase aggregate supply?
    a. an increase in resource prices
    b. a change in technology which increases productivity
    c. an increase in the price level
    d. a decrease in the price level
    e. anticipated higher prices

8.   Which of the following will decrease aggregate supply?
   a.   a decrease in foreign price levels
   b.   new government regulations which require an expensive new technology to reduce pollutants
   c.   appreciation of the domestic currency
   d.   an increase in government spending
   e.   a decrease in foreign incomes

Section 5: Aggregate Demand and Supply Equilibrium

1.   A temporary increase in the equilibrium price level and the equilibrium level of income can result from a(n)
   a.   increase in aggregate demand.
   b.   decrease in aggregate demand.
   c.   increase in aggregate supply.
   d.   decrease in aggregate supply.
   e.   change in the price of resources.

2.   A permanent decrease in inflation coupled with an increase in the equilibrium level of income can only result from a(n)
   a.   increase in aggregate demand.
   b.   decrease in aggregate demand.
   c.   increase in aggregate supply.
   d.   decrease in aggregate supply.
   e.   decrease in government spending.

3.   Which of the following statements is true?
   a.   In the long run, the short-run aggregate demand curve shifts so that changes in aggregate supply determine the price level, not the equilibrium level of income.
   b.   In the long run, the short-run aggregate demand curve shifts so that changes in aggregate supply determine the equilibrium level of income, not the price level.
   c.   In the long run, the equilibrium level of output never changes.
   d.   In the long run, there is a positive relationship between the level of prices and the level of output
   e.   In the long run, the short-run aggregate supply curve shifts so that changes in aggregate demand determine the price level, not the equilibrium level of income.

PRACTICE QUESTIONS AND PROBLEMS

Section 1: Aggregate Demand, Aggregate Supply, and Business Cycles

1.   _____ represents the total spending in the economy at alternative price levels.

2.   _____ represents the total output of the economy at alternative price levels.

3.   _____ inflation is inflation caused by increasing demand for output.

4.   If aggregate demand falls, the equilibrium level of income _____.

5.   A(n) _____ in aggregate supply leads to an increase in the equilibrium level of national income.

6.   An increase in the price level caused by increased costs of production is called _____ inflation.

7. The slope of the aggregate demand curve is _____.

8. The slope of the aggregate supply curve is _____ (in the short run).

Section 2: Factors That Influence Aggregate Demand

1. If wealth decreases, consumption _____.

2. _____ is spending by households.

3. If households expect an economic expansion, _____ increases.

4. If demographics change so that a greater percentage of the population consists of older households, consumption _____.

5. As foreign income rises, net exports _____.

6. If a new trade agreement with Japan succeeds in opening Japanese markets to U.S. goods, net exports will _____.

7. _____ (Price effects, Nonprice effects) are reflected in movements along the aggregate demand curve; _____ (price effects, nonprice effects) are shifts in aggregate demand.

8. _____ equal exports minus imports.

9. When consumers expect future income to increase, consumption _____ (increases, decreases, does not change).

10. All other things being equal, economists expect consumption to _____ (rise, fall, not change) as the population increases.

11. As taxation increases, consumption _____ (rises, falls, does not change).

12. _____ is business spending on capital goods and inventories.

13. As household wealth increases, consumption _____ (increases, decreases).

14. List the five determinants of consumption.

    _____

    _____

    _____

    _____

    _____

15. As the interest rate falls, the rate of return from an investment _____ (rises, falls).

16. As the cost of capital goods rises, the amount of investment _____ (rises, falls).

17. When capacity utilization is high, investment tends to _____ (rise, fall).

18. List the four determinants of investment.

    _____

    _____

    _____

    _____

19. When the domestic currency depreciates, imports _____ (rise, fall).

20. The higher the domestic income, the _____ (higher, lower) the net exports.

21. List the four determinants of net exports.

_____

_____

_____

_____

22. When domestic income increases, imports _____ (increase, decrease).

Section 3: The Aggregate Demand Curve

1. As the level of prices increases, the purchasing power of money _____ (increases, decreases), and the real value of assets _____ (increases, decreases). The _____ effect, or real-balance effect, predicts that the real value of aggregate expenditures will then (rise, fall).

2. When prices increase, people _____ (buy, sell) bonds to get money. Bond prices _____ (increase, decrease), and interest rates _____ (rise, fall). The _____ effect suggests that aggregate expenditures will then _____ (rise, fall).

3. If domestic prices rise while foreign prices and foreign exchange rates remain constant, domestic goods will become _____ (less expensive, more expensive) for foreigners. Net exports will _____ (rise, fall), causing aggregate expenditures to _____ (rise, fall).

4. When the price level falls, aggregate expenditures _____ (rise, fall).

5. The _____ shows how the equilibrium level of expenditures changes as the price level changes.

6. If foreign prices fall, foreign goods become _____ (less expensive, more expensive), which causes _____ (a movement along the aggregate demand curve, a shift to the left of the aggregate demand curve).

7. A fall in the domestic price level causes _____ (a movement along the aggregate demand curve, a shift in aggregate demand to the left).

8. List the three types of price-level effects on total spending.

_____

_____

_____

9. Positive expectations about the economy increase _____ and _____, which in turn _____ (increases, decreases) aggregate demand.

10. Higher foreign incomes cause _____ to rise, causing _____ (a movement along the aggregate demand curve, a shift in aggregate demand to the right).

Section 4: Aggregate Supply

1. The _____ shows the quantity of national output (or income) produced at different price levels.

2. The slope of the short-run aggregate supply curve is _____ because of the effect of changing prices on _____ .

3. If the prices of output increase while all other prices remain unchanged, business profits will _____ (increase, decrease), and producers will produce _____ (more, less) output.

4. The _____ is the period of time when costs are variable.

5. The _____ is the period of time when all production costs remain constant.

6. List the three nonprice determinants of short-run aggregate supply.

   _____

   _____

   _____

7. When the prices of resources fall, the short-run aggregate supply curve shifts to the _____ (right, left).

8. The _____ of the short-run aggregate supply curve reflects the fact that some sectors of the economy are approaching capacity.

9. Where the capacity output is reached, the short-run aggregate supply curve is a _____ line.

10. The _____ curve is a vertical line at the potential level of national income.

11. Draw a short-run aggregate supply curve on the following graph. Label your axes.

Section 5: Aggregate Demand and Supply Equilibrium

1. The equilibrium level of income is at the point where _____ equals _____ .

2. The short equilibrium level of income on the following graph is _____ .

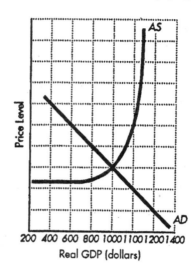

200 400 600 800 1000 1100 1200 1400
Real GDP (dollars)

3. In the long run, there _____ (is, is not) a relationship between the level of prices and the level of output.

4. In the short run, changes in aggregate demand determine the level of prices and income. In the long run, changes in aggregate demand determine only the _____ .

THINKING ABOUT AND APPLYING MACROECONOMIC EQUILIBRIUM: AGGREGATE DEMAND AND SUPPLY

I.   Aggregate Demand and Its Determinants

Now that you have finished this chapter, you should be able to predict the effect on aggregate demand when one of its determinants changes. In the exercise below, decide which of the spending components each event affects, whether it increased or decreased the component, and whether it increased or decreased aggregate demand. Remember the determinants of each component of aggregate demand:

Consumption: income, wealth, expectations, demographics, taxes

Investment: interest rate, cost of capital goods, technology, capacity utilization

Government spending: set by government authorities

Net exports: foreign and domestic income, prices; exchange rates, government policy

Events
1. Interest rates increase.

2. The dollar depreciates against foreign currencies.

3. The government increases its spending.

4. Foreign incomes rise.

5. The population increases more quickly.

6. Factories note a decline in the rate of capacity utilization.

7. The government imposes a nationwide sales tax on retail goods and services.

8. The cost of capital goods decreases.

Component	Effect on Component	Effect on Aggregate Demand
1.		
Investment	Decrease	Decrease
2.		
3..		
4..		
5..		
6..		
7..		
8..		

II.   Aggregate Demand and Supply Equilibrium

Assume that the following are short-run situations.

1. On the following graph, show how an increase in aggregate demand could produce a higher output with no change in prices.

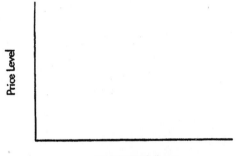

Real GDP (dollars)

2. On the following graph, show a decrease in aggregate demand that produces a lower price level and lower real GDP.

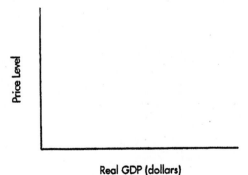

Real GDP (dollars)

3. On the following graph, show how an increase in aggregate demand could result in higher prices at the same level of real GDP.

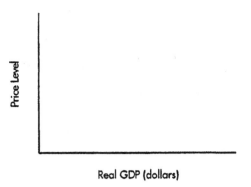

Real GDP (dollars)

III.   A Long-Run Analysis of the Effects of a Slump in Productivity

Many people have been concerned about the slower growth of productivity in recent years. Suppose that the growth of productivity in the United States not only slows, but actually decreases. This could result from declines in basic skills that some educators believe are surfacing in the nation's high schools. What will happen to the equilibrium price level and real GDP in the long run? Use the following graph to analyze this problem. Be sure to label your axes.

IV. Sorting Out the Determinants of Aggregate Demand and Aggregate Supply

Place each of the items under the proper category. Some items can be placed in more than one category.

Wealth effect	Wealth	Domestic income
Resource prices	Expectations	Foreign income
Income	Interest rate effect	Domestic prices
Taxes	Price level	Foreign prices
Interest rates	Demographics	Exchange rate
International trade effect	Cost of capital goods	Government policies
Changes in technology	Capacity utilization	Government spending

Shifts Aggregate Demand   **Shifts Aggregate Supply**

_____ _____   _____ _____

_____ _____   _____

_____ _____

_____ _____

_____ _____

_____ _____

_____ _____

Movements Along *AD*   **Movements Along *AS***

_____ _____   _____

_____ _____

ANSWERS

QUICK-CHECK QUIZ

Section 1: Aggregate Demand, Aggregate Supply, and Business Cycles

1. a;

2. d;

3. a;

4. d;

5. a

If you missed any of these questions, you should go back and review Section 1 of Chapter 12.

Section 2: Factors That Influence Aggregate Demand

1. d;

2. c;

3. a;

4. b;

5. b;

6. e;

7. b;

8. d;

9. b

If you missed any of these questions, you should go back and review Section 2 of Chapter 12.

Section 3: The Aggregate Demand Curve

1. e;

2. b;

3. e;

4. c;

5. d;

6. a;

7. b;

8. b;

9. b

If you missed any of these questions, you should go back and review Section 3 of Chapter 12.

Section 4. Aggregate Supply

1. b;

2. d;

3. e;

4. e;

5. c;

6. b;

7. b;

8. b

If you missed any of these questions, you should go back and review Section 4 of Chapter 12.

Section 5: Aggregate Demand and Supply Equilibrium

1. a;

2. c;

3. e

If you missed any of these questions, you should go back and review Section 5 of Chapter 12.

PRACTICE QUESTIONS AND PROBLEMS

Section 1: Aggregate Demand, Aggregate Supply, and Business Cycles

1. Aggregate demand

2. Aggregate supply

3. Demand-pull

4. falls

5. increase

6. cost-push

7. negative (downward-sloping)

8. positive (upward-sloping)

Section 2: Factors That Influence Aggregate Demand

1. decreases

2. Consumption

3. consumption

4. increases

5. increase

6. increase

7. Price effects; nonprice effects

8. Net exports

9. increases

10. rise

11. falls

12. Investment

13. increases

14. income wealth;
    expectations;
    demographic;s
    taxes

15. rises

16. falls

17. rise

18. interest rate;
    technology;
    cost of capital goods;
    capacity utilization

19. fall

20. lower

21. foreign and domestic income;
    foreign and domestic prices;
    exchange rates;
    government policy

22. increase

Section 3: The Aggregate Demand Curve

1. decreases; decreases; wealth; fall

2. sell; decrease; rise; interest rate; fall

3. more expensive; fall; fall

4. rise

5. aggregate demand curve

6. less expensive; a shift to the left of the aggregate demand curve

7. a movement along the aggregate demand curve

8. wealth effect;
   interest rate effect;
   international trade effect

9. consumption; investment; increases

10. exports; a shift in aggregate demand to the right

Section 4: Aggregate Supply

1. aggregate supply curve

2. positive; expected profits

3. increase; more

4. long run

5. short run

6. resource prices;
   technology;
   expectations

7. right

8. upward slope

9. vertical

10. long-run aggregate supply

11.

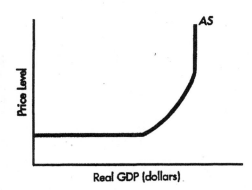

Section 5: Aggregate demand and Supply Equilibrium

1. aggregate demand; aggregate supply

2. 1,000

3. is not

4. level of prices

THINKING ABOUT AND APPLYING MACROECONOMIC EQUILIBRIUM: AGGREGATE DEMAND AND SUPPLY

I.   Aggregate Demand and Its Determinants

Component	Effect on Component	Effect on Aggregate Demand
1. Investment	Decrease	Decrease
2. Net exports	Increase	Increase
3. Government	Increase	Increase

		Increase	Increase
	spending		
4.	Net exports	Increase	Increase
5.	Consumption	Decrease	Decrease
6.	Investment	Decrease	Decrease
7.	Consumption	Increase	Increase
8.	Investment		

II.   Aggregate Demand and Supply Equilibrium

1. You need to draw your aggregate demand curves so that the shifts are confined to the horizontal region of the short-run aggregate supply curve.

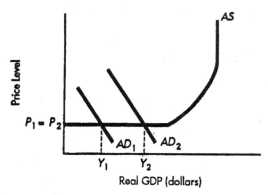

2. You need to draw your aggregate demand curves so that the shifts are confined to the upward-sloping region of the short-run aggregate supply curve.

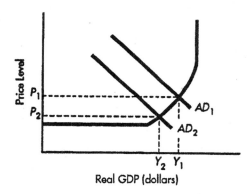

3. You need to draw your aggregate demand curves so that the shifts are confined to the vertical region of the short-run aggregate supply curve.

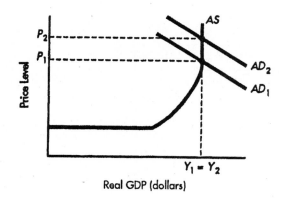

III.   A Long-Run Analysis of the Effects of a Slump in Productivity

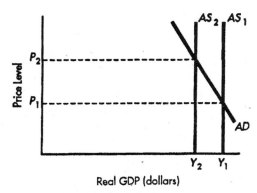

A decrease in productivity causes the long-run aggregate supply curve to shift to the left. If aggregate demand does not change, equilibrium real GDP will be lower and the price level will be higher—a very sorry prospect indeed.

IV.   Sorting Out the Determinants of Aggregate Demand and Aggregate Supply

Shifts Aggregate Demand		Shifts Aggregate Supply	
Income	Domestic income	Resource prices	Expectations
Taxes	Foreign income		Changes in technology
Interest rates	Domestic prices		
Wealth	Foreign prices		
Expectations	Exchange rate		
Demographics	Government policies		
Cost of capital goods	Government spending		
	Capacity utilization		

Movements Along *AD*		Movements Along *AS*
Wealth effect	Interest rate effect	Price level
International trade effect	Price level	

CHAPTER 13

Fiscal Policy

FUNDAMENTAL QUESTIONS

1. How can fiscal policy eliminate a GDP gap?

   Fiscal policy can eliminate a GDP gap by increasing government spending (which directly increases aggregate demand) or by decreasing taxes (which increases consumption). The changes in government spending and taxes have a multiplier effect on income.

2. How has U.S. fiscal policy changed over time?

   Government spending has increased from 3 percent of the GDP before the Great Depression to approximately 18 percent of the GDP in 2000.

3. What are the effects of budget deficits?

   Budget deficits can be harmful to the economy. If the deficit is financed by borrowing, interest rates may be driven up and private domestic investment may be crowded out. Higher interest rates make U.S. financial instruments attractive to foreigners, and the resulting increase in the demand for dollars may cause the dollar to appreciate. The appreciation of the dollar decreases net exports. Greater interest costs as a result of the deficit may decrease national wealth if the debt is held by foreign residents, and the debt did not increase investment and productive capacity in the United States.

4. How does fiscal policy differ across countries?

   Industrial countries spend more of their budgets on social programs than do developing countries and they depend more on direct taxes and less on indirect taxes as sources of revenue. Developing countries rely more on government than the private sector to build their infrastructure and for investment spending. Industrial countries rely on direct taxes on individuals and firms, while developing countries use indirect taxes on goods and services.

KEY TERMS

crowding out	progressive tax	value-added tax (VAT)
discretionary fiscal policy	progressive tax	value-added tax (VAT)
automatic stabilizer	proportional tax	regressive tax

QUICK-CHECK QUIZ

Section 1: Fiscal Policy and Aggregate Demand

1. Which of the following affects aggregate demand only *indirectly?*
    a. consumption
    b. investment
    c. taxes
    d. government spending
    e. net exports

2. Taxes affect the level of aggregate demand primarily through changing the level of
    _____, which alters _____.
    a. disposable income; consumption
    b. disposable income; investment
    c. disposable income; government spending
    d. government spending; consumption
    e. government spending; investment

3. A(n) _____ in government spending or a(n) _____ in taxes lowers
    the level of expenditures at every price and shifts the aggregate demand curve to the
    _____.
    a. decrease; increase; right
    b. decrease; increase; left
    c. increase; decrease; right
    d. increase; decrease; left
    e. decrease; decrease; left

4. Assuming no effects on aggregate supply, if the government decreases government spending
    and increases taxes in an attempt to reduce the federal government budget deficit, aggregate
    demand will shift to the _____, the price level will either remain constant or
    _____, and the level of national income will _____.
    a. left; increase; increase
    b. left; increase; decrease
    c. left; decrease; increase
    d. left; decrease; decrease
    e. right; decrease; decrease

5. A decrease in taxes may cause aggregate supply to shift to the _____, causing the
    level of prices to _____ and the level of national income to _____.
    a. right; fall; rise
    b. right; fall; fall
    c. right; rise; rise
    d. left; fall; rise
    e. left; rise; fall

6. Government spending financed by _____ will have a greater expansionary effect than government spending financed by _____ if the public _____ base current spending on future tax liabilities.
    a. taxes; issuing money; does
    b. taxes; borrowing; does not
    c. taxes; borrowing; does
    d. borrowing; taxes; does
    e. borrowing; taxes; does not

7. Increases in government spending financed by _____ may drive _____ interest rates and decrease _____.
    a. taxes; up; consumption
    b. taxes; down; consumption
    c. borrowing; down; investment
    d. borrowing; up; investment
    e. borrowing; down; net exports

8. Expansionary fiscal policy refers to
    a. decreasing government spending and decreasing taxes.
    b. decreasing government spending and increasing taxes.
    c. increasing government spending and increasing taxes.
    d. increasing government spending and decreasing taxes.
    e. increasing government spending and increasing the money supply.

9. An increase in government spending
    a. has the same effect on aggregate demand as an increase in taxes.
    b. will result in a lower level of prices if the aggregate supply curve is horizontal
    c. shifts aggregate demand to the right.
    d. decreases aggregate expenditures.
    e. is not likely to result in higher prices or a higher level of real GDP.

10. If the aggregate supply curve slopes up before reaching potential real GDP,
    a. the effect of government spending on real GDP is enhanced.
    b. the government must increase its spending by more than the recessionary gap to reach potential real GDP.
    c. the government must increase its spending by the amount of the recessionary gap to reach real GDP.
    d. prices will remain constant as government spending increases.
    e. prices will decrease as government spending increases.

11. Which are the following statements is true?
    a. If the price level rises as real GDP rises, the multiplier effects of any given change in aggregate expenditures are larger than they would be if the price level remained constant.
    b. Spending and tax multipliers overestimate the change in expenditures needed to close a recessionary gap.
    c. If aggregate supply shifts in response to an increase in government spending financed by an increase in taxes, the effects of government spending may be enhanced.
    d. Economists have demonstrated conclusively that government spending crowds out private spending.
    e. The spending multiplier overestimates the expansionary effect of an increase in government spending unless the economy is in the Keynesian region of short-run aggregate supply.

Section 2: Fiscal Policy in the United States

1. Discretionary fiscal policy refers to
    a. government spending at the discretion of the president.
    b. government spending at the discretion of the Congress.
    c. elements of fiscal policy that automatically change in value as national income changes.
    d. government spending at the discretion of the president and the Congress.
    e. changes in government spending and taxation aimed at achieving an economic policy goal.

2. Which of the following is *not* a harmful effect of government deficits?
    a. lower private investment as a result of crowding out
    b. lower net exports as a result of the appreciation of the dollar
    c. increased investment caused by foreign savings placed in U.S. bonds
    d. an increase in saving caused by anticipated future increases in taxes
    e. an increase in imports

3. Which of the following is *not* an example of an automatic stabilizer?
    a. unemployment insurance
    b. lump-sum taxes
    c. progressive taxes
    d. food stamps
    e. welfare benefits

4. The following tax table represents a _____ tax schedule.
    a. regressive
    b. progressive
    c. proportional
    d. lump-sum
    e. constant rate

Income	Tax Payment
$100	$ 45
200	80
300	105
400	120

5. Which of the following is *not* an expected result of government budget deficits?
    a. increases in saving
    b. increases in imports
    c. decreases in investment
    d. increases in consumption
    e. decreases in exports

Section 3: Fiscal Policy in Different Countries

1. Which of the following statements is false?
    a. Historically, government spending has played an increasingly larger role over time in industrial countries.
    b. Government plays a larger role in investment spending in developing countries.
    c. Developed countries rely more on their governments to provide the infrastructure of the economy than do developing countries.
    d. State-owned enterprises account for a larger percentage of economic activity in developing countries than in developed countries.
    e. Industrial nations spend a larger percentage of their budgets on social programs than do developing countries.

2. Which of the following statements is true?
    a. Developing countries rely more heavily on direct taxes than do developed countries.
    b. Developing countries rely more heavily on indirect taxes than do developed countries.
    c. Developing countries rely more heavily on personal income taxes than do developed countries.
    d. Developing countries rely more heavily on social security taxes than do developed countries.
    e. Developed countries rely more heavily on import and export taxes than do developing countries

3. Which of the following statements is true?
    a. The United States imposes value-added taxes.
    b. An export tax is an example of a direct tax.
    c. Developing countries spend more on social programs than industrial nations, because the need is greater.
    d. Personal taxes are hard to collect in agricultural nations.
    e. Personal income taxes are indirect taxes.

PRACTICE QUESTIONS AND PROBLEMS

Section 1: Fiscal Policy and Aggregate Demand

1. Fiscal policy is changing _____ and _____ .

2. The _____ gave the federal government the responsibility for creating and maintaining low inflation and unemployment.

3. Assume the economy is in equilibrium at Y_e. In an attempt to reduce the federal government budget deficit, the government reduces government spending and increases taxes. Further assume that changes in fiscal policy *will* affect aggregate supply and that the change in aggregate demand will be greater than the change in aggregate supply. Show the effects of deficit reduction on the following graph.

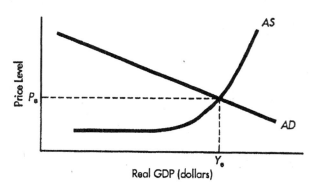

a. Aggregate demand will shift to the _____ (right, left) and aggregate supply will shift to the _____ (right, left).

b. The equilibrium level of national income will _____ (rise, fall) and the equilibrium price level will _____ (rise, fall).

4. Taxes affect aggregate expenditures indirectly by changing _____. This change alters _____.

5. Increases in government spending may drive interest rates _____ thereby _____ investment.

6. If government spending increases by the same amount as taxes, the effect is _____ (expansionary, contractionary).

7. An increase in government spending or a decrease in taxes causes the aggregate demand curve to shift to the _____.

8. When prices go up, the multiplier effect of an increase in spending is _____ (enhanced, reduced). The spending and tax multipliers _____ (understate, overstate) the effect of a change in aggregate expenditures.

9. List the three ways government spending may be financed.

_____

_____

_____

10. An increase in taxes may shift aggregate supply to the _____.

11. The graph below shows equilibrium at Y_1 and P_1. Show the effect of government spending financed by taxes if the aggregate supply curve *is* affected by the change in t

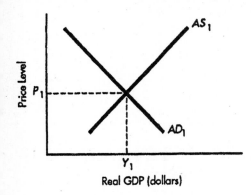

12. A government borrows funds by _____ (buying bonds from, selling bonds to) the public.

13. An increase in government spending that reduces private spending is called

    _____.

14. Crowding out may occur if government borrowing drives up _____.

Section 2: Fiscal Policy in the United States

1. Fiscal policy in the United States is a product of the budget process, which involves the _____ and _____ branches of government.

2. As part of the budget process, federal agencies submit their budgets to the _____ (OMB) which reviews and modifies each agency's requests and consolidates all of the proposals into a single budget.

3. The _____ (CBO) reports to Congress on the validity of the economic assumptions made in the president's budget.

4. The federal budget is determined as much by _____ as by economics.

5. List the two kinds of fiscal policy.

   _____

   _____

6. _____ refers to changes in government spending and taxation aimed at achieving a policy goal.

7. _____ are elements of fiscal policy that automatically change in value as national income changes.

8. Historically, except in times of war, the federal government deficit increased the most during

   _____.

9. Government deficits can harm the economy by dampening _____ and

   _____.

10. As income falls, automatic stabilizers _____ spending.

11. _____ are taxes that are a flat dollar amount regardless of income.

12. With _____ taxes, as income rises, so does the rate of taxation.

13. With _____ taxes, the tax rate falls as income rises.

14. With _____ taxes, the tax rate is constant as income rises.

15. Look at the tax payment schedules below.

Which is progressive? _____

Regressive? _____

Proportional? _____

	A	B	C
Income	Tax Payment	Tax Payment	Tax Payment
$100	$10	$50	$10
200	20	80	30
300	30	90	60
400	40	100	100

16. _____ taxes are an example of an automatic stabilizer.

17. In the year 2000, federal spending was about _____ percent of the GDP.

Section 3: Fiscal Policy in Different Countries

1. Government plays a bigger role in investment spending in the _____ (developing, industrial) countries. Give two reasons why this should be so.

_____

_____

2. Low-income countries _____ (do, do not) spend a greater percentage of their budgets on social programs as compared with industrialized countries.

3. Over time, government spending as a percentage of output has _____ (increased, decreased) in industrial countries.

4. _____ taxes are taxes on individuals and firms.

5. _____ taxes are taxes on goods and services.

6. _____ taxes are hard to collect in developing countries because so much of household production is for personal consumption.

7. In general, developing countries rely more heavily on _____ (direct, indirect) taxes than do developed countries.

8. VAT stands for _____, an indirect tax imposed on each sale at each stage of production.

THINKING ABOUT AND APPLYING FISCAL POLICY

I.   Reducing the Deficit

Your text discusses the possible harmful effects of budget deficits. Since a budget deficit results from government spending that is greater than tax revenues, reducing the deficit implies reducing government spending, increasing taxes, or both. But to quote Publius Syrus, "There are some remedies worse than the disease" (Maxim 301). Since reducing government spending and increasing taxes reduces aggregate demand, the economy might be thrown into a recession if spending cuts and tax increases are adopted.

1. Consider the following graph, where the economy is at equilibrium at P_1 and Y_1. Show what will happen if spending cuts and tax increases are implemented.

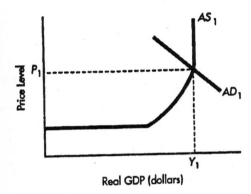

What will happen to equilibrium real GDP and price level?

_____

_____

_____

_____

2. Now consider an economy operating in the vertical region of the aggregate supply curve. Can you draw a curve that illustrates tax increases and spending cuts but does *not* throw the economy into a recession?

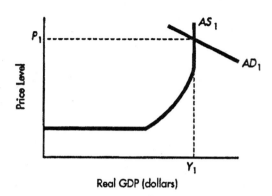

Explain:

_____

_____

_____

_____

II.   Clinton's Economic Stimulus Package

1. President Clinton's initial 1993 budget was referred to as an "economic stimulus package." From what you know about fiscal policy, if the president's goal was economic stimulus, you would expect this package to consist of increases in _____ and decreases in _____ .

2. The plan was also referred to as a "deficit reduction plan." Why might the president want to reduce the deficit?

_____

_____

_____

3. If the goal was to reduce the deficit, _____ would be increased and _____ would be decreased.

4. Does it seem possible to reduce the deficit while stimulating the economy at the same time?

_____

_____

_____

5. The president proposed halving capital-gains taxes for investors in some small businesses and would have expanded the bill's proposed write-off for small businesses' equipment purchases. These tax breaks were intended to _____ (increase, decrease) which component of aggregate expenditures? What effect would that change have on real GDP?

_____

_____

_____

ANSWERS

QUICK-CHECK QUIZ

Section 1: Fiscal Policy and Aggregate Demand

1. c;

2. a;

3. b;

4. d;

5. a;

6. e;

7. d;

8. d;

9. c;

10. b;

11. e

If you missed any of these questions, you should go back and review Section 1 of Chapter 13.

Section 2: Fiscal Policy in the United States

1. e;

2. c;

3. b;

4. a;

5. d

If you missed any of these questions, you should go back and review Section 2 of Chapter 13.

Section 3: Fiscal Policy in Different Countries

1. c;

2. b;

3. d

If you missed any of these questions, you should go back and review Section 3 of Chapter 13.

PRACTICE QUESTIONS AND PROBLEMS

Section 1: Fiscal Policy and Aggregate Demand

1. taxation; government spending

2. Employment Act of 1946

3. You must draw your graph so that the space between *AD* and *AD'* is bigger than the space between *AS* and *AS'*.

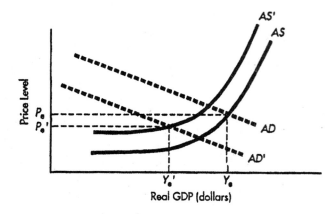

a. left; left

b. fall; fall

4. disposable income; consumption

5. up; decreasing

6. expansionary

7. right

8. reduced; overstate

9. taxes;
change in government debt (borrowing);
change in the stock of government-issued money

10. left

11.

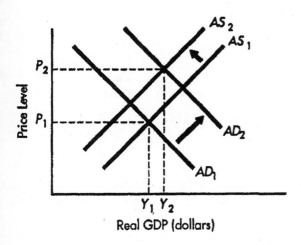

12. selling bonds to

13. crowding out

14. interest rates

Section 2: Fiscal Policy in the United States

1. legislative; executive

2. Office of Management and Budget

3. Congressional Budget Office

4. politics

5. discretionary fiscal policy
   automatic stabilizers

6. Discretionary fiscal policy

7. Automatic stabilizers

8. recessions

9. investment; net exports

10. increase

11. Lump-sum taxes

12. progressive

13. regressive

14. proportional

15. C; B; A

(To determine what kind of tax it is, we must first calculate the tax *rate* at each level of income.)

	A		B		C	
Income	Tax Payment	Tax Rate	Tax Payment	Tax Rate	Tax Payment	Tax Rate
$100	$10	.10	$50	.50	$10	.10
200	20	.10	80	.40	30	.15
300	30	.10	90	.30	60	.20
400	40	.10	100	.25	100	.25

(Since A's tax *rate* is constant at .10, A is a proportional tax schedule. B's tax *rate* decreases with income, so B is a regressive tax. C's tax *rate* increases with income, so C is a progressive tax schedule.

Note: If you look at just the *dollar* amount of taxes paid, all three schedules look "progressive" because the dollar amount of tax payments increases as income increases. But we classify these taxes according to how the tax *rate* changes as income increases.)

16. Progressive

17. 18

Section 3: Fiscal Policy in Different Countries

1. developing

   State-owned enterprises account for a larger percentage of economic activity in developing countries as compared with industrial countries. Also, developing countries rely on their governments, as opposed to private investment, to build their infrastructure.

2. do not

3. increased

4. Direct

5. Indirect

6. Personal income

7. indirect

8. value-added tax

THINKING ABOUT AND APPLYING FISCAL POLICY

I.   Reducing the Deficit

1.

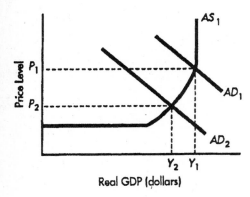

Government spending cuts and tax increases both decrease aggregate demand. If the economy is operating in the Keynesian or intermediate regions, decreasing aggregate demand will decrease real GDP. If the economy is in the intermediate range, the price level will decline. If it is in the Keynesian region, there will be no change in the price level. These are the dire results that the economic analysts fear.

2.

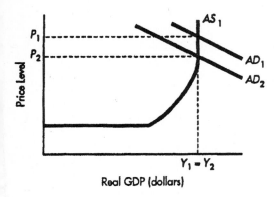

If the economy is operating in the vertical region of short-run aggregate supply (above), a decrease in aggregate demand may bring only a decrease in the price level with no decrease in real

II.   Clinton's Economic Stimulus Package

1. government spending; taxes

2. Many economists argue that deficits raise interest rates, which in turn can depress investment and net exports. Decreases in investment and net exports reduce aggregate demand, which conflicts with the president's goal of stimulating the economy.

3. taxes; government spending

4. Since economic stimulus calls for increasing government spending and decreasing taxes, and deficit reduction calls for decreasing government spending and increasing taxes, the two goals seem incompatible.

5. These tax breaks are intended to increase investment, thereby increasing aggregate demand and equilibrium real GDP.

CHAPTER 14

Money and Banking

FUNDAMENTAL QUESTIONS

1. What is money?

   Money is anything that is generally acceptable to sellers in exchange for goods and services. Money serves as a medium of exchange, a unit of account, a store of value, and a standard of deferred payment.

2. How is the U.S. money supply defined?

   There are three definitions of the U.S. money supply. The narrowest definition, the **M1 money supply**, consists of currency, travelers' checks, demand deposits, and other checkable deposits. M2 adds savings and small-denomination time deposits, and retail money market mutual fund balances. M3 equals M2 plus large time deposits, repurchase agreements, Eurodollar deposits, and institution-only money market mutual fund balances.

3. How do countries pay for international transactions?

   Countries use the foreign exchange market to convert national currencies to pay for trade. They also use **international reserve assets**, like gold, or **international reserve currencies**, like the dollar.

4. Why are banks considered intermediaries?

   Banks act as middlemen between savers and borrowers. They accept deposits from savers and use those deposits to make loans to borrowers.

5. How does international banking differ from domestic banking?

   Domestic banking is heavily regulated, whereas international banking is not. Because they are not restricted by regulations, international banks can usually offer depositors and borrowers better terms than domestic banks.

6. How do banks create money?

   Banks create money by making loans up to the amount of their excess reserves. The banking system can increase the money supply by the **deposit expansion multiplier** times the **excess reserves** in the system.

KEY TERMS

money	**Federal Deposit Insurance Corporation (FDIC)**	hawala
liquid asset	**Eurocurrency market (offshore banking)**	**fractional reserve banking system**
currency substitution	**international banking facility (IBF)**	**required reserves**
credit	**ROSCAS**	**excess reserves**
M1 money supply		**deposit expansion multiplier**

transactions account

international reserve asset

international reserve currency

QUICK-CHECK QUIZ

Section 1: What is Money?

1. Which of the following is *not* one of the functions of money?
    a. a medium of exchange
    b. a unit of account
    c. a resource for production
    d. a store of value
    e. a standard of deferred payment

2. A $34 price tag on a sweater is an example of money functioning as a
    a. medium of exchange.
    b. unit of account.
    c. resource for production.
    d. store of value.
    e. standard of deferred payment.

3. For money to function as a store of value, it is most important that it have which of the following properties?
    a. durability
    b. divisibility
    c. portability
    d. ability to be easily identified as genuine
    e. optimal scarcity

4. Which of the following is *not* a component of the M1 money supply?
    a. demand deposits
    b. other checkable deposits
    c. currency
    d. savings accounts
    e. travelers' checks

5. Which of the following is *not* a transactions account?
   a. negotiable order of withdrawal
   b. credit union share draft account
   c. savings account
   d. automated transfer system account
   e. demand deposit at a commercial bank

6. In late 2001 currency represented _____ percent of the M1 money supply.
   a. 1
   b. 49
   c. 35
   d. 36
   e. 10

7. Which of the following accounts are offered by savings and loans?
   a. negotiable orders of withdrawal
   b. credit union share draft accounts
   c. travelers' checks
   d. automated transfer system accounts
   e. demand deposits at commercial banks

8. Demand deposits made up _____ percent of the M1 money supply in 2001.
   a. 1
   b. 28
   c. 35
   d. 71
   e. 37

9. Which of the following is *not* a component of the M2 money supply?
   a. retail money market mutual fund balances
   b. small-denomination time deposits
   c. currency
   d. savings deposits
   e. large time deposits

10. Which of the following is *not* a component of the M3 money supply?
    a. Eurodollar deposits
    b. value of stocks and bonds
    c. RPs
    d. institution-only money market mutual fund balances
    e. M2

Section 2: Banking

1. Which of the following statements is false?
   a. National banks are banks chartered by the federal government.
   b. The 1980 Depository Institutions Deregulation and Monetary Control Act narrowed the distinctions between commercial banks and thrifts.
   c. Almost all states permit entry to banks located out of state.
   d. The 1980 Depository Institutions Deregulation and Monetary Control Act created the Federal Deposit Insurance Corporation.
   e. The 1980 Depository Institutions Deregulation and Monetary Control Act permitted thrift institutions to offer many of the same services as commercial banks.

2. Which of the following statements is true?
   a. The laws regulating international banks typically are very restrictive, whereas domestic banks go relatively unregulated.
   b. Offshore banking, called the Eurocurrency market, refers to international banking transactions among the seven Western European industrial powers.
   c. Offshore banks are typically able to offer better terms to their customers than domestic banks.
   d. Most ATM transactions occur at banks that are not the customer's own bank.
   e. U.S. banks that participate in international banking on U.S. soil are subject to the same regulations as domestic banks.

3. Which of the following statements is false?
   a. The FDIC does not permit banks to fail for fear of causing a bank panic.
   b. Almost all states permit entry to banks located out of state.
   c. A Eurodollar is a dollar-denominated deposit outside the U.S. banking industry.
   d. International banking facilities are not subject to the same reserve requirements as domestic banks.
   e. International banking facilities are not physical entities.

Section 3: Banks and the Money Supply

1. Deposits at the Third National Bank are $200,000, and the reserve requirement is 10 percent. Cash reserves equal $50,000. Required reserves equal
   a. $40,000.
   b. $20,000.
   c. $50,000.
   d. $30,000.
   e. $10,000.

2. Deposits at the ABC Bank are $600,000, and the reserve requirement is 20 percent. Cash reserves equal $160,000. Excess reserves equal
   a. $120,000.
   b. $160,000.
   c. $32,000.
   d. $40,000.
   e. $128,000.

3. Deposits at the XYZ Bank are $400,000, and the reserve requirement is 20 percent. Cash reserves equal $6,000. The deposit expansion multiplier is
   a. .20.
   b. .80.
   c. 5.
   d. 1.25.
   e. 1.

4. The deposit expansion multiplier will be larger the
   a. smaller the reserve requirement.
   b. greater the currency drain.
   c. greater the percentage of excess reserves held by banks.
   d. larger the bank.
   e. greater the value of the assets held by the bank.

5. The Golden State Bank has cash reserves of $110,000, deposits of $200,000, and loans of $90,000. The reserve requirement is 5 percent. This bank can make additional loans up to the amount of _____.
    a. $4,500.
    b. $10,000.
    c. $5,500.
    d. $100,000.
    e. $190,000.

6. Suppose that excess reserves in the First National Bank are $15,000, and the reserve requirement is 4 percent. The maximum amount that the money supply can be increased is
    a. $60,000.
    b. $600.
    c. $375,000.
    d. $15,000.
    e. $72,000.

7. Banks increase the money supply by
    a. cashing checks.
    b. making loans.
    c. providing currency.
    d. printing money.
    e. printing money and coining currency.

8. A bank has $200,000 in deposits and $10,000 in cash. The reserve requirement is 4 percent. The bank's required reserves are _____, and its excess reserves are _____.
    a. $400; $199,600
    b. $199,600; $400
    c. $8,000; $192,000
    d. $2,000; $8,000
    e. $8,000; $2,000

9. Which of the following types of informal financial arrangements was investigated as a possible source of funding for terrorist activities?
    a. the hawala network
    b. tandas
    c. susu
    d. hui
    e. chits

PRACTICE QUESTIONS AND PROBLEMS

Section 1: What is Money?

1. _____ is anything that is generally acceptable to sellers in exchange for goods and services.

2. A(n) _____ asset is an asset that can easily be exchanged for goods and services.

3. List the four functions of money.

_____

_____

_____

4. _____ is the direct exchange of goods and services for other goods and services.

5. The use of money as a medium of exchange lowers _____ costs.

6. Money eliminates the need for a _____, which is necessary for barter to work.

7. For money to be an effective medium of exchange, it must be _____ and _____.

8. The use of money as a unit of account lowers _____ costs.

9. For money to be an effective store of value, it must be _____.

10. _____ is the use of foreign money as a substitute for domestic money when the domestic money has a high rate of inflation.

11. _____ is available savings that are lent to borrowers to spend.

12. List the four components of the M1 money supply.

_____

_____

_____

_____

13. A checking account at a bank or other financial institution that can be drawn on to make payments is called a _____ account.

14. Currency represented _____ percent of the M1 money supply in late 2001.

15. The U.S. dollar is backed by _____. This type of monetary system is called a _____ monetary system.

16. Money that has intrinsic value is called _____ money.

17. Travelers' checks accounted for _____ percent of the M1 money supply in late 2001.

18. _____ pay no interest and must be paid immediately on the demand of the depositor.

19. _____ are checking accounts at financial institutions that pay interest and give the depositor check-writing privileges.

20. _____ (NOW) accounts are interest-bearing checking accounts offered by savings and loan institutions.

21. _____ (A TS) accounts are accounts at commercial banks that combine an interest bearing savings account with a non-interest-bearing checking account.

22. Credit unions offer their members interest-bearing checking accounts called _____.

23. _____ are nonprofit savings and loan institutions.

24. Demand deposits made up _____ percent of the M1 money supply in 1998.

25. List the four components of the M2 money supply.

_____

_____

_____

_____

26. An _____ is an agreement between a bank and a customer under which the customer buys U.S. government securities from the bank one day and sells them back to the bank the next day.

27. Deposits denominated in dollars but held outside the U.S. domestic bank market are called _____ deposits.

28. _____ deposits are deposits at banks and at savings and loans that earn interest but offer no check-writing privileges.

29. Small-denomination time deposits are also called _____.

30. _____ combine the deposits of many individuals and invest them in government Treasury bills and other short-term securities.

31. List the five components of the M3 money supply.

_____

_____

_____

_____

_____

32. Sales contracts between developed countries are usually invoiced in the national currency of the _____, whereas sales between a developed and a developing country are usually invoiced in the currency of the _____.

33. An asset used to settle debts between governments is called a(n) _____ asset.

34. Currencies that are held to settle debts between governments are called _____ currencies.

35. The _____ is a unit of account used by the industrial nations of Western Europe to settle debts between them.

36. A _____ currency is a unit of account whose value is an average of the values of certain national currencies.

37. The value of the _____ is an average of the values of the U.S. dollar, the French franc, the German mark, the Japanese yen, and the U.K. pound.

Section 2: Banking

1. Thrift institutions include _____, _____, and _____.

2. _____ banks are banks chartered by the federal government, whereas _____ banks are chartered under state law.

3. _____ banks operate in only one location.

4. The _____ is a federal agency that insures deposits in commercial banks so that depositors do not lose their deposits when a bank fails.

5. The international deposit and loan market is often called the _____ or _____.

6. Typically, domestic banks are subject to _____ regulations, whereas offshore banks are subject to _____ regulation.

7. _____ (Domestic, Offshore) banks are usually able to offer better terms to their customers.

8. Eurodollar transactions are _____ (more risky, less risky) than domestic transactions in the United States because of the lack of regulation and deposit insurance.

9. A bank _____ occurs when depositors, fearing a bank's closing, rush to withdraw their funds.

10. _____ are permitted to take part in international banking activities on U.S. soil.

11. The _____ (1980) eliminated many of the differences between commercial banks and thrift institutions.

Section 3: Banks and the Money Supply

1. In a _____ banking system, banks keep less than 100 percent of their deposits on reserve.

2. A financial statement that records a firm's assets and liabilities is called a _____.

3. _____ are what the firm owns, and _____ are what the firm owes.

4. In the United States, reserve requirements are set by the _____.

5. _____ reserves are the cash reserves a bank must keep on hand or on deposit with the Fed.

6. _____ reserves are total reserves minus required reserves.

7. A bank is _____ when it as zero excess reserves.

8. The deposit expansion multiplier equals _____ (formula).

9. The deposit expansion multiplier tells us the _____ (maximum, minimum) change in total deposits when a new deposit is made.

10. If people withdraw deposits from banks, _____ occurs, and the deposit expansion multiplier will be less than the reciprocal of the reserve requirement.

11. Any single bank can lend only up to the amount of its _____.

12. Banks increase the money supply by _____.

13. McDougall Bank and Trust has vault cash in the amount of $300,000, loans of $900,000, and deposits of $1,200,000.

   a. Prepare a balance sheet for this bank.

   _____

   _____

   _____

   _____

   b. If the bank maintains a reserve requirement of 5 percent, what is the largest new loan it can make? _____

   c. What is the maximum amount the money supply can be increased by the banking system due to McDougall Bank and Trust's new loan? _____

14. The State Bank of Oswald has cash reserves of $5,000, loans of $495,000, and deposits of $500,000. The bank maintains a reserve requirement of 1 percent.

a. Calculate this bank's excess reserves.

_____

_____

b. The bank receives a new deposit of $100,000. What is the largest loan the bank can make?

_____

c. What is the maximum amount the money supply can be increased as a result of the State Bank of Oswald's new loan? _____

THINKING ABOUT AND APPLYING MONEY AND BANKING

I.   Sorting Out the Monetary Aggregates

Put *M3* next to items that are included only in M3, *M2* next to items included in M2 and M3, and *M1* next to items common to all three monetary aggregates.

_____ RPs

_____ Demand deposits

_____ Savings deposits

_____ Large time deposits

_____ Institution-only money market mutual funds

_____ Currency

_____ Eurodollars

_____ Small-denomination time deposits

_____ Demand deposits

_____ Retail money market mutual funds

_____ Other checkable deposits

_____ Travelers' checks

II.   The Components of the Monetary Aggregates

The table below lists the components of the monetary aggregates in billions of dollars.

Large time deposits	356.7
Travelers' checks	8.1
Institution-only money market mutual funds	178.0
Savings deposits	1,135.0
Demand deposits	406.5
Other checkable deposits	420.0
Eurodollars	52.2
Currency	357.3
RPs	100.8
Retail money market mutual funds	372.1
Small-denomination time deposits	826.9

Calculate M1 , M2, and M3.

M1

M2

M3

ANSWERS

QUICK-CHECK QUIZ

Section 1: What is Money?

1. c;
2. b;
3. a;
4. d;
5. c;
6. b;
7. a;
8. b;
9. e;
10. b

If you missed any of these questions, you should go back and review Section 1 of Chapter 14.

Section 2: Banking

1. d;
2. c;
3. a

If you missed any of these' questions, you should go back and review Section 2 of Chapter 14.

Section 3: Banks and the Money Supply

1. b;
2. d;
3. c;
4. a;
5. d;
6. c;
7. b;
8. e;
9. a

If you missed any of these questions, you should go back and review Section 3 of Chapter 14.

PRACTICE QUESTIONS AND PROBLEMS

Section 1: What is Money?

1. Money

2. liquid

3. medium of exchange;
   unit of account;
   store of value;
   standard of deferred payment

4. Barter

5. transactions

6. double coincidence of wants

7. portable; divisible

8. information

9. durable

10. Currency substitution

11. Credit

12. currency;
    travelers' checks;
    demand deposits;
    other checkable deposits (OCDs)

13. transactions

14. 49

15. the confidence of the public; fiduciary

16. commodity

17. less than 1

18. Demand deposits

19. Other checkable deposits (OCDs)

20. Negotiable order of withdrawal

21. Automated transfer system

22. share drafts

23. Mutual savings banks

24. 37

25. M1;
    savings deposits;
    small-denomination time deposits (certificates of deposit, or CDs);
    retail money market mutual fund balances

26. repurchase agreement

27. Eurodollar

28. Savings

29. certificates of deposit

30. Retail money market mutual fund balances

31. M2;
    large time deposits;
    RPs;
    Eurodollar deposits;
    institution-only money market mutual fund balances

32. exporter; developed country

33. international reserve

34. international reserve

35. European currency unit (ECU)

36. composite

37. special drawing right (SDR)

Section 2: Banking

1. savings and loans; mutual savings banks; credit unions

2. National; state

3. Unit

4. Federal Deposit Insurance Corporation (FDIC)

5. Eurocurrency market; offshore banking

6. restrictive; little or no

7. Offshore

8. more risky

9. panic

10. International Banking Facilities (IBFs)

11. Depository Institutions Deregulation and Monetary Control Act

Section 3: Banks and the Money Supply

1. fractional reserve

2. balance sheet

3. Assets; liabilities

4. Federal Reserve Board

5. Required

6. Excess

7. loaned up

8. 1/reserve requirement

9. maximum

10. currency drain

11. excess reserves

12. making loans

13.

    a.

Assets		Liabilities	
Cash	$ 300,000	Deposits	$1,200,000
Loans	900,000		
Total	$1,200,000	Total	$1,200,000

    b. $240,000 (Required reserves = .05($1,200,000) = $60,000. Excess reserves = total reserves – required reserves = $300,000 – $60,000 = $240,000. Since a bank can make loans up to the amount of its excess reserves, this bank can loan out $240,000.)

    c. $4,800,000 (The deposit expansion multiplier = 1/reserve requirement = 1/.05 = 20. Change in the money supply = deposit expansion multiplier × excess reserves = 20($240,000) = $4,800.000.)

14.

    a. Required reserves = .01($500,000) = $5,000. Excess reserves = $5,000 – $5,000 = 0.

    b. $99,000 (Cash = $105,000. Deposits = $600,000. Required reserves = .01($600,000) = $6,000. Excess reserves = $105,000 – $6,000 = $99,000.)

    c. $9,900,000 (Deposit expansion multiplier = 1/.01 = 100. Maximum amount of money that can be created = deposit expansion multiplier × excess reserves = 100($99,000) = $9,900,000.)

THINKING ABOUT AND APPLYING MONEY AND BANKING

I.   Sorting Out the Monetary Aggregates

M3   RPs

M1   M3 M1 Demand deposits

M2   M2 Savings deposits

M3   M3 Large time deposits

M3   M3 Institution-only money market mutual funds

M1   M1 Currency

M3   M3 Eurodollars

M2   M2 Small-denomination time deposits

M1   M1 Demand deposits .

M2   M2 Retail money market mutual funds

M1   M1 Other checkable deposits

M1   M1 Travelers' checks

II.   The Components of the Monetary Aggregates

M1   = Currency + travelers' checks + demand deposits + other checkable deposits

          = 347.3 + 81 + 406.5 + 420.0

          = 1,191.9

M2   = M1 + savings deposits + small-denomination time deposits + retail money market mutual
funds

          = 1,191.9 + 1,135.0 + 826.9 + 372.1

          = 3,525.9

M3   = M2 + large time deposits + RPs + Eurodollars + institution-only money market mutual
funds

          = 3,525.9 + 356.7 + 100.8 + 52.2 + 178.0

          = 4,213.6

CHAPTER 15

Monetary Policy

FUNDAMENTAL QUESTIONS

1. What does the Federal Reserve do?

   The Federal Reserve is the central bank of the United States. As such, the Fed provides currency, accepts deposits from and makes loans to financial institutions, acts as a banker for the federal government, supervises the banking system, and controls the money supply.

   The **Federal Open Market Committee (FOMC)** is the policy-making body of the Federal Reserve. It consists of the seven-member Federal Reserve Board and five of the twelve Federal Reserve Bank presidents, who serve on a rotating basis. The FOMC issues directives to the Federal Reserve Bank of New York, which implements its directives.

2. How is monetary policy set?

   The Fed's ultimate policy objective is economic growth with stable prices, but it cannot control output or the price level directly. Instead the Fed uses the money supply as an intermediate target. It controls the money supply, which in turn affects real GDP and the level of prices.

3. What are the tools of monetary policy?

   The tools of monetary policy are the reserve requirement, the discount rate, and open market operations. The reserve requirement is the percentage of deposits that financial institutions must keep on hand or at the Fed. The higher the reserve requirement, the smaller the amount of deposits banks can create and the smaller the money supply. The **discount rate** is the rate of interest that the Fed charges banks. If the Fed wants to increase the money supply, it lowers the discount rate. **Open market operations** are the buying and selling of bonds to change the money supply. The Fed buys bonds if it wants to increase the money supply and sells bonds to decrease the money supply. Open market operations are the Fed's most important tool.

4. What role do central banks play in the foreign exchange market?

   Central banks may intervene in the foreign exchange market to stabilize or change exchange rates. For example, the Fed might buy euros to bolster the price of the euro if U.S. goods and services become too expensive for the Europeans.

5. What are the determinants of the demand for money?

   There are three aspects to the demand for money. Consumers and firms demand money in order to conduct transactions—the **transactions demand for money**, to take care of emergencies—the **precautionary demand for money**, and to be able to take advantage of a fall in the price of an asset that they want—the **speculative demand for money**.

   The amount of money held depends on the interest rate and nominal income. Increases in nominal income generate a greater volume of transactions, so more money is needed. The demand for money is therefore positively related to nominal income. The interest rate is the opportunity cost of holding money. A higher interest rate means that it costs more to hold money, so less money will be held. The demand for money is negatively related to the interest rate.

6. How does monetary policy affect the equilibrium level of real GDP?

    Monetary policy refers to controlling the money supply. An increase in the money supply decreases interest rates, which increases consumption and investment. The increases in consumption and investment increase aggregate demand, which increases the equilibrium level of real GDP. A decrease in the money supply increases interest rates, which decreases consumption and investment. The decreases in consumption and investment decrease aggregate demand, which decreases the equilibrium level of real GDP. So increases in the money supply are expansionary, whereas decreases in the money supply are contractionary.

    a. What does the ECB do?

    The ECB is the central bank of the 12 nations adopting the euro as their national currency. As such, it conducts monetary policy for the euro region.

KEY TERMS

Federal Open Market Committee (FOMC)	federal funds rate	foreign exchange market intervention
intermediate target	FOMC directive	sterilization
equation of exchange	legal reserves	transactions demand for money
velocity of money	federal funds rate	precautionary demand for money
quantity theory of money	discount rate	speculative demand for money
	open market operations	

QUICK-CHECK QUIZ

Section 1: The Federal Reserve System

1. Which of the following is *not* a function of the Fed?
    a. accepting deposits from banks
    b. making loans to banks
    c. controlling taxes
    d. acting as a banker for the federal government
    e. controlling the money supply

2. The _____ is(are) the policy-making entity of the Fed.
    a. Federal Reserve chairman
    b. Federal Reserve Board
    c. twelve Federal Reserve district banks
    d. twelve Federal Reserve Bank presidents
    e. FOMC

3. The Fed's most important function is to
    a. provide services to the banking community.
    b. control the money supply.
    c. supervise the banking community.
    d. clear checks.
    e. hold bank reserves.

4. Federal Reserve Board governors are appointed by
   a. the President.
   b. the Senate.
   c. the House of Representatives.
   d. the Congress.
   e. the Comptroller of the Currency.

5. Federal Reserve Board governors are appointed for _____ year terms.
   a. two
   b. four
   c. five
   d. ten
   e. fourteen

Section 2: Implementing Monetary Policy

1. The ultimate goal of monetary policy is
   a. economic growth with stable prices.
   b. stable exchange rates.
   c. stable interest rates.
   d. a low federal funds rate.
   e. steady growth in bank reserves.

2. According to the equation of exchange,
   a. if the money supply increases and velocity is constant, real GDP must rise.
   b. if the money supply increases and velocity is constant, nominal GDP must rise.
   c. an increase in the money supply causes an increase in the price level.
   d. an increase in the money supply causes an increase in real GDP and higher prices
   e. if the money supply increases, nominal GDP must rise.

3. To increase the money supply, the Fed would
   a. increase the reserve requirement, increase the discount rate, and sell bonds.
   b. increase the reserve requirement, increase the discount rate, and buy bonds.
   c. decrease the reserve requirement, decrease the discount rate, and sell bonds.
   d. decrease the reserve requirement, decrease the discount rate, and buy bonds.
   e. increase the reserve requirement, decrease the discount rate, and buy bonds.

4. Consider the First National Bank of Rozzelle. The bank has deposits of $600,000, loans of $500,000, vault cash of $30,000, and deposits at the Fed of $70,000. The reserve requirement is 4 percent. The bank's legal reserves are _____, and excess reserves are _____. The deposit expansion multiplier is _____, and the banking system could create a maximum of _____ in new money.
   a. $30,000; $6,000; 25; $150,000
   b. $30,000; $26,000; 25; $650,000
   c. $100,000; $96,000; 25; $2,400,000
   d. $100,000; $76,000; 4; $304,000
   e. $100,000; $76,000; 25; $1,900,000

5. If the Fed wants to decrease the money supply, it can
    a. buy bonds.
    b. sell bonds.
    c. lower the reserve requirement.
    d. lower the federal funds rate.
    e. lower the discount rate.

6. Suppose that the U.K. pound is currently equivalent to $1.596 and that the Fed wants the dollar to depreciate versus the pound. The Fed will most likely
    a. buy dollars.
    b. buy pounds.
    c. sell dollars.
    d. sell pounds.
    e. ask the U.S. central bank to buy pounds.

7. If the Fed intervened in the foreign currency market to buy another currency, the domestic money supply would _____, and the Fed might _____ bonds to offset its foreign currency operations. This process is called c.
    a. decrease; buy; sterilization
    b. decrease; sell; sterilization
    c. increase; sell; sterilization
    d. increase; buy; sterilization
    e. increase; sell; depreciation

8. In recent years, the Fed's short-run operating target has been
    a. M1.
    b. M2.
    c. M3.
    d. the federal funds rate.
    e. the level of reserves held by commercial banks.

9. If the money supply is $500, the price level is 3.00, and the velocity of money is equal to six, Q will be _____ and nominal GDP will be _____.
    a. 250; $1,500
    b. 3,000; $9,000
    c. 18; $54
    d. 1,000; $3,000
    e. 100, $3,000

Section 3: Monetary Policy and Equilibrium Income

1. A student who cashes a check at the student union in order to go shopping is an example of the
    a. transactions demand for money.
    b. speculative demand for money.
    c. precautionary demand for money.
    d. income effect.
    e. substitution effect.

2.   An increase in the interest rate will cause a(n)
     a.   increase in the demand for money.
     b.   increase in the quantity demanded of money.
     c.   decrease in the demand for money.
     d.   decrease in the quantity demanded of money.
     e.   increase in the supply of money.

3.   A decrease in nominal income will cause a(n)
     a.   increase in the demand for money.
     b.   increase in the quantity demanded of money.
     c.   decrease in the demand for money.
     d.   decrease in the quantity demanded of money.
     e.   decrease in the supply of money.

4.   The supply of money is
     a.   a positive function of interest rates.
     b.   a negative function of interest rates.
     c.   a positive function of income.
     d.   a negative function of income.
     e.   independent of income and interest rates.

5.   A bond selling for $998 pays $54.89 in interest annually. The current interest rate is
     a.   .18.
     b.   .055.
     c.   .82.
     d.   .945.
     e.   .125.

6.   If the interest rate is above the equilibrium rate, there is an excess _____ of money. People will _____ bonds, and the interest rate will _____.
     a.   demand; sell; rise
     b.   demand; sell; drop
     c.   demand; buy; drop
     d.   supply; buy; drop
     e.   supply; sell; rise

7.   If the Fed wants to increase equilibrium income, it should _____ the supply of money, which will _____ interest rates. The change in interest rates will _____ consumption and investment, causing aggregate demand to _____.

     a.   decrease; increase; decrease; decrease
     b.   decrease; decrease; increase; increase
     c.   increase; decrease; increase; increase
     d.   increase; increase; decrease; decrease
     e.   increase; increase; increase; increase

8. Consider the following graph. The demand for money is Md_1, and the supply of money is Ms_1. The equilibrium interest rate is i_1, and the equilibrium quantity of money is M_1. If income decreases,
   a. the demand for money shifts to Md_2, and the interest rate and equilibrium quantity rise.
   b. the demand for money shifts to Md_2, and the interest rate rises.
   c. the demand for money shifts to Md_3, and the interest rate and equilibrium quantity fall.
   d. the demand for money shifts to Md_3, and the interest rate falls.
   e. the supply of money shifts to the left, the interest rate rises, and the equilibrium quantity of money falls.

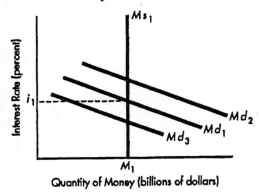

9. A bond sells for $990 and has a yield of 8.5 percent. The bond must be paying _____ in interest annually.
   a. $84.15
   b. $8,415
   c. $8.415
   d. $116.47
   e. $1,164.71

PRACTICE QUESTIONS AND PROBLEMS

Section 1: The Federal Reserve System

1. The Federal Reserve System was intended to be a _____ (centralized, decentralized) system.

2. There are _____ Federal Reserve districts, each with its own Federal Reserve Bank.

3. Monetary policy is largely set by the _____.

4. The chairman of the Federal Reserve Board of Governors is appointed by the _____ and serves a _____-year term. Governors serve _____-year terms.

5. Each of the Fed's twelve district banks has a _____-member board of directors.

6. The _____ is the official policy-making body of the Federal Reserve System. It consists of the Board of Governors plus _____ of the Federal Reserve Bank presidents.

7. List the six main functions of the Fed.

    _____

    _____

    _____

    _____

    _____

    _____

8. The most important function of the Fed is _____ .

9. The Federal Reserve is the _____ bank of the United States.

10. The _____ has been called the second most powerful person in the United States.

11. The president of the _____ Federal Reserve Bank is always a member of the FOMC.

Section 2: Implementing Monetary Policy

1. The goal of monetary policy is _____ with _____ .

2. An _____ is an objective used to achieve some ultimate policy goal.

3. $MV = PQ$ is the _____ .

4. The _____ of money is the average number of times each dollar is spent on final goods and services in a year.

5. The _____ states that if the money supply increases and the velocity of money is constant, nominal GDP must rise.

6. In the late 1970s and early 1980s, the M1 velocity of money _____ (fluctuated erratically, remained relatively stable).

7. The Federal Reserve Bank of _____ implements monetary policy for the Fed.

8. A(n) _____ is the instructions issued by the FOMC to the Federal Reserve Bank in New York to implement monetary policy.

9. List the three tools the Fed uses to change reserves.

    _____

    _____

    _____

10. Large banks must hold a _____ (greater, smaller) percentage of deposits in reserve than do small banks.

11. Legal reserves consist of _____ and _____ .

12. The Fed can reduce the money-creating potential of the banking system by _____ (raising, lowering) the reserve requirement.

13. The _____ rate is the rate of interest the Fed charges banks. In other countries, this rate is often called the _____ rate.

14. Banks borrow from other banks in the _____ market.

15. If the Fed wants to increase the money supply, it _____ (raises, lowers) the discount rate.

16. _____ are the buying and selling of government bonds by the Fed and are the Fed's major monetary policy tool.

17. To increase the money supply, the Fed _____ (buys, sells) bonds.

18. _____ indicate how the money supply should react to a change in the short-run target.

19. In recent years, the Fed has been using _____ as its short-run operating target.

20. _____ is the buying and selling of foreign exchange by a central bank in order to move exchange rates up or down.

21. If the Fed wants the dollar to appreciate against the yen, it will buy _____ (dollars, yen).

22. _____ is the use of open market operations to offset the effects of a foreign exchange market intervention on the domestic money supply.

23. If the Fed wishes to support a foreign currency, it _____ (increases, decreases) the domestic money supply, unless offsetting operations are undertaken.

24. If $M = \$300$, $P = 2$ and $V = 5$, real output (Q) will be _____ and nominal income will be $ _____.

25. The Bank of McDonald has the following balance sheet:

Assets		Liabilities	
Vault cash	$20,000	Deposits	$400,000
Deposits in the Fed	30,000		
Loans	350,000		

If this bank's reserve requirement is 5 percent,

a. legal reserves are _____.

b. required reserves are _____.

c. excess reserves are _____.

d. the deposit expansion multiplier is _____.

e. this bank can create _____ of additional deposits.

f. the banking system could create a maximum of _____.

Section 3: Monetary Policy and Equilibrium Income

1. The _____ demand for money is a demand to hold money in order to spend it on goods and services.

2. The _____ demand for money is a demand to hold money to take care of emergencies.

3. The _____ demand for money is created by uncertainty about the value of other assets.

4. The demand for money depends on _____ and _____.

5. There is a(n) _____ relationship between the interest rate and the quantity of money demanded.

6. The greater the nominal income, the _____ (greater, smaller) the demand for money.

7. The _____ sets the money supply.

8. The supply of money _____ (does, does not) depend on interest rates and nominal income.

9. The formula for the current interest rate of a bond is _____.

10. A bond pays $200 a year in interest and sells for $2,500. The current interest rate is _____.

11. As bond prices increase, the current interest rate _____.

12. A decrease in the money supply causes interest rates to _____ (rise, fall), which causes consumption and investment to _____ (rise, fall). The changes in consumption and investment cause aggregate demand to _____ (increase, decrease), which causes equilibrium income to _____ (rise, fall). Use the following graphs to illustrate the sequence of events following a decrease in the money supply.

(a)

Quantity of Money (billions of dollars)

(b)

Real GDP (dollars)

13. Norm and Debbie keep 1.5 months' income in a NOW account for emergencies. This is an example of the _____ demand for money.

14. A young couple cashes in a bond to buy a crib and changing table to prepare for the birth of their first child. This is an example of the _____ demand for money.

15. If nominal income increases, the demand for money _____ (shifts to the left, does not change, shifts to the right).

16. You read in *The Wall Street Journal* that the bond markets rallied yesterday (bond prices increased). Interest rates must have _____ (increased, decreased).

17. A bond sells for $975 and pays $68.25 in interest annually. The current rate of interest is _____. If the bond market plummets (demand falls), the price of this bond will _____ (rise, fall), and the interest rate will _____ (rise, fall).

THINKING ABOUT AND APPLYING MONETARY POLICY

I.   More on Foreign Exchange Market Intervention

If the Fed feels that the price of the dollar in terms of U.K. pounds is unacceptably high, it may choose to intervene directly in the foreign exchange markets. To bolster the pound, the Fed will _____ (buy, sell) pounds. In the process, the domestic money supply will _____ (increase, decrease).

In the absence of any sterilization actions by the Fed, domestic interest rates will _____ (increase, decrease) as a result of the change in the money supply. The change in domestic interest rates will _____ (increase, decrease) the demand for U.s. securities. The dollar will _____ (appreciate, depreciate) in value. The effect of the change in the money supply has _____ (reinforced, opposed) the Fed's actions in the foreign exchange market.

II.   Bond Prices and Interest Rates

Fill in the gaps in these typical articles from *The Wall Street Journal*.

a. "The benchmark 10-year Treasury bond rose more than ¼ point to 106, a gain of more than $2.50 for a bond with a $1,000 face amount. Its yield, which moves in the _____ (same, opposite) direction from the price, _____ (rose, fell) to 6.65% . . ."

b. "More investors and economists are beginning to believe that interest rates are headed higher, although many think long-term bond yields won't move as fast as short-term rates . . . . Mr. Olsen . . . believes there will be a significant sell-off in the bond market."

   Why would higher interest rates precipitate a significant sell-off in the bond market?

   _____

   _____

ANSWERS

QUICK-CHECK QUIZ

Section 1: The Federal Reserve System

1. c;

2. e;

3. b;

4. a;

5. e

If you missed any of these questions, you should go back and review Section 1 of Chapter 15.

Section 2: Implementing Monetary Policy

1. a;

2. b (Answer a is false, and the others are true only if certain assumptions are made. For c to be true, velocity must be constant and the economy must be at full employment, so that Q cannot rise. For d to be true, velocity must be constant and there must be some unemployment in the economy. Answer e may be true if velocity is constant.);

3. d;

4. e $(LR$ = vault cash + deposits at the Fed = \$30,000 + \$70,000 = \$100,000. $RR = rD =$ .04[\$600,000] = \$24,000. $ER = LR - RR$ = \$100,000 − \$24,000 = \$76,000. The deposit expansion multiplier = $1/r$ = 1/.04 = 25. The change in the money supply = $1/r[ER]$ = 25[\$76,000] = \$1,900,000.);

5. b;

6. b (The Fed can keep this up indefinitely, since it can create dollars to buy pounds. It does not need the help of the U.K. central bank to depreciate the dollar.);

7. c;

8. d;

9. d

If you missed any of these questions, you should go back and review Section 2 of Chapter 15.

Section 3: Monetary Policy and Equilibrium Income

1. a;

2. d;

3. c;

4. e;

5. b;

6. d;

7. c;

8. d;

9. a

If you missed any of these questions, you should go back and review Section 3 of Chapter 15.

PRACTICE QUESTIONS AND PROBLEMS

Section 1: The Federal Reserve System

1. decentralized

2. 12

3. Board of Governors

4. president; 4; 14

5. 9

6. Federal Open Market Committee (FOMC); 5

7. provides currency;
    holds reserves;
    clears checks;
    supervises commercial banks;
    acts as a banker for the federal government;
    controls the money supply

8. controlling the money supply

9. central

10. Fed chairperson

11. New York

Section 2: Implementing Monetary Policy

1. economic growth; stable prices

2. intermediate target

3. equation of exchange

4. velocity

5. quantity theory of money

6. fluctuated erratically

7. New York

8. FOMC directive

9. reserve requirement;
    discount rate;
    open market operations

10. greater

11. vault cash; deposits in the Fed

12. raising

13. discount; bank

14. federal funds

15. lowers

16. Open market operations

17. buys

18. Short-run operating targets

19. the federal funds rate

20. Foreign exchange market intervention

21. dollars

22. Sterilization

23. increases

24. 750; 1,500

25.

    a. $50,000 *(LR* = vault cash + deposits in the Fed = $20,000 + $30,000)

    b. $20,000 *(RR = rD* = .05[$500,000])

    c. $30,000 *(ER = LR − RR* = $50,000 − $20,000)

    d.   20 (1/*r* = 1/.05)

    e. $30,000 (the amount of *ER)*

    f. $600,000 (change in money supply = deposit expansion multiplier × excess reserves = 20[$30,000])

Section 3: Monetary Policy and Equilibrium Income

1. transactions

2. precautionary

3. speculative

4. nominal income; interest rates

5. inverse

6. greater

7. Federal Reserve

8. does not

9. annual interest payment/bond price

10. .08 (annual interest payment/bond price = $200/$2,500 = .08)

11. decreases

12. rise; fall; decrease; fall

(a)

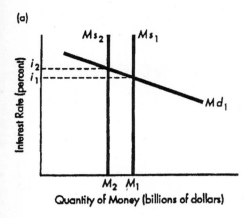

(b)

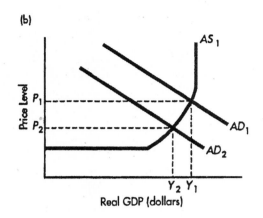

13. precautionary

14. transactions

15. shifts to the right

16. decreased

17. .07 (annual interest payment/bond price = $68.25/$975 = .07); fall; rise

THINKING ABOUT AND APPLYING MONETARY POLICY

I.   More on Foreign Exchange Market Intervention

buy; increase; decrease; decrease; depreciate; reinforced

II.   Bond Prices and Interest Rates

a.   opposite; fell

b.   Bond prices drop as interest rates rise. If owners of bonds expect higher interest rates, they will want to sell their bonds before the prices of the bonds decrease.

CHAPTER 16

Macroeconomic Policy, Business Cycles, and Growth

FUNDAMENTAL QUESTIONS

1. Is there a tradeoff between inflation and the unemployment rate?

    The **Phillips curve** is a graph showing the relationship between the inflation rate and the rate of unemployment. In the short run, the Phillips curve has a downward slope, indicating a possible tradeoff between inflation and unemployment. In the long run, the Phillips curve is vertical, indicating that no such tradeoff is possible.

2. How does the tradeoff between inflation and the unemployment rate vary from the short to the long run?

    The short-run downward slope of the Phillips curve is caused by shifts in aggregate demand while aggregate supply stays constant. In the long run no tradeoffs are possible because adaptations are made and the aggregate supply curve shifts.

3. What is the relationship between unexpected inflation and the unemployment rate?

    Unexpected inflation can decrease unemployment in three ways. If workers have constant **reservation wages** and constant expectations about inflation, an unexpected increase in inflation raises nominal wages without raising real wages. Workers do not realize that inflation has increased, so they accept smaller real wages and unemployment decreases.

    When aggregate demand is greater than expected, inventories fall and prices on remaining goods in stock are higher. Businesses hire new workers to increase production to offset the falling inventories.

    If wage contracts exist, employers must adjust employment to changing conditions. If revenues fall, employers must reduce costs, either by lowering wages or by getting rid of workers. If a wage contract precludes lowering wages, a decrease in inflation will result in unemployment.

4. How are macroeconomic expectations formed?

    Adaptive expectations are expectations based on past experience. People expect things to be as they were before, and they take nothing else into account. **Rational expectations** are formed using all available information, including, but not limited to, past events.

5. Are business cycles related to political elections?

    Some economists believe in the existence of a political business cycle, in which the incumbent administration stimulates the economy just before the election. After the election, unemployment and inflation rise. There is no conclusive evidence of political business cycles in the United States.

6. How do real shocks to the economy affect business cycles?

The economy can expand or contract as a result of changes in real economic variables, such as the weather, technology, and so forth. These real **shocks** are to be distinguished from discretionary fiscal and monetary policies.

7. How is inflationary monetary policy related to government fiscal policy?

The government must finance its spending through taxes, borrowing, or changes in the money supply. If the government cannot or will not borrow and deficits continue, monetary policy must be inflationary.

8. How are economic growth rates determined?

Economic growth means a shift rightward of the aggregate supply curve, increasing the potential output of the economy. A country's economic growth rate is determined by the factors that determine the aggregate supply curve: the amount of productive resources available and technology. The faster the growth of productive resources and technological advancement, the higher a country's growth rate will be.

9. What is productivity?

Productivity is one way to look at the impact of advances in **technology** on economic growth. Productivity is the ratio of output produced to the amount of input used. Improvements in technology mean that productivity increases as we find new and better ways to use inputs to produce output. More specifically, **total factor productivity (TFP)** is a nation's output divided by its stock of labor and capital. Economic growth is the sum of the growth rate of total factor productivity and the growth rate of available resources.

KEY TERMS

Phillips curve	**rational expectation**	**total factor productivity (TFP)**
reservation wage	**shock**	
adaptive expectation	**technology**	

QUICK-CHECK QUIZ

Section 1: The Phillips Curve

1. According to the short-run Phillips curve,
    a. inflation is inversely related to unemployment.
    b. inflation is positively related to unemployment.
    c. inflation is not related to unemployment.
    d. high inflation necessarily requires high unemployment.
    e. low inflation and low unemployment can occur at the same time.

2. The long-run Phillips curve is
   a. downward-sloping, illustrating the possibility of trading off higher inflation for lower unemployment.
   b. upward-sloping, indicating that high unemployment is associated with rising prices.
   c. horizontal, indicating that no tradeoff is possible between unemployment and inflation in the long run.
   d. vertical, indicating no relationship between inflation and unemployment in the long run.
   e. horizontal, indicating an infinite number of tradeoffs between inflation and unemployment.

3. Which of the following statements is false?
   a. In the long run, as the economy adjusts to an increase in aggregate demand, there is a period in which national income falls and the price level rises.
   b. The tradeoff between unemployment and inflation worsened from the 1960s through the 1970s.
   c. A decrease in aggregate supply is reflected in a movement along the Phillips curve.
   d. The long-run Phillips curve is a vertical line at the natural rate of unemployment.
   e. The tradeoff between unemployment and inflation disappears in the long run.

4. Unemployment and inflation data is consistent with an _____ shift of the Phillips curve in the 1960s and 1970s, and an _____ shift in the 1980s. These shifts show that the tradeoff between inflation and unemployment _____ in the 1960s and 1970s and _____ in the 1980s.
   a. inward; outward; improved; worsened
   b. inward; outward; worsened; improved
   c. outward; outward; worsened; worsened
   d. outward; inward; improved; worsened
   e. outward; inward; worsened; improved

Section 2: The Role of Expectations

1. Unexpected inflation can affect the unemployment rate through
   a. the income effect.
   b. the substitution effect.
   c. the wealth effect.
   d. wage contracts.
   e. the interest rate effect.

2. Which of the following could *not* cause a movement along the Phillips curve?
   a. a change in inflation that is not expected by workers
   b. an unexpected increase in inflation that causes inventories to decline
   c. wage contracts that did not correctly anticipate the inflation rate
   d. an anticipated rise in nominal wages
   e. All of the above cause movements along the short-run Phillips curve.

3. Which of the following is an example of rational rather than adaptive expectations?
    a. The crowd expects a 95 percent free-throw shooter to sink the free throw to win the state basketball championship.
    b. A professor has been 10 minutes late to class three times in a row. Students come to the fourth class 10 minutes late.
    c. The fans of a pro football team that had four wins, ten losses, and one tie last year find another team to root for this year.
    d. Stockholders of a firm that had losses three years in a row sell off their stocks.
    e. A company with a poor earnings record over the past five years finds itself swamped by investors when word of its new superproduct leaks out.

4. Which of the following is false?
    a. The short-run effect of unexpected disinflation is rising unemployment.
    b. The short-run Phillips curve assumes a constant reservation wage and a constant expected rate of inflation.
    c. The tradeoff between inflation and unemployment comes from expected inflation.
    d. Inventory fluctuations may cause a movement along the Phillips curve.
    e. If wages were flexible, unexpected changes in aggregate demand might be reflected more in wage adjustments than in employment adjustments.

5. Unexpected increases in aggregate demand _____ inventories and _____ prices. Unemployment _____.
    a. lowers; raises; decreases
    b. lowers; raises; increases
    c. lowers; lowers; increases
    d. raises; lowers; increases
    e. raises; lowers; decreases

Section 3: Sources of Business Cycles

1. Which of the following statements is true?
    a. Economists have clear evidence that political business cycles occur in the United States.
    b. Real shocks can have expansionary effects on the economy.
    c. The end result of the political business cycle is that the economy returns to its original equilibrium price level and output after the election.
    d. Real business cycles are caused by discretionary monetary policy.
    e. Real business cycles are caused by discretionary fiscal policy.

2. Which of the following would *not* be a cause of a real business cycle?
    a. a decrease in government borrowing
    b. a drought in the Midwest
    c. oil prices skyrocketing as a result of an accident on the world's largest offshore oil rig
    d. a labor strike that cripples the steel industry
    e. an improvement in the technology for solar energy that yields a lightweight solar battery that can be used to power cars for long trips

3. The existence of a political business cycle implies that, prior to the election, the incumbent administration would
   a. increase aggregate demand by increasing government spending and the money supply.
   b. increase aggregate demand by increasing government spending and decreasing the money supply.
   c. increase aggregate demand by decreasing government spending and the money supply.
   d. decrease aggregate demand by increasing government spending and the money supply.
   e. decrease aggregate demand by increasing government spending and decreasing the money supply.

4. A drought in the Midwest would cause _____ to shift _____, which would _____ real GDP.
   a. aggregate demand; left; decrease
   b. aggregate demand; right; increase
   c. aggregate supply; left; increase
   d. aggregate supply; left; decrease
   e. aggregate supply; right; increase

Section 4: The Link Between Monetary and Fiscal Policies

1. The government budget constraint
   a. always holds true.
   b. demonstrates that there is no link between fiscal and monetary policy.
   c. demonstrates that an expansionary fiscal policy implies a contractionary monetary policy.
   d. shows that the change in the money supply equals government spending minus borrowing.
   e. demonstrates that monetary reform will always halt inflation.

2. Which of the following is false?
   a. In most developed countries, monetary and fiscal policies are conducted by separate independent agencies.
   b. Fiscal policy can impose an inflationary burden on monetary policy.
   c. In typical developing countries, monetary and fiscal policies are controlled by the same central authority.
   d. Using money to finance deficits has produced severe deflation in many countries.
   e. Monetary control is not possible until fiscal policy is under control.

Section 5: Economic Growth

1. In terms of the aggregate demand-aggregate supply model, economic growth is shown as a(an)
   a. rightward shift in the aggregate demand curve.
   b. rightward shift in the aggregate supply curve.
   c. leftward shift in the aggregate demand curve.
   d. leftward shift in the aggregate supply curve.
   e. upward shift in both aggregate demand and aggregate supply.

2. An abundance of natural resources
   a. is always necessary for economic growth.
   b. is necessary for economic growth only in capitalist countries.
   c. is necessary for economic growth only in developing countries.
   d. has no effect on economic growth.
   e. can contribute to economic growth but is not necessary for growth.

3.   Growth in a country's capital stock is tied to
   a.   increases in the amounts of natural resources available.
   b.   current and future saving.
   c.   improvements in technology.
   d.   increases in the amount of labor available.
   e.   decreases in the labor force participation ratio.

4.   Which of the following is *not* one of the determinants of economic growth?
   a.   the size and quality of the labor force
   b.   the amount of capital goods available
   c.   technology
   d.   natural resources
   e.   the shape of the aggregate demand curve

5.   Total factor productivity is the ratio of a
   a.   firm's marginal revenue to its marginal cost.
   b.   firm's total revenues to its total costs.
   c.   nation's total income divided by its total output.
   d.   nation's output to its stock of labor and capital.
   e.   nation's labor supply to its capital stock.

6.   Economic growth is the sum of
   a.   total factor productivity and resources.
   b.   total factor productivity and marginal factor productivity.
   c.   growth in total factor productivity and growth in resources.
   d.   real GDP and national output.
   e.   GNP and GDP.

PRACTICE QUESTIONS AND PROBLEMS

Section 1: The Phillips Curve

1.   The _____ illustrates the inverse relationship between inflation and the unemployment rate.

2.   The Phillips curve tradeoff between inflation and unemployment _____ (does, does not) persist over the long run.

3.   Over the long run, the Phillips curve is _____.

4. Plot the following unemployment and inflation data on the following graph. Be sure to label your axes.

Year	Inflation Rate	Unemployment Rate
1974	14.6	5.6
1975	13.5	8.5
1976	9.3	7.7
1977	11.0	7.1
1978	13.9	6.1

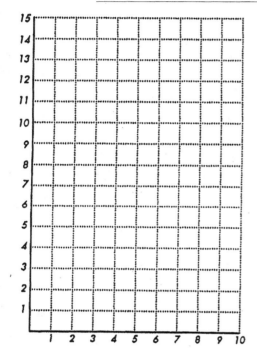

Does your graph imply the existence of a short-run Phillips curve during this period?
_____

5. The downward slope of the short-run Phillips curve is caused by shifts in _____, with _____ remaining constant.

Section 2: The Role of Expectations

1. A(n) _____ is the lowest wage that an unemployed worker is willing to accept.

2. List the two assumptions underlying the short-run Phillips curve.

_____

_____

3. If people's expectations about inflation do not change, the short-run effect of disinflation is rising _____.

4. The short-run tradeoff between inflation and unemployment comes from _____ inflation.

5. Unexpected inflation can affect the employment rate in the following three ways:

   _____

   _____

6. As economic conditions change, firms with expiring wage contracts can adjust _____ to those conditions; firms with existing contracts must adjust _____ to those conditions.

7. _____ expectations are expectations that are determined by what has happened in the recent past.

8. _____ expectations are based on all available relevant information.

9. Your economics professor bases her first exam solely on material from the textbook. Before the second exam, she announces that this exam will be based primarily on lecture material. If you only study the textbook, you are acting on the basis of _____ expectations.

10. When the inflation rate is unexpectedly high, unemployment _____.

11. If wages were always flexible, unexpected changes in aggregate demand would be met by _____ adjustments rather than by _____ adjustments.

Section 3: Sources of Business Cycles

1. The _____ refers to macroeconomic policy used to promote the reelection of incumbent politicians.

2. The _____ refers to a business cycle that is not related to discretionary policy actions.

3. The political business cycle argument suggests that incumbent administrations follow _____ macroeconomic policies just before an election.

4. Economists _____ (do, do not) agree on whether a political business cycle exists in the United States.

5. A(n) _____ is an unexpected change in a variable.

6. A(n) _____ is an expansion and contraction of the economy caused by a change in the weather, technology, or other real factors.

7. List some examples of real shocks.

   _____

   _____

   _____

   _____

Section 4: The Link Between Monetary and Fiscal Policies

1. Write the equation for the government budget restraint.

   _____

2. The only way to reduce the amount of money being created is to reduce the _____ minus _____.

3. The government can finance its spending by _____, _____, or _____.

Section 5: Economic Growth

1. Economic growth shifts the aggregate _____ (demand, supply) curve to the _____ (right, left).

2. The long-run growth of the economy rests on growth in productive resources such as _____, _____, _____, and on advances in _____.

3. The size of a country's labor force is determined by the _____ and the _____ of the population in the labor force.

4. Growth in a country's capital stock depends on current and future _____.

5. Technology is ways of combining _____ to produce _____.

6. What are two factors that cause developing countries to lag behind in the development and implementation of new technology?

    _____

    _____

7. Productivity is the ratio of _____ to the amount of _____.

8. _____ is the nation's real GDP divided by its stock of labor and capital.

9. In the United States, labor receives about 70 percent of national income and capital receives about 30 percent. If total factor productivity increases by 1 percent, labor increases by 1 percent, and capital increases by 3 percent, by what percentage will national income increase?

    _____

THINKING ABOUT AND APPLYING MACROECONOMIC POLICY, BUSINESS CYCLES, AND GROWTH

I.   Expectations and Government Spending Cuts

In an editorial titled, "Hurry Up and Wait," former president Ronald Reagan complained that the Clinton administration wanted to "hurry up" with tax increases but that the deficit reduction through spending cuts wasn't scheduled to take place for four or five years. Mr. Reagan urged the budget makers to put spending cuts in the same year as tax increases, not at some point down the road. He implied that people should not believe in future spending cuts because, when he was president, Congress agreed to make such cuts but never did *(The Wall Street Journal*, 7/8/93, page A12).

1. Mr. Reagan expected this Congress to renege on its promise to cut government spending down the road because Congress did not follow through with spending cuts promised in 1982. Expectations formed in this way are called _____ expectations.

2. At the time of the editorial's publication, the Clinton administration hoped to persuade the public to believe that the deficit would be reduced through cuts in government spending in the future. Mr. Clinton said he learns from mistakes. The Clinton administration hoped that the public would consider new information and have _____ expectations.

II.   War on Inflation

The leader of a developing nation has declared war on inflation by issuing a series of belt-tightening measures. Capital gains taxes will be enforced, lending and deposit rates at banks will be raised, and government spending will be slashed.

Use the government's budget constraint to explain how these measures will affect inflation.

_____

_____

III.   Government Policy and Growth

Government policies that hold down interest rates have adverse effects on economic growth in developing countries. Although low interest rates are intended to make it cheaper for local businesses to invest in new capital goods, they have the effect of drying up the supply of savings, since savers can get a higher return by taking their money out of the country or by making less productive investments on their own. Similar policies are sometimes followed in other economic sectors, with similarly bad results.

For example, many developing countries require farmers to sell their crops to the government, which resells the food to city dwellers. To keep the city dwellers happy, the prices charged for food are set very low, as are the prices paid to farmers. Think about the farmers' opportunity costs of growing food for sale, and predict what is likely to happen to the food supply in countries adopting this policy.

_____

_____

_____

_____

ANSWERS

QUICK-CHECK QUIZ

Section 1: The Phillips Curve

1. a;
2. d;
3. c;
4. e

If you missed any of these questions, you should go back and review Section 1 of Chapter 16.

Section 2: The Role of Expectations

1. d;
2. d (Only unanticipated inflation makes the inflation-unemployment tradeoff possible.);
3. e;
4. c;
5. a

If you missed any of these questions, you should go back and review Section 2 of Chapter 16.

Section 3: Sources of Business Cycles

1. b;
2. a;
3. a;
4. d

If you missed any of these questions, you should go back and review Section 3 of Chapter 16.

Section 4: The Link Between Monetary and Fiscal Policies

1. a;
2. d

If you missed either of these questions, you should go back and review Section 4 of Chapter 16.

Section 5: Economic Growth

1. b;
2. e;
3. b;
4. e;
5. d;

6. c

If you missed any of these questions, you should go back and review Section 5 of Chapter 16.

PRACTICE QUESTIONS AND PROBLEMS

Section 1: The Phillips Curve

1. Phillips curve

2. does not

3. vertical

4.

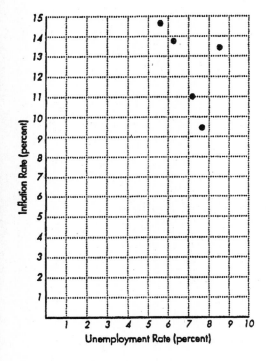

> Yes. (Since the curve does slope down, there is evidence of a short-run Phillips curve tradeoff between inflation and unemployment.)

5. aggregate demand; aggregate supply (Note that aggregate supply does shift in the long run.)

Section 2: The Role of Expectations

1. reservation wage

2. constant expected rate of inflation;
   constant reservation wage

3. unemployment

4. unexpected

5. wage expectations;
   inventory fluctuations;
   wage contracts

6. wages; employment

7. Adaptive

8. Rational

9. adaptive

10. decreases

11. wage; employment

Section 3: Sources of Business Cycles

1. political business cycle

2. real business cycle

3. expansionary

4. do not

5. shock

6. real business cycle

7. technological change;
    changes in tastes;
    labor strikes;
    weather

Section 4: The Link Between Monetary and Fiscal Policies

1. $G = T + B + \Delta M$

2. fiscal deficit; borrowing

3. taxing; borrowing; creating money

Section 5: Economic Growth

1. supply; right

2. labor; capital; natural resources; technology

3. working-age population; percentage

4. saving

5. resources; output

6. low levels of education
    limited funds for research and development

7. output produced; inputs

8. Total factor productivity

9. 2.6 percent (Growth is growth in TFP plus growth in each resource × that resource's share of national income. For this case, growth = 1 (TFP growth) + .7 (1 percent growth in labor × labor's .7 share of national income) + .9 (3 percent growth in capital × capital's .3 share of national income.)

THINKING ABOUT AND APPLYING MACROECONOMIC POLICY, BUSINESS CYCLES, AND GROWTH

I.   Expectations and Government Spending Cuts

1.   adaptive

2.   rational

II.   War on Inflation

$\Delta M = (G - T) - B$

If G is decreased and T is increased, $(G - T)$ will be smaller. If there is no change in government borrowing, the change in the money supply will be negative and inflation will decrease.

III.   Government Policy and Growth

If the price paid for food crops is low enough, farmers will decide to do something else with their resources than grow food crops. They may switch to cash crops sold for export or just take more leisure, growing only enough to feed themselves and their families. Either way, the amount of food produced for sale to city dwellers will drop substantially. The low prices charged to city dwellers will not help them much when there is no food available for sale.

CHAPTER 17

Issues in International Trade and Finance

FUNDAMENTAL QUESTIONS

1. What determines the goods a nation will export?

   A nation exports those goods for which it has a *comparative advantage* over other nations—that is, those goods for which its opportunity costs are lower than the opportunity costs of other nations.

2. What are the sources of comparative advantage?

   There are two major sources of comparative advantage: productivity differences and factor abundance. Productivity differences come from differences in labor productivity and human capital and from differences in technology. Factor abundance affects comparative advantage because countries have different resource endowments. The United States, with a large amount of high-quality farmland, has a comparative advantage in agriculture.

   Productivity differences and factor abundance explain most, but not all, trade patterns. Other sources of comparative advantage are human skills differences, product life cycles, and consumer preferences. Consumer preferences explain **intraindustry trade**, in which countries are both exporters and importers of a product. Some consumers prefer brands made in their own country; others prefer foreign brands.

3. Why do countries restrict international trade?

   Most countries follow some sort of **commercial policy** to influence the direction and volume of international trade. Despite the costs to domestic consumers, countries frequently try to protect domestic producers by restricting international trade.

   To help hide the special-interest nature of most trade restrictions, several arguments commonly are used. These include saving domestic jobs, creating fair trade, raising revenue through tariffs, protecting key defense industries, allowing new industries to become competitive, and giving **increasing-returns-to-scale industries** an advantage over foreign competitors. Although a few of these arguments have some validity, most have little or no merit.

4. How do countries restrict the entry of foreign goods and promote the export of domestic goods?

   Several tactics are used for these purposes. **Tariffs**, or taxes on products imported into the United States, protect domestic industries by raising the price of foreign goods. Quotas restrict the amount or value of a foreign product that may be imported; **quantity quotas** limit the amount of a good that may be imported, and **value quotas** limit the monetary value of a good that may be imported.

   Subsidies, payments made by the government to domestic firms, both encourage exports and make domestic products cheaper to foreign buyers. In addition, a wide variety of other tactics, among them health and safety standards, are used to restrict imports.

5. What kinds of exchange-rate arrangements exist today?

At the present time, nations use a variety of exchange-rate arrangements, including fixed exchange rates, freely floating exchange rates, and managed floats or other types of systems.

KEY TERMS

absolute advantage	**strategic trade policy**	**quantity quota**
intraindustry trade	**increasing-returns-to-scale industry**	**value quota**
commercial policy	**tariff**	**subsidies**

QUICK-CHECK QUIZ

Section 1: An Overview of World Trade

1. A nation has an absolute advantage in producing a good when
    a. it can produce a good for a lower input cost than can other nations.
    b. the opportunity cost of producing a good, in terms of the forgone output of other goods, is lower than that of other nations.
    c. it can produce a good for a higher input cost than can other nations.
    d. the opportunity cost of producing a good, in terms of the forgone output of other goods, is higher than that of other nations.
    e. the nation's export supply curve is below its import demand curve.

2. A nation has a comparative advantage in producing a good when
    a. it can produce a good for a lower input cost than can other nations.
    b. the opportunity cost of producing a good, in terms of the forgone output of other goods, is lower than that of other nations.
    c. it can produce a good for a higher input cost than can other nations.
    d. the opportunity cost of producing a good, in terms of the forgone output of other goods, is higher than that of other nations.
    e. the nation's export supply curve is below its import demand curve.

3. The productivity-differences explanation of comparative advantage stresses
    a. differences in labor productivity among countries.
    b. the advantage that comes to a country that is the first to develop and produce a product
    c. the relative amounts of skilled and unskilled labor in a country.
    d. differences in the amounts of resources countries have.
    e. differences in tastes within a country.

4. The factor-abundance explanation of comparative advantage stresses
    a. differences in labor productivity among countries.
    b. the advantage that comes to a country that is the first to develop and produce a product.
    c. the relative amounts of skilled and unskilled labor in a country.
    d. differences in the amounts of resources countries have.
    e. differences in tastes within a country.

5. The human-skills explanation of comparative advantage stresses
   a. differences in labor productivity among countries.
   b. the advantage that comes to a country that is the first to develop and produce a product.
   c. the relative amounts of skilled and unskilled labor in a country.
   d. differences in the amounts of resources countries have.
   e. differences in tastes within a country.

6. The product-life-cycle explanation of comparative advantages stresses
   a. differences in labor productivity among countries.
   b. the advantage that comes to a country that is the first to develop and produce a product.
   c. the relative amounts of skilled and unskilled labor in a country.
   d. differences in the amounts of resources countries have.
   e. differences in tastes within a country.

7. The consumer-preferences explanation of comparative advantage stresses
   a. differences in labor productivity among countries.
   b. the advantage that comes to a country that is the first to develop and produce a product.
   c. the relative amounts of skilled and unskilled labor in a country.
   d. differences in the amounts of resources countries have.
   e. differences in tastes within a country.

Section 2: International Trade Restrictions

1. The basic objective of commercial policy is to
   a. promote free and unrestricted international trade.
   b. protect domestic consumers from dangerous, low-quality imports.
   c. protect domestic producers from foreign competition.
   d. protect foreign producers from domestic consumers.
   e. promote the efficient use of scarce resources.

2. Using trade restrictions to save domestic jobs
   a. usually forces consumers to pay higher prices.
   b. usually redistributes jobs from other industries to the protected industry.
   c. may provoke other countries to restrict U.S. exports.
   d. does all of the above.
   e. does only b and c above.

3. Some arguments for trade restrictions have economic validity. Which of the following arguments has *no* economic validity?
   a. the infant industry argument
   b. the national defense argument
   c. the government revenue creation from tariffs argument
   d. the creation of domestic jobs argument
   e. All of the above have some economic validity.

4. The objective of strategic trade policy is to
   a. protect those industries needed for national defense.
   b. provide domestic decreasing-cost industries an advantage over foreign competitors.
   c. develop economic alliances with other countries.
   d. carefully develop free trade areas to counteract customs unions.
   e. increase government revenues through tariffs.

5.   A tariff is a
      a.   tax on imports or exports.
      b.   government-imposed limit on the amount of a good that can be imported.
      c.   government-imposed limit on the value of a good that can be imported.
      d.   payment by government to domestic producers.
      e.   payment by government to foreign producers.

6.   A subsidy is a
      a.   tax on imports or exports.
      b.   government-imposed limit on the amount of a good that can be imported.
      c.   government-imposed limit on the value of a good that can be imported.
      d.   payment by government to domestic producers.
      e.   payment by government to foreign producers.

7.   A quantity quota is a
      a.   tax on imports or exports.
      b.   government-imposed limit on the amount of a good that can be imported.
      c.   government-imposed limit on the value of a good that can be imported.
      d.   payment by government to domestic producers.
      e.   payment by government to foreign producers.

8.   A value quota is a
      a.   tax on imports or exports.
      b.   government-imposed limit on the amount of a good that can be imported
      c.   government-imposed limit on the value of a good that can be imported.
      d.   payment by government to domestic producers.
      e.   payment by government to foreign producers.

Section 3: Exchange Rate Systems and Practices

1.   In the world today, exchange rates are determined by
      a.   the United Nations.
      b.   the government of the United States.
      c.   the same method in all countries.
      d.   one of two methods.
      e.   several diverse methods.

2.   The two main methods of determining exchange rates are
      a.   set and non-set exchange rates.
      b.   fixed and floating exchange rates.
      c.   monetary and fiscal exchange rates.
      d.   dollar and non-dollar exchange rates.
      e.   European and Asian exchange rates.

3.   The exchange rate system whereby central banks try to influence exchange rates by
      intervening in floating foreign exchange markets is called
      a.   a managed floating exchange rate.
      b.   a manipulated fixed exchange rate.
      c.   the multiplied-float arrangement.
      d.   the EMS.
      e.   a clean float.

4. The exchange rate system in which the exchange rate is fixed against a major currency or some basket of currencies is called
    a. crawling pegs.
    b. managed floating.
    c. a fixed peg.
    d. horizontal bands.
    e. a currency board.

PRACTICE QUESTIONS AND PROBLEMS

Section 1: An Overview of World Trade

1. _____ (Comparative, Absolute) advantage is based on the relative opportunity costs of producing goods in different countries.

2. _____ (Comparative, Absolute) advantage occurs when a country can produce a good for a lower input cost than can other nations.

3. The following table shows the output per worker per day in either mangos or papayas in Samoa and in Fiji.

	Samoa	Fiji
Mangos (in tons)	6	2
Papayas (in tons)	12	6

   a. The country that has an absolute advantage in producing mangos is _____.

   b. The country that has an absolute advantage in producing papayas is _____.

   c. The opportunity cost of 1 ton of papayas in Samoa is _____.

   d. The opportunity cost of 1 ton of papayas in Fiji is _____.

   e. The country that has a comparative advantage in papayas is _____.

   f. The opportunity cost of 1 ton of mangos in Samoa is _____.

   g. The opportunity cost of 1 ton of mangos in Fiji is _____.

   h. The country that has a comparative advantage in mangos is _____.

   i. The limits on the terms of trade are 1 ton of mangos for between _____ and _____ tons of papayas.

4. Name the comparative-advantage theory that matches each explanation of comparative advantage listed below.

   a. Differences in labor productivity among countries: _____

   b. The advantage that comes to a country that is the first to develop and produce a product: _____

   c. The relative amounts of skilled and unskilled labor in a country: _____

   d. Differences in the amounts of resources countries have: _____

   e. Differences in tastes within a country: _____

5. Differences in consumer tastes within a country explain _____, in which a country is both an exporter and an importer of a differentiated product.

Section 2: International Trade Restrictions

1. The main reason governments restrict foreign trade is to protect _____ producers from _____ competition.

2. Governments can generate revenues by restricting trade through _____; this is a common tactic in _____ (industrial, developing) countries.

3. The argument that new industries should receive temporary protection is known as the _____ argument.

4. Strategic trade policy aims at identifying industries with _____ and giving them an advantage over their foreign competitors.

5. Trade restrictions usually _____ (create more, redistribute) domestic jobs within the economy.

6. Tariffs are _____ on imports or exports. In the United States, tariffs on _____ (imports, exports) are illegal under the Constitution.

7. Quotas can be used to set limits on the _____ or _____ of a good allowed to be imported into a country.

Section 3: Exchange Rate Systems and Practices

1. In the world today, exchange rates are based on _____ exchange rates, _____ exchange rates, or some combination of these methods.

2. In a _____ exchange rate system, a government tries to keep their country's exchange constant over time.

3. In a _____ exchange rate system, a government allows their exchange rate to shift according to the forces of demand and supply.

4. A country is said to _____ its currency when the value of its currency is tied to another country's currency.

5. What type of exchange rate system does the United States use? _____

THINKING ABOUT AND APPLYING ISSUES IN INTERNATIONAL TRADE AND FINANCE

Tax Effects of Import Restrictions

According to *Newsweek:*

Lower-income families are hit hardest by trade restrictions, because they spend a far greater share of their earnings at the store. In 1989, for example, households earning more than $50,000 laid out 3.3 percent of their disposable incomes on clothing, but households in the $20,000-to-$30,000 bracket spent 4.6 percent—and families earning $10,000 to $15,000 spent 5.4 percent. The quotas and tariffs that force import prices up to protect U.S. apparel jobs don't matter much in Beverly Hills, but they put a big dent in pocketbooks in Watts. (July 12, 1993, p. 45)

Let's look more closely at the effects of tariffs and quotas on apparel on different income groups. Assuming that 20 percent of the price of clothing is due to tariffs and quotas, calculate the dollar cost of tariffs and quotas on families making the incomes given below. Then calculate the percentage of its income each family pays due to tariffs and quotas.

1. Family income = $50,000; Cost: _____; Percentage of income: _____

2. Family income = $25,000; Cost: _____; Percentage of income: _____

3. Family income = $10,000; Cost: _____; Percentage of income: _____

4. Do tariffs and quotas hit lower-income families the hardest, as *Newsweek* says? _____

ANSWERS

QUICK-CHECK QUIZ

Section 1: An Overview of World Trade

1. a;
2. b;
3. a;
4. d;
5. c;
6. b;
7. e

If you missed any of these questions, you should go back and review Section 1 in Chapter 17.

Section 2: International Trade Restrictions

1. c;
2. d;
3. d;
4. b;
5. a;
6. d;
7. b;
8. c

If you missed any of these questions, you should go back and review Section 2 in Chapter 17.

Section 3: Exchange Rate Systems and Practices

1. e;
2. b;
3. a;
4. c

If you missed any of these questions, you should go back and review Section 3 in Chapter 17.

PRACTICE QUESTIONS AND PROBLEMS

Section I: An Overview of World Trade

1. Comparative
2. Absolute

3.

    a.   Samoa (One Samoan worker can produce more mangos than one worker in Fiji.)

    b.   Samoa (One Samoan worker can produce more tons of papaya than one worker in Fiji.)

    c.   1/2 ton of mangos (6 mangos = 12 papayas, so 12/12 papayas = 6/12 mangos)

    d.   1/3 ton of mangos (2 mangos = 6 papayas, so 6/6 papayas = 2/6 mangos)

    e.   Fiji (Fiji has the lower opportunity cost; it has to give up only 1/3 ton of mangos to get a ton of papayas, whereas Samoa has to give up 1/2 ton.)

    f.   2 tons of papayas (6 mangos = 12 papayas, so 6/6 mangos = 12/6 papayas)

    g.   3 tons of papayas (2 mangos = 6 papayas, so 2/2 mangos = 6/2 papayas)

    h.   Samoa (Samoa has the lower opportunity cost; it has to give up only 2 tons of papayas to get a ton of mangos, whereas Fiji has to give up 3 tons.)

    i.   2; 3

4.

    a.   productivity differences

    b.   product life cycle

    c.   human skills

    d.   factor abundance

    e.   consumer preferences

5.   intraindustry trade

Section 2: International Trade Restrictions

1.   domestic; foreign

2.   tariffs; developing

3.   infant industry

4.   increasing-returns-to-scale

5.   redistribute

6.   taxes; exports

7.   quantity; value

Section 3: Exchange Rate Systems and Practices

1.   fixed; floating

2.   fixed

3.   floating

4.   peg

5.   United States dollar

THINKING ABOUT AND APPLYING ISSUES IN INTERNATIONAL TRADE AND FINANCE

Tax Effects of Import Restrictions

1. $330 (3.3 percent of $50,000 = $1,650 spent on clothing; 20 percent of $1,650 = $330); 0.66 percent ($330/$50,000 = .0066 = 0.66 percent)

2. $165 (4.6 percent of $25,000 = $1,150 spent on clothing; 20 percent of $1,150 = $230); 0.92 percent ($230/$25,000 = .0092 = 0.92 percent)

3. $108 (5.4 percent of $10,000 = $540 spent on clothing; 20 percent of $540 = $108); 1.08 percent ($108/$10,000 = .0108 = 1.08 percent)

4. Yes. (The percentage of income paid in the "tax" is highest for low-income families and then decreases for higher-income families.)